Having passed threescore years and ten, and ha\
memories of childhood and adolescence (most\ ... war South West
London), the author thought that she had material that might be of interest to others.
Despite her self-confessed egotistical, opinionated style of writing, and despite
displaying some immaturity and paranoia, she believes she has outlined a culture and
lifestyle unique to London from 1945 to 1967 – the time between her birth and
occupation. In her autobiography, she outlines the feelings she experienced and the
scenes she witnessed as a rebellious child and teenager, and naïve young woman.
Later commentary has been added in the form of historical and personal footnotes to
put the work in context and add to its authenticity. She says she has been as factual
as her memory will allow and is confident of 95% accuracy, but apologises if any
incidents have been misunderstood or misinterpreted, and also apologises for her
constant "whinges".

Maureen Katrina Wilson

London War Trophy

"Warts 'n' All"

AUSTIN MACAULEY PUBLISHERS™

LONDON • CAMBRIDGE • NEW YORK • SHARJAH

A CIP catalogue record for this title is available from the British Library.

ISBN 9781528908054 (Paperback)
ISBN 9781528908061 (Hardback)
ISBN 9781528958790 (ePub e-book)

www.austinmacauley.com

First Published (2020)
Austin Macauley Publishers Ltd
25 Canada Square
Canary Wharf
London
E14 5LQ

Contents

Chapter 1

Gauden Road, Clapham, S.W.4. 1945-1949

Like many children – but in my case justifiably – I felt there was something different about me throughout my childhood. I wondered if I had been adopted, or in my more fanciful moments if I was a changeling. In my teens I often tried to discuss these feelings with my mother, particularly when the relationship with my father began to break down in my early teens, but she laughed off such notions. It was only when I had reached the age of 29, and my mother 54, that she actually told me the facts that had been kept hidden from me since birth – and even then it was only after Aunty Kit let a cryptic clue "out-of-the-bag" that could not be ignored, otherwise I am not sure whether my mother would ever have come round to telling me the truth.

The new revelation was that my mother had only lived with her husband Len, my dad, for two years after their marriage in June 1939. Many couples separated during the war, some for long periods of time, but according to my mother she and Len made a complete break from their marriage in 1941 and they began to live as single individuals once more. In 1943 my mother met my natural father, a Canadian soldier with whom she lived in a common-law marriage situation for the final two years of the war until his premature death. I never talked much to my stepfather about his separation from my mother when I knew the truth. I think his version may have been a little different from my mother's. I suspect he may not have wanted the separation, or realised for some time that she had a new partner.

My natural father was Warrant Officer 2nd class Walter Edward Doyle RCEME. He was known in England as "Mick" and was born on 12 February 1917 at 99, Harrison Avenue, Etobicoke, Twp Ontario. His pre-war occupation from 1937 to 39 was automobile mechanic at the Pneumatic Insulating Company 24, Adelaide Street, East Toronto. He died in Enschede, Holland (army records wrongly quote Belgium) on 26 May 1945 following a car accident, and was subsequently buried in Almelo Civil Cemetery, Holland. According to army records my father and a friend had been on an army errand somewhere in the Netherlands where they were stationed, and then had continued on to a local dance. As they were returning to base the jeep that my father was driving hit a tree at a known dangerous spot on a bend in the road; my father was killed and his passenger injured. This happened just three and a half months after my birth in London.

My natural father's gravestone in Almelo, Holland

The following photographs are a few of those my father left in London with my mother that were eventually passed on to me.

Staff-Sgt. W. E. Doyle
Toronto.

Old Canadian newspaper cutting kept by my mother, with a picture of my natural father taken before his commission, when he was still staff sergeant

Photograph of Mick (Walter) taken on a London common – probably Streatham Common or Tooting Bec Common – both close to Sternhold Avenue where he and my mother lived when he was not in mainland Europe.

This is Mick's mother and adopted younger brother, Glen, in Canada. It looks as though Glen was about 10 years old when the photo was taken on Sunday 4 January 1942.

I was told by my mother that Mick's sister Florence had always been in poor health. She died in Canada 1943, having a year earlier given birth to a son who she named John. John was adopted soon after his mother's death.

Ethel, (Florence and my father's mother,) had immigrated to Canada as a teenager in 1908, together with her parents and sister.

While in the UK Mick visited his mother's Uncle James, Aunt Elizabeth and their daughter at Warney Mill, Derbyshire, their home.

Mick's sister Florence with adopted brother Glen

Mick's relatives in Derbyshire, James and Elizabeth Walton, with their daughter Elizabeth standing behind them, in front of the mill house

My mother always kept my birthday and other cards, for which I am now grateful. Among them is a 1945 Valentine Card. I never knew who it was from. Was it sent to me by my father from the Netherlands, was it one of the few sentimental gestures my mother made towards me, or was it from Uncle Cyril?

The Valentine Card that was sent to me when I was two weeks old had been manufactured in England, and had been left unsigned, as was the custom.

Later enquires never revealed who the sender was.

Baby's first Valentine!
See what it brought—
A HEART FULL
OF LOVE
To a dear little tot!

In July having not heard from her partner for some time, my mother wrote to Mick's commanding officer asking for information, and received the tragic news of his death. Further communication with the Canadian army resulted in my mother being advised not to contact Mick's family in Canada. His widowed mother was elderly the officials said (she was only 53!), and hearing about us would cause her further anxiety. My natural father had begun divorce proceedings from his former wife back in Canada, (confirmed in army records) and so he had kept news of his new relationship away from his mother and the army to avoid complicating the legal proceedings. Learning of me and my mother's existence so soon after the death of her son and close to the death of her daughter, would have been too traumatic for Mrs Doyle the army insisted; there was little Mrs Doyle could do to help anyway they emphasised.

Following is the first correspondence my mother received after her initial enquiry-

First Cdn A Trs Wksp RCEME
Cdn Army Overseas
30 Jul'45

Dear Miss G Lewis,

I have received your letter of 26 Jul'45 concerning B94212 AQM5 Doyle W E. I regret to inform you that Walter Edward Doyle was killed instantly in a car accident 26 May'45. He was buried in the civilian cemetery in the beautiful Dutch town of Almelo on Monday 28 May. Captain F G Stewert, our padre, conducted the ceremony and a large group of comrades attended the service.

Such news is always heart breaking but doubly so after the conclusion of hostilities. There is little we can say to bring comfort except to tell you that your fiancé has been a splendid soldier and fulfilled his duty throughout the weary years of this war.

I send to you the sympathy of myself personally and my entire unit, and may your faith and hope be sufficient for your need in this hour.

I regret that I did not know of your relationship so that I may have written to you sooner

Most sincerely,
A C Drysdale Major

Not long after discovering about her partner's death in Holland my mother's family – in particular Cyril her brother – contrived and was successful in gaining reconciliation between her and her legal husband, Len. The couple were back together again before the end of October 1945. Len, the dad I grew up knowing as a child, had been in North Africa with "Monty" for at least part of the war, but other than that my knowledge of his wartime experience is sketchy. I heard odd snippets of information but never strung them together properly. I believe he may have been wounded and left the war-arena to convalesce back home at some point, and at another time was allowed compassionate leave to try and sort out his marital problems. My mother claimed he found comfort in a nurse during their separation, but as her claims were sometimes misleading or self-protecting, I never accepted them at face value. I wish I had been more inquisitive and asked more questions because with hindsight I believe my dad was basically a good man, if perhaps weak and lacking in confidence, self-esteem and self-control. At the very beginning he did try to be a good father to me.

Knowledge of my mother's marriage, separation, new relationship, bereavement and subsequent reconciliation with Len, did much to help me understand scenes I had witnessed as a child. For instance there was a time during one of my parents' heated rows when my dad tore up some old photographs that my mother had kept hidden. He must have become incensed by something my mother had said or done, making him feel inadequate and playing second fiddle to a ghost. I now realise these photos had probably been connected to my natural father, and Len was attempting to show my mother that the past was the past and could not be retrieved. Another time as a baby I remember standing up in my cot beside my mother and stepfather's bed as they slept. For some reason I felt like a stranger even though I had not yet reached my first birthday. I suppose my mother must have wanted to keep me close to her for the first few months of her reunion with Len. The situation could not have been easy for her or my dad and I as a baby must have been picking up the negative vibes around me. I also now know why one of my mother's favourite songs during my childhood, was **"My Bonny Lies Over the Ocean".**

1.
My Bonnie lies
over the Ocean
My Bonnie lies
over the Sea
My Bonnie lies
over the Ocean
Oh bring back my Bonnie to
me

CHORUS
Bring back, bring back
Bring back my Bonnie to
me to me
Bring back, bring back
Bring back my Bonnie to
me.

2.
Last night as I lay on
my pillow,
Last night as I lay on
my bed,
Last night as I lay on
my pillow,
I dreamt that my
Bonnie was dead.
CHORUS

3.
Oh blow ye the winds
o'er the Ocean And blow
ye the winds o'er the Sea.
Oh blow ye the winds
o'er the Ocean And bring
back my Bonnie to me.
CHORUS

4.
The winds have blown
over the Ocean, The
winds have blown over
the Sea. The winds have
blown over the Ocean,
And brought back my
Bonnie to me.
CHORUS

Five decades later, not long before my mother's death in 1996, when she and I were trying to build some sort of trust in each other, I visited her unexpectedly one day with my husband. By then she was living in a retirement flat in Beckenham, Kent. She looked a little embarrassed on seeing us and hurriedly went over to move something from her sideboard; as she did so a group of old photographs fell to the floor. They were of young men in World War Two military uniforms. My mother muttered something about them being acquaintances from the war years, and servicemen from various countries; I remember Finland in particular being mentioned. It confirmed my suspicion that my mother had led anything but a nun's life following her estrangement from Len. She would have liked me to think she was the injured party in the separation, had not been promiscuous but had led a disciplined existence before eventually meeting her soul mate, my natural father. She used to maintain that early on in the marriage she and Len discovered they were incompatible, and after a couple of years separation from each other she had unexpectedly found happiness with Mick who she met at a dance in the Locarno Ballroom, Streatham, a place I later frequented myself as a teenager.

The following is an account my mother gave me when I was 29 years old of how she and Mick met for the very first time. She told she had been to a dance at the Locarno Ballroom, when Mick and some of his friends came over and joined her group. During conversation it emerged that Mick needed a bed for the night as he had left it too late in the evening to return to his military base. My mother offered him a bed in her spare room and did not expect to see him again after she left her flat for work the next morning. However on leaving her office at the end of her work-shift her lodger was waiting for her outside and their intimate relationship began. She said that during their two-year affair both she and my natural father decided they wanted a child and my conception was no accident. I have known my mother to cover up inconvenient situations with misinformation and lies, or to romanticise events, but I think this claim probably had some credence, if somewhat "stage-managed".

Old photograph of Streatham Hill, looking north. The Locarno Dance Hall is in the foreground second from the left. It was opened in 1929 by the bandleader, Billy Cotton.
© Ideal Homes/28dayslater – Wikimedia

An Armistice Ball, was held at the Locarno in November 1930, when the ballroom was one of the most popular purpose-built dance halls in south London.

The Streatham Hill Theatre, (built 1928,) is seen just beyond the Locarno. The two establishments were part of an entertainment complex built along Streatham High Road around the 1930s. The Locarno has undergone many refurbishments since then. It was re-opened as "The Cats Whiskers" in 1969, "The Studio" in 1984, and "The Ritzy" in 1990 and in 1995, it became "Caesars Night Club". Streatham Theatre also underwent changes, at one time becoming a bingo hall.

Before the war, my mother had been a shoe-shop assistant, but the war enabled London women to be quickly promoted up the ranks to more important jobs. Women were needed to fill the rapidly increasing job-vacancies to be found in the West End and City. By the 1940s my mother was working for the Civil Service doing clerical work at the Ministry of Supplies in the Strand. The extra prestige and money this brought with it meant she could enjoy a reasonable social life between air raids and other wartime horrors. I know she went to the Stork Club off Regent Street on several occasions, and dined out frequently. One wartime story she used to tell our family was of her enjoying a meal with friends in a restaurant when she happened to mention to the other guests how tasty the pie was. She was taken by surprise when told that it was a pigeon pie. Pigeons had not been part of my mother's previous cultural diet. The only pigeons she knew were the dirty ones that hung around Trafalgar Square, but in those days of food shortage wood pigeon had become a delicacy on restaurant menus. It was a pity my mother did not continue to appreciate the pie; apparently she rushed out to the cloakroom and was violently sick.

Following the trauma of war, news of Mick's death, and my mother's reconciliation with her husband, she and Len managed through the council to rent a ground floor flat in Gauden Road, Clapham, S.W.4, (possibly number 37 – the number scratched on the pillar in a photograph to follow, or maybe 53 – the house number these photos had been assigned to at a local developing-and-printing shop). I was nine months old when we moved in, and we continued to live at this address until I was four and a half years old. The house was a fair way down Gauden Road on the right-hand side as you walked away from the main road towards Larkhall Rise. My memories of this period are to say the least patchy. I was too young to attach significance to situations that were presented to me at the time, but I do remember the building and our flat in great detail together with a few scenes that occurred in or near it. I suppose it is only human to assume that if we have some vivid baby and early childhood memories it is a sign of a well-developed brain, good intuition and perception, but I believe most individuals are able to recall some images from infancy, and this appears to be particularly true of war babies. Perhaps the emotional upheaval of war with its unpredictable situations and strained relationships trigger a greater degree of mental observation. My friend Lesley Knill, who is mentioned later and became Mrs Lesley Osman on marrying and immigrating to Australia in the 1960s, also lost her father in the war. Like me she had no time to be with her natural father, and as a toddler had to adapt to a new family situation. She has similar baby and early childhood memories to my own.

In addition to our ground floor flat in the Gauden Road house there was also a basement flat and another above us with possibly a fourth flat on our level. I remember the flight of steps at the front of the house leading up to the front door (now confirmed in the photographs I have since received from my sister). The front door led straight into a hallway and then there was another door into our flat on the right. There was also a flight of stairs in the hallway which led up to the first floor flat. In my mind's eye, I can still see my mother standing at the bottom of these stairs talking to the upstairs neighbour, both women wearing housework-pinafores and headscarves tied up in the turban-style fashion of the day. Another clear memory I have is of the garden at the back of the Gauden Road house. It had a huge tree at the far end. On a warm day, I would sit under its branches making mud-pies. Once while doing this, a large daddy-longlegs spider crawled over my foot and startled me. I did not know what it was or what it was doing, and so ran to my mother, but was too young to put into words what had happened and so could not tell her of my encounter.

The above photos were given to me around 1990, and confirm my early memories of Gauden Road, Clapham. They show me with my adopted father and mother outside our home around the year 1948. The bike at the top of the stairs is my dad's.

Weirdly, I can remember one or two scenes on Clapham Common; one involves Uncle Cyril pushing me in my pram across the common. I can see the pond we passed and a couple of small canvas-type stalls or kiosks, in which I presume people were trading – though what they were selling I have not the faintest idea.

CLAPHAM COMMON
© Wikipedia

Clapham Common is a large triangular urban park in Clapham, south London. It was originally common land for the parishes of Battersea and Clapham. It is overlooked by large Georgian and Victorian mansions and nearby Clapham Old Town.

Apart from my pram memory with Uncle Cyril, I remember little else about him in my early years, but I know he must have played a prominent part in my life right from the beginning. He felt responsible for ensuring my parents' reconciliation was a success and was trying to do his fair share of baby-minding and so on. This sense of responsibility partly came from earlier conversations he had had with them when he pointed out to them that they had both been left on their own after the traumatic years of the war, and were both in need of support and companionship – conversations he later confided and shared with me. In my childhood, Uncle Cyril must have been one of the more stable elements in my life. For many years, his pet name for me was "Stinker", a result I believe of him one day having to change one of my particularly unsavoury baby's nappies. In 1951 I received the following birthday card from him confirming this embarrassing pet name. I was six years old when I received it, but he had not forgotten the earlier incident.

I have at least one other pram memory which must even predate our move to Gauden Road, because the surroundings are completely different. It involves me lying in a pram that was parked on a landing at the top of a flight of stairs inside a house. A couple of inquisitive women peer in at me through a net placed over the pram. My mother later confirmed that she did in fact use a cat-net over the hood and chassis of my pram to prevent cats, bees and other creatures getting in. This memory may have been from our days in Reading, Berkshire. On discovering the death of her partner Mick, my mother was approached by her Aunt Lizzie who suggested it might be a good idea if my mother went to stay with some of her relatives (or possibly friends), who lived in Reading. Not knowing what else to do at that time my mother agreed, but according to her she did not stay there long. She felt she was being organised by the older women of the house and wanted time to herself to run her own life, especially where provision and care for me was concerned. I now suspect that these women may have been Aunt Lizzie's stepsisters Ada and Jessie, my half great aunts.

My most dramatic early memory is of an accident I had at Gauden Road. I was about eighteen months old and remember being outside on the balcony at the back of our house. This balcony overhung the basement flat, whose subterranean back door and window looked out onto a small dugout concreted area below normal ground level. Somehow, I managed to get through the balcony's widely spaced iron railings and began to fall. For a few seconds I held on to the balcony railings, dangling over the thirteen-foot drop. I remember crying out and catching sight of my mother as she came through the French doors onto the balcony – then BLANK! Apparently I had fallen onto the concrete below, with my head inches away from a concrete step that could have broken my neck. My mother said it was a serious accident, but having had me taken to hospital by ambulance, examined and patched up by medical staff, she insisted I should not stay in hospital overnight. I was allowed home on the understanding that for the foreseeable future my mother would return with me on a daily basis to the hospital for the required check-ups and treatment. This she did, wheeling me along in a pushchair right through the rest of the summer, and then periodically through the autumn and that terrible arctic-type winter of 1946/7 (January to March 1947 was particularly bad!). I still retain a small scar under my lip from the accident. The hospital used plastic strips to hold together a small wound there. It was a technique that had been successfully pioneered on injured soldiers in the war. I now find it curious that I never quite knew what other injuries I had sustained in the accident. I do not think I had any broken bones or organ damage.

There are several things about this accident that do not seem to add up. Discussing the event with my mother in later years she claimed to have been talking to someone in the flat earlier that day. When this person left by the French door, they forgot to shut the gate which divided the balcony from the steps leading down to the garden. I suppose it is possible that I could have gone past this gate then poked myself through the railings on the stairs beyond, but my mental picture is of falling through the bars of the actual balcony, and in any case the steps were closer to garden-level. My mother also believed she did not see me when I fell whereas my recollection is of her coming out of the French doors and stepping on the balcony as I held on to the railings for the last few seconds. Perhaps my memory is faulty, perhaps my mother was confused, or perhaps our two accounts can be knitted together. There is a small chance my mother may have been feeling guilty because she was involved elsewhere at the time of the accident, and tried to modify details to compensate for being distracted and forgetting to keep her eye on me. I will never know the truth. I know of other occasions where my mother's accounts of events have been far from accurate.

I had regular yearly hospital check-ups throughout my childhood. I do not know if they were associated with the accident because the reason was never explained to me. It might have been a requirement of the Canadian authorities, with me being the dependent of a dead Canadian soldier. (I now know my mother received a monthly pension for me from the Canadian Government. Originally she had told me these payments were the result on an endowment she had taken out for me before my birth.) Perhaps my mother had to prove to the Canadian authorities she was still my guardian, and that I was in good health. In my more negative moods I have wondered if the annual medical check-ups were the British authorities checking up on my mother's child-rearing and coping strategies, especially if it had been suspected that my accident was linked to some parental neglect. My mother's half-hearted explanation once was that these check-ups were connected to a lump on my ribs that required monitoring. It is true my ribs are slightly out-of-true, one side protruding a little further than the other, but it has never been a problem and I have never seen medical reports concerning the matter.

Guy's Hospital was one of the institutions I visited as a child, and may have been the place of my annual check-up. I remember travelling there on an old-fashioned tram with its road rails and overhead cables. These trams were solid and dependable and compared favourably with today's mismatch of public transport with impractical seating arrangements, dirty appearance and regular mechanical failures.

As a child, I was certainly not the healthiest of individuals. I suffered bouts of severe bronchitis, bad constipation and I had regular gastric upsets. Travelling made me particularly sick. My mother and Aunt Lizzie had to take extra bags and towels with them when they went on a coach outing with me. Roughly once a month I woke up in the middle of the night and was violently sick. I can still recall the horrors of sitting up in my bed with my stomach heaving away. I hated it. Even at a young age I realised I did not have control of my body and found this frightening. These episodes may have been a precursor to the later anxiety and panic attacks that I experienced as an adult. Turbulence in aeroplanes, or on the sea, or being dehydrated or feverish have all been known to trigger off some very severe stress-related reactions. I wondered recently whether these childhood monthly vomit-attacks might have been an emotional reaction to my mother's menstrual problems. She suffered from a disturbed menstrual cycle having only three or four proper periods a year, but she still had regular monthly tension during which times she could be extremely irritable and irrational. Violent rows at home were inevitable during these periods. When I was a teenager my mother told me the cause of her disturbed cycle was the sudden death of her father, when she was 17 years old. It came unexpectedly and was a shock to her because she had been particularly close to him. This menstrual irregularity made her pleasantly surprised when she discovered she was pregnant with me she said in one of her more thoughtful and caring moments in her later life. Apparently, although she and Mick wanted a child, they did not know whether this would be possible.

Dr Menon was our family doctor during those days at Gauden Road. He was one of the few Indian doctors practising in London immediately after the war and his ability and skills were greatly respected. In addition to his obvious expertise he came from a well-established Indian family at the centre of Indian politics. Ill health however was the least of problems for post-war children. The authorities made sure we were well looked after with free quotas of malt, cod-liver oil, school milk and strong-tasting concentrated orange juice that our mothers collected from the clinic each week, and we never had a problem getting an appointment with a doctor or a dentist in those days!

When I was just three years old, I went into hospital to have my tonsils and adenoids removed. Afterwards my mother sent me to Bournemouth for two week's convalescence. I was sent to a place I did not know and felt lonely and completely lost. I remember my mother and father waving me off at a London train station and from then on being surrounded by strange faces. I was terribly miserable throughout the whole time in Bournemouth and began wetting the bed in my sleep. One morning one of the carers lifted up my wet sheets for all in the dormitory to see. I felt ashamed and embarrassed as the other children looked on.

I remember little else about my stay in Bournemouth. I do not know if I was taken down to the beach, or out for trips. I think I received a goodies-parcel from my parents one day, but there is little else I remember. When older I told my mother how unhappy I had been in Bournemouth. She said it was an opportunity she could not miss, as she had been able to claim the cost of my convalescence from an insurance policy (or more likely from the Canadian pension fund as I now believe it to have been). She considered it an additional holiday for me, while rightly or wrongly I sensed her reason might have been to have a little time to herself without responsibility for me. The one good thing I remember about Bournemouth was seeing a red squirrel from the dormitory window. It was on a pine tree in the grounds of the large house where we were staying. A carer pointed it out to us and explained how red squirrels were becoming rare in England with the American grey squirrel taking over.

Some more 1940s photographs recently passed on to me by my sister.

Me sitting on our Gauden Road balcony, which looks as though it had been boarded up behind following the accident	-playing in the garden on a tricycle with another girl, possible one of those with whom I went to tea (described later).	-sitting on an air-raid shelter in one of the Gauden Road gardens, holding our family's pet cat.

I could never really communicate with my parents. Eventually I heard that my mother and father had gone to counselling and therapy sessions in the early days of their reconciliation to strengthen their relationship and cope with emotional problems and broken trust. My mother later put many of the marriage problems down to my father's sexual inadequacy and did not seem to take any responsibility herself.

As a toddler I saw my mother occasionally going into deep faints. Once when I was walking with my father and one or two of his friends along Gauden Road, (it must have been summer because he and his friends were not wearing jackets, only slacks and shirts with rolled up sleeves, and I must have been about three or four years old because I was able to reason a little in my head by then) I turned to him in front of his friends and said something about Mummy being "on the floor", because that is how I remember her being when we left the flat. He did not seem terribly concerned, and muttered something to suggest she was being dramatic, or what I would now understand to be attention-seeking. I do not know if he was right but with hindsight, I suspect my mother may have had some deep-seated neurological problems that needed addressing. I certainly felt my dad should have been more sympathetic on this particular occasion. I will never know the real ins-and-outs of my parents' troubles but they certainly left me with some bad memories, including the terrible arguments that went on in our home, some ending in mild physical violence – nothing too serious I am pleased to say, just a few pieces of crockery being thrown about the place now and again, and so on. At a later home, in Greyhound Lane, Streatham, I secretly used to get out of bed on occasions to go out onto the landing and watch my parents rowing in the hallway below.

It is possible my mother used me as an infant to get the attention she craved for herself. Having lost both her own parents, and the man she thought she loved, she was obliged to give all her consideration to my adopted dad and his parents, Harold and Lucy Lewis. Mr and Mrs Lewis senior lived in Tremaine Road, Anerley, London, S.E.20. One of the stories my mother used to tell me was of a visit we paid to dad's parents in the early days of their reconciliation. Apparently during this visit my adopted grandparents suggested I should be disciplined a little more than I was. My mother's immediate reaction was to put on my hat and coat and whisk me out of the house leaving it for my father to follow after us, searching the streets to try and find us again. As a child, I did not know what adult games were being played; I certainly found it difficult to understand the adult world.

Grandma and Granddad Lewis were not a worry to me personally I am glad to say. I did not fear them, in fact on occasions I stayed with them in Anerley without my parents. Granddad liked making things, especially from wood. He made me a couple of children's jigsaw puzzles and other toys in a work-shed at the bottom of the garden. Grandma was good at crochet and needlework and she used to make me little pastel-coloured socks in a crocheted shell-pattern which I can still see in my mind's eye. I think I found Dad's parents more credible than my own mother who in my mind always wanted to be the centre of attention. All things meaningful and worthwhile had to be related back to her. When I was a pupil at grammar school, and brought home some dishes from my cookery lessons, she would never praise my efforts, but would immediately refer back to the Sunday dinners we used to have at Gauden Road where she "would always make a special apple pie". She might have made the odd one or two but all I can remember is having tinned evaporated milk with tinned fruit for our Sunday dessert – and as for Sunday breakfast it was Dad who stood over the frying pan to give us our only proper cooked breakfast of the week. I must admit I do recall my mum's tasty butterbean sauce that she used to make and pour over our Sunday roasted joint of meat, and she certainly knew how to present a good dining table for guests. She made the tables look particularly festive at Christmas and for other celebrations. "Image" and "presentation" were my mother's hallmark. She was proud of the fact that as a little girl she was not allowed to sit at the table unless the flared skirt of her dress was arranged just so on her chair. She also could not bear to eat cucumber unless it was cut wafer-thin, as it had been when she was little. Being a traditional English woman of the early 20th century she claimed she could not bear even the slightest hint of garlic in or near her food, but the culture she had inherited could not have been nearly as important to her as she made out, because in later life, when she could afford to go on frequent package holidays abroad she would of necessity have consumed a large and regular quantity of garlic – and as for being lady-like I can recall her sipping her cups of tea, coffee and cocoa very loudly and unsociably in her dressing-gown most mornings. My mother could almost quote word for word from an imaginary book of dos-and-don'ts. Most were normal polite practice and good manners, but you would think she had some special mastery on "The Art of Gentility", and this gave her the air of importance she wanted.

My grandparents' house in Tremaine Road was lovely. It had all sorts of trappings, which were above the standard I was used to in my own home. There was a special billiards room, a leaded glass window in the front door, tasteful art-deco ornaments and decorations, and a long back garden separated into sections with trellises and beds of scented flowers with Granddad's large shed at the far end. I can still smell the lily-of-the-valley in the garden, which, although not a rare plant – growing, as it does like a weed – smelt better than I have ever smelt lily-of-the-valley since. There was a country-like alley leading down the side of their house and to me it all suggested space and opulence.

Apart from the billiards room downstairs in the house there was also the front room, a living room (or lounge) which opened out to the back garden through French windows, and a large kitchen-dining room with fitted wooden cupboards and a large kitchen table. This too had access to the garden via the back door. Upstairs in the house there were three or four bedrooms and a bathroom. When I stayed there, I slept in the bedroom at the front of the house. It had been Dad's bedroom when he was a little boy. I always felt safe and cosy there with the warm eiderdown on top of the bed and the little Lucky White Heather and Crested ornaments on the windowsill. Dad and his brother, Uncle Ken, had brought these ornaments back from the seaside-outings they had been on as boys with their parents.

I learnt later from family-tree research that Granddad's family came from Gillingham, in Kent, and Grandma had been born in Whitstable, Kent, probably the reason they made frequent visits back to the Kent coast in the 1920s and '30s. Granddad Lewis had been a manager of a shoe factory before the war, possibly a shoe repair and cobbling business, although it might have been a shoe manufacturing business. He came from a fairly affluent background but unfortunately either his father or grandfather had lost much of the family fortune and then committed suicide. (This at least was my mother's belief, but I have been unable to confirm it from public records.) Grandma Lewis was a few years older than Granddad and had an aura of graciousness and amenability about her. If she was two-faced as my mother claimed it was kept well hidden from me.

This more recent photo of houses in Tremaine Road, Anerley, shows them as now mostly
divided into maisonettes, with two front doors to each property.
I remember these houses as being single dwellings in the 1940s/50s.

It was here in Anerley while staying with my grandparents that I probably began to show signs of social mal-adjustment. I would love to excuse myself because of my family situation but excuses do not eradicate personal responsibility. One occasion that I remember in particular occurred when I was playing in my grandparents' back garden with some neighbouring children. I must have been really horrible to one of the little girls because I made her cry. I cannot remember what I said or did but I really upset her.

19

I certainly did not want anyone to find out what had happened, and the distress I had caused, especially my mother when she called to pick me up. Mum always made me feel so inadequate and useless when things went wrong. I put all my effort into trying to pacify the girl and encourage her not to tell anyone but she did not cooperate and remained upset. I felt guilty and trapped and I was not very popular with her, my mother or grandparents for some time afterwards.

Another incident of social inappropriateness at my grandparents' house, one that my mother loved to remind me about, happened when I was a toddler and went over to Anerley with her and Dad for tea one day. The table was beautifully laid for the occasion and in the centre was a cake-stand with a variety of pretty little fairy cakes placed on the stand's layered plates. It must have been quite an achievement for my grandmother to provide this in those days of post-war austerity, with luxury commodities being in short supply. As soon as I saw the fairy cakes, I assertively pointed out the two I wanted reserved for me. My mother was absolutely disgusted at my declaration and showed it in the way she looked and spoke to me. She never let me forget the incident. I was only two or three years old and had not realised I was being selfish. Apart from my great-aunt Lizzie Dad's parents were the only two other older relatives I knew as a toddler. My mother's parents had died before I was born, and I had few mature role models to observe and learn from.

Despite some of these early negative memories I do recall some good times. I especially enjoyed going to a big departmental store called Kennards, in Croydon. Here, together with other children, I was treated to a ride on a horse or donkey that trotted around a small indoor-arena. I went to Kennards specifically to have my hair cut for the first few years of my life. The store had a good reputation for this and my mother was exceptionally snobby about such things as to who should style a child's hair, and what sort of shoes a child should wear (namely Clarks Shoes – which in those days were made by skilled English crafts-people in Somerset).

Photo of the old Kennards Store, Croydon
©Bygone Croydon

In the Clapham garden with my much-loved doll's pram.

My mother's high ideals were practised on me in my early years but later, when older, I was dressed more soberly in handouts and cheap quality clothes. My mother even began to cut part of my hair herself, resulting in me having a permanently wonky fringe seen in later photographs. I do not think diminishing financial funds were the prime reason for this; I believe it was more to do with me beginning to acquire an independent streak at a very early age. I began to question some of her statements and actions and became very self-willed, challenging her authority. Being spoilt and pampered only appeared to be an option if I remained submissive, pliable and an extension of her ego. Almost thirteen years later my half-sister fared much better where our mother's generosity was concerned. By nature my sister is less argumentative and more trusting than I ever was.

Another happy memory I have is of the dolls' pram that was bought for me one Christmas or birthday. I loved wheeling it up and down the Gauden Road pavement. I had all the correct matching accessories for it, made by my mother and grandmother. Unfortunately the cover from the pram-set was lost on one of these trips and my mother made me feel guilty about it for a long time afterwards. I was not allowed to forget this or similar incidents. For most of my childhood we kept a pet cat and I can recall dressing one of the poor creatures up in the dolls' clothes knitted for me by my grandmother. With great difficultly I then tried to lie the cat down in the dolls' pram – not very animal-friendly – but I thought I was doing the cat a favour and no one told me any different until I was badly scratched one day.

In my first few years, while still at Gauden Road, I received regular parcels from the Canadian Red Cross containing some very stylish American children's clothes. Most London girls were dressed modestly after the war of necessity, and so I do not know how my mother with her image to maintain managed to explain the clothes away to her friends and neighbours, most of whom did not know I was illegitimate and receiving additional support on account of my natural father's death.

A special magical memory I have is of spending a few days in Kent one Christmas. I think it was just before my third birthday. Every time I recall it, I immediately return to an enchanted world. I had gone to Kent with my parents to stay in a large country house with several other people. I believe my mother knew the woman who was housekeeper there. This woman had taken up her post either during or immediately after the war, and the owners of the house were making their home open and available for the festive season to all friends and relatives of anyone associated with their staff and property.

One meal we enjoyed at the house remains indelible in my mind. The adults were sitting at a large dinner table in a large hall-like room while we children sat nearby on children's chairs at a smaller, lower table. Food was brought in to us by a maid. I could not believe my eyes when a certain dessert was brought to the children's table. It was the biggest blancmange I had ever seen, layered in different colours and flavours with an assortment of glace fruit and confectionary decorating the outside of its moulded shape. It looked and tasted absolutely wonderful.

During this Christmas break in Kent I remember going down country lanes collecting cobnuts with my mother, and being back at the big house playing hide-and-seek with the other children and some adults. I especially remember Christmas night. I was in a little box-room on my own, and heard – and almost saw (I thought) – "Father Christmas". He entered the room and put some parcels on my bed. I kept my eyes tightly closed pretending to be asleep in case he went away before completing his task. This made me sleepy and so I did in fact doze off again. The next thing I knew it was Christmas morning and I woke up to a pile of presents at the end of my bed waiting to be opened. The biggest was a beautiful dolls' house. I learned later that my dad had made it with his father in Anerley. It had everything – a smart front door, real glass in the bay windows, wooden furniture decorated with miniature hand-painted motifs, a Bakelite radiogram etc. It was named Katrina Villa, with the name painted on the front surrounded by a posy of painted flowers.

A few years later I asked why the dolls' house was called by my second Christian name instead of my first one. My mother said it was because she and Dad thought at one point they might prefer to call me Katrina rather than Maureen. I now know that Maureen was the name chosen for me by my natural father who had some Irish ancestry on his paternal side. Perhaps it was considered too much of a sad reminder for his common-law widow – or perhaps my newly adopted father felt uncomfortable with a name chosen by his rival. Katrina had in fact been suggested for my second name by a nurse at Kings College Hospital, Dulwich S.E.5. where I was born, surprisingly (considering my mother's menstrual complications) exactly at the predicted time, the end of January. My mother's pregnancy was over-seen by John Peel, who almost three years later assisted in the birth of Prince Charles, and eventually became the queen's official gynaecologist; he was knighted as such in 1960. Following my delivery, and on realising my mother was looking for a second name for her baby, a Scottish nurse or midwife suggested Katrina. My mother immediately liked the name and accepted it. As time went by my original first-name was retained as the main one, with Katrina kept for the second.

Thinking back to the situation of my birth I suppose it must have been a difficult time for my mother. Although my birth was reasonably straightforward there was still a stigma attached to mothers who were not married to their baby's father, and especially for the girlfriends of GIs. I expect my mother was grateful she had a marriage certificate to make my birth appear conventional and part of a marriage arrangement. There was no need either for her to explain the absence of a father at the bedside in January 1945. Partners of many new mothers were still serving abroad, unable to be home for the birth or available for post-natal hospital visits. Some photographs were taken of me soon after my birth and my mother says she sent copies of these to Mick in the Netherlands. She wondered whether following his death they might have been forwarded on to his mother back in Canada together with his other belongings. Among some of these early photographs I have seen, one is of my mother leaving hospital with me in her arms. She was wearing a hat that had a light net veil that covered half her face, and disguised the jaundiced condition she was suffering at the time.

Continuing with the theme of my early childhood magical feelings, another I had was linked to a book I received. Along with the doll's house and other presents I found at the bottom of my bed that memorable Christmas in Kent was a large fairy book. Images of the pictures and print have remained in my head ever since. Following retirement from a teaching career I spent hours trying to find a similar book on E-Bay or other websites. I remembered the book as being cardboard backed and about four times the size of most other children's books of the day. It had large text inside, around which were woven illustrations of fairies, flowers, mushrooms, insects, animals and so on. These were all delicately drawn and coloured. Only recently have I discovered the book's identity. It is "A Day in Fairyland" by Sigrid Rahmas, and was illustrated by Ana Mae Seagren. The book held super-natural significance for me as did another ordinary everyday item, bindweed. I was standing one day with my mother at the Clapham Road end of Gauden Road looking at the large white trumpet-like flowers straddling the railings near the railway bridge. My mother was talking to a railway worker who was wearing dirty dark-coloured work-clothes and a cap. As a result of something I said he explained the flowers were poisonous and a weed, but this did not spoil the romantic feeling I had for them.

I have since wondered whether these magical feelings were peculiar to me or common to most children. As a city girl, I always felt I had a special link with nature and loved creating make-believe objects from twigs, leaves and flowers. It would keep me engrossed for hours, and was far more interesting than making things from manufactured materials. One day in 1953 when my mother was walking with me and my baby brother in his pushchair, we stopped at the corner of Clarence Avenue in the Clapham Park area of S.W.4. There was a patch of grass with some trees and a wooden bench on which my mother decided to sit for a while. My brother seemed quite happy chuckling to himself in his pushchair, and my mother was lost in her thoughts, so I began selecting different leaves to mould and knit together to create a range of miniature pots and pans – an odd occupation, but one that kept me amused and hypnotised for a while. Much later in my teens my favourite activity at youth-camp was the "Hanging Basket Challenge" – making and arranging a hanging basket from natural items found in a neighbouring wood.

Another surrealistic experience I had (but unfortunately not a pleasant one), happened one holiday. Our two-week annual summer holiday to the coast – usually the south coast, but occasionally Norfolk – was a luxury my parents would not forego. My mother would have preferred to go to more exotic destinations and constantly harangued my father about this. His poor pay and lack of ambition were the constant bane of her life. As has been said, Dad's family were financially sound and received respectable incomes even after the loss of family assets decades earlier. Before the war and his marriage my father had joined the Cooperative movement, becoming a grocery assistant with plenty of opportunity for job development and promotion. The Cooperative Society in the thirties and forties was a prestigious firm offering excellent career prospects for the well-motivated – but the war, marital problems and my mother's pushiness had helped nurture my father's laid-back attitude and lack of assertion. He was never fully promoted to shop-manager during his whole time with the Co-op, and consequently we lived more humbly than my mother would have wished. Holidays were restricted to caravan sites, or sometimes holiday-camps such as Maddieson's Littlestone Holiday Camp in Sussex, where this next childhood memory took place.

I must have been about two and a half years old when this incident occurred. Once again, I was too young to communicate properly in words to people around me, but I nevertheless retain a strong memory of the scene. I can recall being brought back to the holiday camp chalets by one of the camp leaders. He was wearing slacks and a blazer, (the equivalent I imagine of the better-known Redcoat Outfits worn by Butlin's Holiday Camp staff). He was holding my hand and leading me across some sort of putting green where campers were relaxing and playing mini-golf together in the sun. I had been found lost and wandering about in a confused state, and the leader was taking me back to find my parents. When I queried the incident with my parents in later years it was once again something that was never properly explained. I do not know why I had wandered off and how I had come to be lost. Did I panic? Was I afraid? Had I been mischievous? Why had my parents not missed me, because I think they were still in their chalet when I was returned to them? It is a real mystery, and the details have never come to light, but the rescue remains vivid in my memory and has definitely not been influenced by any later accounts I may have heard.

It is possible my parents went on this particular holiday with a couple called Lillian and John. We saw a lot of Lillian and John in my childhood. Apart from spending several holidays with them we saw them back home in London too. They lived in Lewisham, Kent, now London S.E.13., not far from our own home in South West London. Lillian was a sewing machinist working in the so-called "Rag Trade". Her sweat-shop, or small factory outlet, was situated in Peckham Rye, S.E.15.

As I grew older, I found Lillian's personality rather overpowering and oppressive. Recently, without prompting, my sister mentioned feeling the same way. I am not sure what John did for a living. He was certainly more easy-going and better to get along with than his wife. Lillian and John did not have children of their own. Mum said it was through choice. "Children are too much trouble, and Lillian and John want to enjoy themselves" she took delight in telling me. The couple certainly seemed to make the most of their leisure-time. My first memories of them are with their motorbike. They used it constantly, visiting friends and going out on pleasure-trips together. John was always in the driving seat. There was a sidecar to the motorbike which was attached when Lillian wanted to use it rather than sit in the passenger seat behind him. Only in middle age did Lillian and John succumb to the comfort of a car, giving my mother yet more ammunition to tell Dad how poor we were in comparison to their car-owning friends.

A man dressed in drag for a holiday camp themed party-night (1948 or 1949).

My mother in a camp sack race

My father with me and a friend on a camp bike, 1949.

☐Holiday camp group photograph taken 1948. My mother is holding me, bottom right hand corner.

Another holiday photograph, but where is it? Does anyone recognise this strand?

I do not know how my parents met Lillian and John, but in my late twenties when talking to Aunty Kit, she muttered something about my mother at one time getting caught up in partner swapping. I do not know whether she meant during or after the war, or both. I did not pursue the subject because there was only a 50% chance Aunty Kit was telling me the truth anyway. Aunty Kit, (otherwise Mrs Catherine Dean) was not a real aunt, but a wartime friend of my mother. During the war the two women had lived in the Criffel Avenue – Telford Avenue – Sternhold Avenue – area of Streatham Hill. It was Aunty Kit who had led me to question the background of my birth when I was twenty-nine years old, but I knew from experience that like my mother Aunty Kit was capable of exaggerating, stirring up trouble and even lying. I was careful not to take everything she said at face value. According to my mother, Aunty Kit was no saint herself when it came to sexual matters. She said that although Aunty Kit had married Uncle Harry some years before the war, and they had never separated, she led a full life during the war while Uncle Harry was serving abroad with the armed forces. Uncle Harry seemed to me to be a kind and inoffensive man. He and Aunty Kit had had a son before the interruption of war, but by the 1950s he was more or less estranged from his parents. Perhaps his mother's extra-marital antics played a part in his loss of parental respect. It is hard to believe now, but despite their mutual point-scoring and backstabbing, my mother and Aunty Kit remained good friends to the end of their lives. I have since reflected on Aunty Kit's claim about partner swapping and wondered whether John and Lillian might possibly have been part of this set-up. Was this the distraction that led to my going "AWOL" at the holiday camp?

A less important memory of mine at the seaside is of a fairly crowded narrow confined beach between cliffs and the sea. Intermittent with the sandy patches on the beach were stretches of rock supporting several rock pools that absolutely teamed with crabs. There were dozens of these creatures. Children and parents were trying to catch them with their nets and buckets. I do not think we joined in but I remember my dad having a bucket and spade and building me a sandcastle. I can still see the beach clearly in my mind, but although I have visited a large part of the English coastline since I have never come across this same stretch again.

A major event in my life at Gauden Road, in 1948, was being bridesmaid at the wedding of Mary Jean Lloyd and Albert George Simcock. It was the one time I was truly put on show. My mother could not be accused of shunning the limelight for herself or her family if the occasion was offered. In following years I learnt my mother had done a lot of politicking to get me into the role of bridesmaid in those days when weddings were of necessity economic, and food and clothing in short supply. My mother offered to lend Jean (as she was known) her 1939 wedding dress and veil, and also agreed to supply and make my bridesmaid's dress if Jean would have me as her bridesmaid. I suppose it was an offer Jean could not refuse. When the day of the wedding arrived, I was duly washed, polished and ready to take my place in the event. Jean was one of Aunty Kit's nieces and younger than my mother. The story I was told sometime later was that during the war my mother allowed Jean to use her flat for courting because Jean's father disapproved of his daughter's relationship with Bert (as he was known) Simcock. The reason for this may have been Bert's much older age; another reason may have been her father's non-acceptance of the war and post-war promiscuous scene that his daughter may have been caught up in.

The scene I remember best from the wedding was my praying. For some odd reason I had confused the breaststroke action in swimming to people praying in a church. Perhaps I had seen newsreel footage of Muslims at prayer, and imagined this was the same as the swimming actions that I had also seen elsewhere. Whatever the reason, at some point in the church service while standing behind the bride and groom, I knelt down on a hassock, then laid flat down on my stomach and began to do the breaststroke. I think I can recall a man coming over to pick me up and put me back on my feet. I must have looked a very strange figure dressed in my pink, frilled, satin dress with my white shoes and little bouquet lying on a hassock, flaying out my arms and legs. I suppose I can be forgiven; I was only three years old and at least I was trying! I have since found the incident highly amusing but my mother never referred to it again. I think once again I had embarrassed her in company, and not lived up to the sophisticated image she would have liked for herself and family.

Uncle Harry and Aunty Kit are standing just to the right of the bride in the photograph, and so I assume Jean's immediate family did not attend the 1948 wedding.

A coloured-in photograph of me in the bridesmaid dress my mother made.

At Jean and Bert's wedding reception, I loved more than anything the icing on the wedding cake. It was rock hard and needed a lot of biting before it disintegrated into smaller hard lumps in the mouth. I suspect in those days it may have been made with egg-white substitute or similar. I have tried to find similar icing since, but always been disappointed. Present day variations of royal, glace, frosted, butter and moulded icing do not have the same challenge as the dense texture of that post-war icing.

The Simcocks went on to have two children, Richard born 1951, and Karen born 1955. Initially the family lived in Brixton, Lambeth – in or near Acre Lane, but after some years they moved to Bideford in Devon on a council-house exchange-scheme. They eventually bought this Devon council house at a very reasonable price. This of course frustrated my mother immensely because she herself had not progressed to home-ownership. Mum kept in touch with Jean and Bert all her life. Some months before my mother's death I took her to stay in the Cornish cottage my husband and I own and drove her one day to Bideford to find and visit Jean and Bert. The friends had kept in touch with Christmas cards and the occasional letter but it was the first time they had seen each other for many years. Jean and Bert had a beautiful home situated above the main town, east of the river. I went shopping for the day leaving my mother and Jean alone, (with Bert in the next room) to relive old times.

Another recollection of these early Clapham days-worth mentioning, for historical reasons if not for any other, is of a visit I made to a post-war prefabricated house, or "prefab" as it was affectionately known. I am not sure whose it was, most likely a friend of my mother's because it was she who took me there. The rooms in these prefabs were light and airy and contained modern appliances that few other properties of the time possessed. I particularly remember the refrigerator in the kitchen. Nearly all prefabs were detached, self-contained, single story homes surrounded by neat little gardens with pathways leading up to the front door. They were highly prized right up to the time when most were dismantled in the late 1950s and 1960s, when councils began to replace them with more permanent housing. Many prefabs had remained as good as the day they were first erected.

Prefabricated Houses – a common sight in the 1950s

©Humphrey Bolton geography – Wikimedia

© Dave Snowden – Wikimedia

© Oosoomonen – Wikipedia

Another memory from my time at Gauden Road is of a neighbour, a young boy called Richard who lived a few doors away from us. He always looked so sad and neglected. I can remember my mum trying to cheer him up, and I think on one occasion she sent around a parcel of useful items for him. I imagine he must have been one of the unwanted war babies. Sometimes my mother would sing the song "Open the Door Richard" as she tried to amuse him and make a light-hearted reference to his name. Despite her personality-defects, my mother could show compassion at times – even to me on the odd occasion.

From different accounts, I have learnt that the hit song, "Open the Door Richard" was recorded by the saxophonist, Jack McVea, in 1947, on a Black and White label. It was recorded at the suggestion of "Artist and Repertoire" man, Ralph Bass, and became an overnight sensation, at one time being number one on the billboard's "Roll of Hits".

The words my mother would sing are......
Open the door, Richard,
Open the door and let me in,
Open the door, Richard,
Richard, why don't you open the door

Apart from Richard there were a few other children who lived near us in Gauden Road. On one occasion I was invited by one of the mothers to go around and have tea with her and her children in their basement-flat. (Perhaps my mother had arranged it to allow her to do something that was best done without me being present.) The woman gave us hot milk to drink and bread and butter to eat. I found the plain hot milk very odd and not very appetising and the bread and butter rather bland. My mother told me the children's mother was trying to make sure we had something nutritious in our stomachs because many foods were still rationed, and scarce. Other than this occasion I cannot remember mixing much with other children in Gauden Road, although each week from the age of three I was taken by some of the neighbouring children to a local church

Sunday school. I have a feeling my mother made this arrangement to get me out of the house and give her and my father some space and time to be alone together because she was not particularly religious herself at this time in her life. I cannot remember the other children at the Sunday school but I do recall the woman who took our group. She was not fat but rather well built with dark hair. She used plasticine figures to illustrate the Bible stories that she was telling, and moved them across a sand board as the story progressed. I can also recall the unusual windows in the church hall where the Sunday school was held.

I was taken on occasions to see my cousins in Streatham. They were the children of my mother's eldest brother, Jack, and his wife, Elsie. John was the eldest of these cousins and fifteen months older than me, and then there was Sheila who was almost two years younger than me, Brenda born 1948, and Richard born 1950. In the early days, they lived with their parents at 28, Penrith Street, Streatham, S.W.16., the house that had been built by my mother's father, another John Benfield. My grandfather was a Master Builder and responsible for the construction of several terraces of houses in the Mitcham-Streatham area of London. He chose, 28, Penrith Street to be the family home for himself, his wife, (my grandmother Maud,) and their children, John (later to be known as Jack), Leslie, Cyril, and after World War One, Gwendoline my mother.

As a successful businessman my grandfather was one of the few in Streatham to own a Ford car in the late 1920s and 1930s. Unfortunately he died unexpectedly in 1937 returning home from work one day. His custom was to travel to work by tram, and he was getting off one of these at the bottom of Streatham Common when he collapsed and died. My grandmother died of a brain tumour four years later in 1941, and so both were dead by the time I was born in 1945. Following the death of these grandparents, 28 Penrith Street became vacant until at some point Uncle Jack moved back into his childhood home with his own family, giving my mother another matter to complain about. She felt that she too should have benefited from the capital that had been tied up in the property. Uncle Jack and his family remained there in residence for several years.

28, Penrith Street, Streatham, in the year 1923, with my mother and Uncle Cyril as children standing in front.

Me with cousin John in the garden of 28, Penrith Street, in the year 1947.

On one of the occasions that my mother took me round to visit Aunty Elsie, and my cousins, I was sent out into the garden to play with John. I remember Sheila also being outside in her pram, so the year was probably early 1947. A hammer was lying on the ground and I picked it up. As I stood with it in my hand John who had been stooping down suddenly stood up and cracked his head on it. Blood appeared and he cried out. Immediately my mother and Aunty Elsie came rushing into the garden. Aunty Elsie lifted John up and mopped the blood away while my mother took me inside, sat me down on a kitchen-top surface and smacked me hard. She had assumed I had hit John with the hammer. It was not unusual for her to blame me for mishaps without investigating first. Once again, I was too young to have the necessary words to explain what had happened. I was very upset and not even comforted when John cheered up and was able to tell them what really happened. I do not think my mother said sorry for jumping to the wrong conclusion and I felt very aggrieved about this injustice for some time after.

Other cousins I saw from time to time were the children of my dad's brother, Ken. He and his wife, another Elsie, had married in 1945 and they had two sons, Michael, born 1948 and Trevor in 1952. The family lived in Norwood, South East London. As a child I did not know they were not my blood cousins, but one incident that occurred when I was about 8 years old has stuck in my mind, and since proved significant. I was walking along a pavement with Aunty Elsie, Michael, one or two other children and a couple of Aunty Elsie's friends, holding on to the handle of Trevor's pram as my aunt pushed it along. Suddenly I realised my aunt was talking to her friends in hushed tones, and I sensed she was talking about me. I could not understand why. Nothing out of the ordinary had happened and for a change I did not seem to be in trouble for anything I had said or done, but somehow I knew that what was being discussed was important. I now realise my aunt and her friends were most likely discussing my paternity, which they could not talk about openly.

My formal education and introduction to a wider social circle of children began when I started state school in Clapham at the age of four. This schooling may have begun in the January of 1949, as soon as I was four years old, or more likely a few months later after the Easter holidays. I do not remember the name of my first school, but I do remember walking there with my mother and it was not a long journey. However I was only a pupil at this school for a short time; soon after we moved and were living in Brixton Hill, S.W.2. by the time of my fifth birthday. Here I was enrolled at the New Park Road Infant School.

At my first Clapham school they tried to teach me to read by the phonic method. It did not suit me at all, and I made little progress until I transferred to New Park Road School. Here the teacher gave me a Ladybird Book. As I held it, she read a page to me then sat me down, told me to look at the words she had just read and try to remember them. When I was ready, I had to return to her desk and read the page back to her. This I did and was away to a flying start with my ability to read. Sight learning was certainly a better teaching method where I was concerned. Since being a teacher myself I have come to appreciate different methods suit different individuals, especially in relation to reading.

The only real mental picture I can retrieve that relates to my first school was when my mother collected me one day. On the way home we stopped at the house of one of her friends, and in the front room children were sitting around a television watching a programme. Televisions were a novelty in the 1940s, and I felt very privileged to be able to join in the viewing of one.

Perhaps over the years, I have come to exaggerate the emotional deprivation I felt as a child. Many of us look for excuses to explain away personal weaknesses and shortcomings. I have frequently blamed my mother and past stress for my present poor attitudes and behaviour – the obvious lack of trust I have in other people and the fact that like my mother I rarely take responsibility for my shortcomings. Thoughts of my mother being continuously disappointed and embarrassed with me loom large in my mind. By now I should have forgotten scenes such as the one where I forgot myself in Gauden Road in front of my parents and their friends Lillian and John. Accidentally, I farted out loud. I could only have been about two but the look of disgust and horror on my mother's face was withering. I felt like a leper. When a few years later my baby half-brother Philip played with some fluff on his penis in his baby-bath, again in front of my parents and the same couple, it was considered highly amusing and the four burst into laughter. I could not see the difference between his innocent act and my earlier natural mishap. When I grew older my mother's constant verbal digs at me, both directly and indirectly and often in the presence of my friends, hurt me immensely. It may have happened because she was utterly miserable and insecure herself, and trying to deflect her sense of inadequacy onto me. Sometimes she would sing the song "You Always Hurt the One you Love" to me. I think it was meant to be poignant, and perhaps deep down she was trying to say sorry, but mere sentiment was not my idea of a good exchange for actual kind and loving words and actions.

From different accounts I have learnt the song, "You Always Hurt the One you Love" was written by Allan Roberts and Doris Fisher, and became a standard pop song. Among the artists who have performed it over the years are listed - The Mills brothers, Connie Francis, Fats Domino, The Impressions, Frankie Laine, Richard Chamberlaine, Peggy Lee, Michael Buble, Kay Starr, Hank Thomas and Clarence "Frogman" Henry.

On 22nd June 1944, it reached the Best Seller Chart in Billboard Magazine, where it stayed for 20 weeks. In 1959 it was number 13 on the UK Singles Chart, and in 1961 it became a top twenty hit.

The words my mother would sing to me are...
You always hurt the one you love;
The one you shouldn't hurt at all,
You always take the sweetest rose,
And crush it till the petals fall.

Chapter 2

Maybury Street, Tooting, S.W.17. 1945-1954

From an early age, I went to stay for the odd week or weekend with Aunt Lizzie at her flat in Maybury Street, Tooting, South West London. (I think it may have been number 23). As has been said, Aunt Lizzie was my great-aunt, my mother's, mother's half-sister. My great-grandmother, (Aunt Lizzie and my grandmother's mother,) was Elizabeth Gilson, who had been born in Fen Ditton, Cambridgeshire in the year 1853; her ancestors were mostly Cambridgeshire farm-labourers. Unfortunately my great-grandmother lost her own mother when only five years old, and was left with her father and nine surviving siblings to fend for herself much of the time.

When old enough, or perhaps sooner because she seems to have added a few years to her actual age, my great-grandmother became a servant in Kensington, London, and then on the 25 February 1873 she married Charles Miller at Wimbledon Parish Church, Kingston, Surrey. I assume this was to give her some status in society, because Charles was a 47-year-old widower with grown-up children and she was only 19, (but erroneously recorded on the marriage certificate as being 23). Two children resulted from the marriage, William James Miller, born 1878, and Aunt Lizzie – registered as Annie Burley Miller – in 1880. Charles Miller died in 1883, three years after Aunt Lizzie's birth, but at least two years before this my great-grandmother had been living apart from him in Westminster with her toddler son and baby daughter. The 1881 census shows her as being a housekeeper to the Margato family and living with her children at the Margato's premises, 9, Charlwood Street, Westminster. Charles was living in Battersea with a daughter from his first marriage, her husband and children. Following widowhood my great-grandmother married my great-grandfather, Thomas Robert Jones who was a widower himself with young children, but this time someone nearer her own age. The new marriage increased the family further with more children, one being my grandmother Maud.

Poor Aunt Lizzie must have had a crisis of identity. Throughout her life, her names changed many times as I have now discovered through my research. At birth, she was registered as Annie Burley Miller. This was slightly altered for the 1881 census where she was registered as Anne N Miller (perhaps an official confused the initial of the middle name), and soon after this she became known by her mother's Christian name, Elizabeth (or Lizzie for short). Following her mother's second marriage in 1884 her surname was altered from Miller to Jones and from then on for formal documents, Anne, or Annie, was sometimes retained, and sometimes forgotten, and her second Christian name, Burley, was corrupted into Burrell, Beryl or just plain B, and then of course Aunt Lizzie's three marriages gave her further surname changes. Her first married surname was Richards; after widowhood, she remarried and became Mrs Reader and lastly, towards the end of her life having been widowed for a second time she married once more and became Mrs Sims.

Aunt Lizzie and her older brother William were raised in Battersea with six surviving Jones siblings, three daughters from the first marriage of Thomas Robert Jones and three children resulting from their mother's second marriage to him. Following my great-grandmother's death in 1899, my great grandfather Thomas Robert Jones, in 1901 married for the third time. His new wife was a young woman called Lily. Unfortunately Lily had only been married twenty months before she too died. She had not long given birth to her first and only child, Ernest Albert Jones and was just 26 years old. My great-grandfather was 48 by then and too old to bring up another child. Baby Ernest was given to Lily's relatives for nurturing and rearing, and his siblings in Battersea saw little of him. Most of the details surrounding Aunt Lizzie's life and family have only come to light in recent years, chiefly through work I have done on our family tree. When I was a child Aunt Lizzie made the occasional comment to me about her past and family history but I was not interested then and did not bother to ask for further details. Now however I would love to hear her personal reminiscences.

For most of my childhood I remember my great-aunt being called Mrs Reader by her friends and neighbours. In the 1940s and '50s, people were friendly but far more formal than we are today. Robert Reader, Aunt Lizzie's second husband, had died in 1940, so my great aunt was on her own again by 1945 when I was born. My mother told me Aunt Lizzie liked children and wanted to have some herself, but as a young woman she would have needed a small operation to become pregnant and this she refused being apprehensive about anything medical. The cause of her anxiety may have been the accident she had as a toddler when she ran into a bucket of boiling water being carried by one of her father's workers. For many months she was on the doctor's danger list, and continued to carry horrific scars on her neck and side until the day she died. Aunt Lizzie's childlessness and lack of personal family commitments was an asset to my mother who was able to deposit me on her doorstep whenever the need arose. At the time I did not appreciate that the war had left my mother and father with deep emotional scars and that they needed time and space on their own to try and re-establish their damaged relationship.

Maybury Street was a typical Victorian street of terraced houses with bay windows on the ground floor. Aunt Lizzie lived in a house the side of the street that was still standing in 2006. The even-number houses that I knew on the other side of the road had by then been demolished to make way for a recreation area. Aunt Lizzie lived in the bottom half of the house, and Mr and Mrs Dobner lived upstairs. It was quite common after the war for people to share their homes. I know my aunt was a tenant, but I'm not sure if the Dobners owned the house or were tenants too. The two flats were not self-contained and each morning Mr Dobner made a pot of tea in his kitchen upstairs. He took one cup of it to his wife in bed then came downstairs with another cup for my aunt who was also still in bed. After this he returned to drink his own cup of tea in his kitchen while reading his newspaper. Not so much with her early morning cup of tea but with later ones through the day Aunt Lizzie would retain one of her quaint habits. She would pour some of the hot tea into the saucer and blow on it to cool it down and then drink it straight from the saucer. These days it would be considered rude and inappropriate but to Aunt Lizzie it was quite normal. She also had another quaint habit. When she had biscuits for elevenses, she would dunk them in her cup of tea before eating them. Those who had endured the war, my mother included, picked up this practice from having to eat wartime biscuits that were often hard and tasteless and needed a good soaking.

A large sugar-bowl was always placed in the centre of Aunt Lizzie's large wooden table in her kitchen. It was made of thick, moulded, Victorian glass and had a sturdy stem supporting its bowl. Inside the bowl were old-fashioned sugar-cube lumps and a set of metal sugar-tongues. This bowl was in constant use, with sugar continually being required for cooking and to sweeten drinks. Aunt Lizzie had been a domestic cook in service before marriage. She may have worked in the Battersea pie and mash shop that had been founded by her blood father, and following his death managed by her older half-brother. Aunt Lizzie had spent much of her teens and twenties working with pots and pans and so her kitchen and its cupboards were important to her. She owned a variety of cooking utensils and accessories, and on the kitchen shelves over the cupboards she displayed her Willow Pattern crockery that fascinated me, as did the colourful art-deco motifs on some of her large pudding bowls. There was a drawer under the top of Aunt Lizzie's kitchen table where she kept her cutlery and serving utensils. She prepared food and did most of her chores on this large table. Her meals tended to be good and wholesome – basic and non-fancy – a legacy of her training in the pie-and-mash business I imagine. I can still recall the taste of her stewed cabbage, corn-flour puddings and pies. As you entered the kitchen from the hallway most of the cupboards and shelves were on the left-hand wall. In one of the bottom cupboards Aunt Lizzie kept her shoes, shoe-cleaning kits, rags and other cleaning items. One day, she showed me how to turn some of the clean rags into a rag-doll. I loved looking at the old shoes she kept in this cupboard. One pair in particular had funny long pointed toes that I considered extremely dated, until some years later as a teenager I wore even more outrageous long-pointed winkle-picker shoes myself. I even had to stuff cotton wool into the toes of these shoes to prevent them curling up too much. On the right-hand wall of the kitchen was a window that looked out onto the side section of the house's small L-shape garden, and after the window, also on the right, was the back door that led into the garden.

Aunt Lizzie slept in the front room of her flat in a big double bed that I shared with her when I stayed. Near the bed by the bay window was a traditional aspidistra plant that stood on its stand; there was also a sideboard in the room and some other items of furniture. Under the bed was an old-fashioned chamber pot that I was permitted to use on the occasions I stayed and needed "to go" in the night. It avoided me having to go out the back door and use the garden toilet, which was only a couple of feet away from the back door, but nevertheless inconvenient at night time. In the mornings after the pot had been used, Aunt Lizzie would ceremoniously cover it with a cloth and take it outside to empty it down the toilet. It was like some ancient ritual.

Behind Aunt Lizzie's front bedroom was her parlour with a small table where we ate and beyond this a larger room that straddled the hallway and stairs that lead up to the Dobners' flat. This was the kitchen that has already been described. At the far end of the kitchen was a small area divided into two providing a small scullery on the left and a bricked off toilet cubical on the right that could only be accessed via the garden. Aunt Lizzie had long grey hair which she kept in Tyrolean style plaits wound around each ear. After washing her hair on summer days she would hang it out of the small scullery window to dry. I was allowed to brush her hair in bed some mornings before we got up. I looked on this as a great honour, probably because my mother never allowed me to tamper with any of her grooming.

In the small L-shaped garden, at the back beyond the house, there was a gooseberry bush. I remember picking gooseberries from it one day with Uncle Cyril, on one of his visits to Maybury Street. He was a very sociable man and as he was picking the gooseberries with me, he started up a conversation with the next-door neighbour over the small dividing fence. I cannot recall the other plants in the garden, but remember it as being a cosy and intimate place. Mr and Mrs Dobner did not seem to use the garden. I presume they had their own bathroom with toilet upstairs, and did not need to use the outside toilet. Apart from my aunt's early morning cup of tea Mr and Mrs Dobner rarely intruded on my aunt's privacy unless they had to use the stairs to and from the front door or had some news to share with her. We knew the Dobners were not far away should we need them any time, and they knew where we were should they need us.

This is a formal photograph of Aunt Lizzie and me that was commissioned by my great aunt in 1949.

The writing on the back says...
'To Gwen and Len, from Maureen and Aunt Lizzie on her Anniversary, 15 September 1949.'

I think the anniversary commemorated by this photograph must be Aunt Lizzie's birthday – her birth registration says she was born 8 September 1880 – because I can find no family wedding anniversary close to this date. Aunt Lizzie's first wedding was on 13 October 1906, her second in the last quarter of 1933 and her third had not yet taken place. My mother and adopted father had married on 21 June 1939, and therefore the date was not relevant to my parents either.

Kenlor Road, Tooting, was not far from Maybury Street, and was where Aunt Ada moved to after the war. Aunt Lizzie took me to visit her once in the late 1940s. I did not understand why I had to call her aunt when I was expected to call Aunt Lizzie's other neighbours and friends Mr, Mrs or Miss with their surname, but research into family history reveals Aunt Ada was Aunt Lizzie's step sister; the first daughter of Thomas Robert Jones by his first wife. Like Aunt Lizzie she was a half great-aunt to me. I can still recall her home when I visited it with Aunt Lizzie. It was full of lace, quaint textiles, large wood-framed photographs, chiming clocks, taxidermy displays and so on, all reflective of the Victorian-Edwardian era, the period of Aunt Lizzie's and Aunt Ada's youth.

Aunt Ada appeared a kind lady, but rather reserved and self-contained, wanting to keep her dignity. When I realised my relationship with her I wondered why my mother seemed to have no contact with this lady, because it must have been she who sent the following card to my mother after my birth, and possibly one of the two ladies who lived in Reading, Berkshire in 1945, with whom my mother and I stayed for a month or two before my mother became annoyed at the interference she felt she was experiencing and left. At least my mother kept Aunt Ada's card and I still have it. The faded wording inside says, "Love from Auntie Ada, Barbara and Colin". In recent years I have tried to find out who Barbara and Colin were. Aunt Ada and her deceased husband had had three sons but none was named Colin. On meeting a descendant of Aunt Ada more recently I asked him who the couple might be, but he too had no knowledge of the pair. Perhaps they were wartime lodgers.

Aunt Ada's card sent to my mother – The faded writing at the bottom says "Love from Auntie Ada, Barbara and Colin"

Delighted
to hear of
Baby's arrival.
Accept heartiest
congratulations
and good wishes.

My early impression of Aunt Ada was of a staunch old-fashioned lady, but I have since seen a more up-to-date photograph of her taken in the mid-1950s when she was eighty plus years old. By then, encouraged by her children and grandchildren no doubt, her appearance was far less formal and much more modern.

Another local but more modern home I visited close to Aunt Lizzie's flat was that of Veronica and her grandmother. They lived the other side of Maybury Street, almost opposite Aldis Street, in one of the houses since demolished. Veronica was a couple of years older than me and seemed to be pitied by some people. Eventually I learnt she was the result of an unplanned and unwanted wartime pregnancy. Her American GI father did not want to know his English girlfriend when he was told about the pregnancy, and when the baby was born his girlfriend decided she could not cope, and left her illegitimate daughter with her mother in Tooting. The grandmother brought up Veronica as best she could with the limited resources she had. I went to their house to play with Veronica on a few occasions. We got on quite well but the age gap was a bit of a hindrance to any deeper friendship.

When still very young I wondered why my mother and Aunt Lizzie often compared me to Veronica. I was constantly being told how fortunate I was to have a home and parents who wanted me, unlike Veronica's situation. (At the time of course I did not know or understand Veronica's history and background.) When I reached the age of four or five and beginning to rebel even more, I was told that I would be taken away by the authorities and put into an orphanage if I continued to behave so badly. I suppose my mother, great aunt and others were trying to warn me my situation was not straightforward. Even if my mother was a little neurotic and irrational at times, I suppose she was in her own way trying to fulfil her responsibilities towards me. I don't think my aunt and others meant to be cruel, or to put me down, but I came to feel isolated and unloved at a very early age.

Yet another person I remember from Maybury Street was Rhoda. She was younger than Aunt Lizzie and quite modern in attitude and dress, a bit like my mother I suppose but not so garish. Aunt Lizzie got on well with Rhoda and often stopped to chat and have a laugh with her. A name that was sometimes mentioned in their conversations was Queenie. I thought this an unusual name but have since learnt it was a fairly common nickname at the beginning of the twentieth century. I never met Queenie but I now believe she may have been Jessie, the third daughter of my great-grandfather Thomas Robert Jones – a full sister to Aunt Ada, a half-sister to my grandmother Maud and a stepsister to Aunt Lizzie.

Most of my Maybury Street memories are happy ones, or at least satisfactory, but there were one or two sad occasions. Once while sitting alone in my aunt's front bedroom by the aspidistra plant near her window, I sucked away at my lower arm until a couple of large blood-marks appeared. I was feeling utterly miserable for some reason. I imagine I had probably been in trouble with my aunt or my parents for something since forgotten. When my aunt came into the room, she was shocked at seeing the marks, probably realising they were a sign of an emotionally disturbed child. On another occasion I must have been absolutely miserable once more, because I refused to eat the boiled egg and buttered bread Aunt Lizzie had prepared for me for my lunch. Luckily it was one of Uncle Cyril's visiting days. Being more modern and worldly-wise than Aunt Lizzie he calmed the situation down and encouraged me to continue eating the egg.

My aunt was a true Victorian, prim and proper with limited experience of children, especially those from traumatised family backgrounds. She must have found it difficult to understand my needs. Having said this I instinctively knew from the beginning that she cared for me. She was the one who spent time showing me how to make things like the rag doll already mentioned, and how to make Victorian rose-petal scent-water; she was the one who allowed me to spoon out and lick the remaining custard left in the saucepan, she was the one who made sugar-butter balls for me to eat as a treat in those days of sweet-rationing, and she was the one who went berserk when a neighbour took me on an outing one day and did not return when expected. The kindly Miss Kerr had taken me by bus or coach all the way from Tooting to Hampton Court, not mentioning the destination to my aunt. Aunt Lizzie began to panic when there was no sign of our early return. It was Aunt Lizzie who bought me a Pavlova Cake from a baker's shop one day as another special treat, only to be disgusted when, on breaking open the meringue crust, we found an ants' nest inside. My aunt marched straight back to the bakery and told the staff in no uncertain terms what she thought of their hygiene. She never bought anything from that shop again. It was Aunt Lizzie who spotted the carbuncle under my arm and had it surgically removed for me.

As my great aunt grew older, she mellowed becoming less Victorian and more approachable. She started talking to me about feminine matters such as menstruation and how to wash my face without soap to keep it moist. At the age of 74, when I was nine years old Aunt Lizzie married for a third time, and moved into a small cottage that her new husband bought for them both in Fountains Road, Tooting. It was not far from Maybury Street. Aunt Lizzie had been friends with Arthur Sims and his first wife Eliza for many years. When Eliza died Arthur proposed to my aunt. She was thrilled at the prospect of having company again in old age and becoming a homeowner. My mother on the other hand felt Arthur's motives were calculating, and that all he really wanted was a willing and cheap housekeeper. Whatever the motives Aunt Lizzie was very proud of her new marital status. She had been told some time before that she would remarry, and that her general prospects would improve. This prediction came from a gypsy who was selling lucky-white-heather door-to-door in Maybury Street. At the time Aunt Lizzie laughed at the unsolicited piece of fortune-telling thinking it would never happen. I went to stay at the cottage in Fountains Road once or twice. While there, Aunt Lizzie would give me a little pocket money each morning to go to the local sweet shop and buy an ice cream, some sweets or a lollypop, and later in the day she would give me a second further secret amount of money when Uncle Arthur was out. This meant I could go for a second trip to the sweet shop. I imagine Aunt Lizzie did not want to appear over-indulgent with me in front of her new husband. Instead of becoming self-centred and irritable like many old people do Aunt Lizzie grew more thoughtful and compassionate. Once when I was walking with her along Fountains Road, we passed a young brother and sister walking along the pavement hand in hand. They were very poorly dressed and looked neglected. Aunt Lizzie was genuinely moved by what she saw and commented to me about the way the pair seemed to be looking out for each other and facing the world as best they could.

Perhaps the most lasting effect my aunt had on me was to pass on her Christian faith. She was by no means a "Bible Basher". I cannot remember her ever talking to me about anything serious where religion was concerned, and she certainly did not use God as an excuse to create feelings of guilt or inadequacy in me. My main memories are of the Christian choruses and hymns she sometimes sang while doing her chores around her flat in Maybury Street; "Count your Blessings", "Tell me the Old, Old Story" and so on. She sometimes took me with her to meetings in a small mission hall in Aldis Street around the corner from her flat in Maybury Street (I was pleased to discover this was still standing and used as a place of worship in the year 2000). Immediately after the war this mission hall was run by a man called Mr Walker. He was a happy, smiling, friendly person who would ride up to the mission hall on his bike, dismount, take off his bicycle clips and open up the hall for his small congregation to enter. The services were informal. I can recall the portable wooden seats, the well-used Golden Bells Hymnbooks and the small musical organ played by one of the hall's members. My aunt would help me to read some of the words from the hymnbooks as we sang along together in the weekday services. I also remember the little stamp-texts I was given for attending the children's Sunday school at the mission hall on the Sunday afternoons when I had stayed with my aunt over the weekend. These stamp-texts were stuck into a little booklet, and taken back home to my usual Sunday school where I would receive an attendance mark on their register too. I was never forced to go to the mission hall, and certainly did not mind going. The congregation at the weekday services were mostly middle-aged ladies who were very kind and fussed over me, which I suppose I must have enjoyed. From time to time my aunt would go to whist drives at the mission hall while I went over the road to play with Veronica. Jumble sales were another activity at this hall, and I went to a couple of these with my aunt and remember the big urn that was used to make tea for the stallholders and customers.

My aunt was definitely a Christian, but she still kept some of her old London superstitions. She would throw a pinch of the salt she had spilt over her shoulder to keep misfortune away, touch wood if she was tempting fate and read light-hearted messages from the tealeaves turned out into the saucer from an upturned teacup after its contents had been drunk. Then of course there was the gypsy who told her about her remarriage and future prospects. Aunt Lizzie may have laughed off the prediction but she must have taken it to heart or she would not have remembered it.

Once or twice I went with my aunt for a special service in Tooting parish church. When I think back, I can see myself standing outside the main entrance of the church with worshippers all around me, greeting each other and sharing news. It was like another world; I could not equate it with anything else I knew at the time. It was far more intimate and friendly than the normal domestic situation I found myself in back home. Tooting parish church is the place where I was taken at ten months old to be christened. My mother said I was quite a plump baby and the vicar referred to me as a "right little bruiser". (Was this another attempt by my mother to highlight my imperfections?) I now know that by October 1945 my mother had learnt of my natural father's death in the Netherlands and consequently been persuaded to return to her husband. It was the time my mother and adopted father were trying to start rebuilding their marriage, and my christening must have been a marker in this chain of events; an attempt to be once more a conventional family.

After the christening service at St Nicholas Church a celebration tea was held at Aunt Lizzie's home in Maybury Street, presumably because my parents move to their new home in Gauden Road, Clapham, was still in its early stages and it would have been impractical to have it there. For godparents my mother chose Aunty Kit from Streatham, Uncle Cyril, and a couple she knew during the war years. This couple had some connection with Canada. I believe the woman like my mother had met a Canadian soldier, but in her case had actually married him. The couple might even have known my blood father. It is all speculation because my mother avoided going into any further detail about it. However if my speculation is correct it would explain why my mother quickly lost touch with them. The couple would have reminded her of a tragic episode in her life, one she wished to forget. The pair may also have moved on to live in Canada after the christening. I certainly never had the chance to get to know them, and they had no further contact with me.

In 1956 my mother told me my great aunt had died. She told me this while washing dishes at the sink with tears in her eyes. Aunt Lizzie was buried with her first husband, William Henry Richards, in Streatham Cemetery 14th December 1956.

Aunt Lizzie was confirmed as a Christian in the Church of England just before my birth. In preparation she bought a prayer book that carries the above inscription.

St Nicholas Church, Tooting
© Derek Harper – Wikimedia

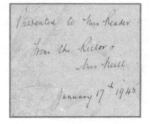

A Bible was presented to my aunt at her confirmation by the rector, the Rev Robert Richard Neill, and his wife. Above is the inscription they wrote on its front page. i.e. Presented to Mrs Reader from the Rector and Mrs Neill, January 17th 1945

Chapter 3

56, Thornbury Road, Brixton Hill, S.W.2. 1949-1952

As noted, my family moved away from Clapham before I was five years old. Our next home was a flat over a Co-op shop in Thornbury Road, Brixton Hill, S.W.2., on the corner of Wingford Road. When I returned there more recently, I found the flat and shop converted into a single dwelling, possibly the home of a city worker. Many professionals from the 1970s onwards found Brixton Hill a convenient place to commute to and from their businesses in Central London.

I imagine my father must have negotiated the tenancy of this flat, working as he did for the South Suburban Cooperative Society. Some of the time we lived in Thornbury Road my father worked as grocery assistant in the shop below our flat, but not all the time; there were occasions when he went to other stores to be acting-manager while the regular one was on holiday or on sick leave. Mum hoped this would lead to permanent promotion for him but it never did. Dad was just not ambitious. He was however a good conscientious worker and popular with his customers. I can still picture him standing at the shop's counter cutting a joint of ham with the meat slicer or exchanging sweets and other items for ration-coupons that were still being used in those early post-war years.

Thornbury Road was where I began to mix more confidently with children my own age. I remember going out to play in the surrounding streets with friends. London streets were reasonably safe and free from excessive traffic in those days. Apart from adults telling us not to go off with strangers and to watch out for moving cars there was little for us to worry about. Some of us even went to the local bombsites to play. They were like adventure parks but we had to be careful to avoid broken glass and jagged metal, and I don't think our parents knew where we were.

It was about this time that I became sexually aware. My mother had become pregnant again when I was five and a half years old. This, together with playground gossip nurtured my curiosity. I cannot remember ever talking to my mother about personal and intimate matters but I do remember sharing odd bits of information with friends in the school playground and cloakroom. On one occasion a few of us decided to play the risqué game of nurses and doctors in the backyard that belonged to my family's flat and the Co-op shop. The yard was a concreted area surrounded by a brick wall topped with barbed wire and jagged glass – security for the shop I suppose; there were no health and safety restrictions for using such materials in those days. A shed was at the far end of the yard where Dad kept his tools. It was in this, one Sunday morning, that five or six of us boys and girls went to play this game that we had heard about from others. Before we went too far with our undressing and investigations my father came into the yard to put some rubbish in the dustbin and we cried off, which is just as well because I think we all felt uncomfortable about the proposed activity. We didn't attempt it again. Another incident I recall was when I was with some friends – probably the same ones – walking along Thornbury Road. One of our group spotted a toddler inside the house, standing by the downstairs bay window. He was partially holding back the net curtains and we could hear adult giggling coming from inside the room. Vaguely we could distinguish a bed with a young couple romping about on it. We tried to encourage the toddler to hold the curtains back further so we could see better what was going on, but he did not understand, and in any case the couple appeared to be dressed and the plants in the small front garden were preventing us having a better view of the flirtation.

Perhaps it was these same friends who I was with one snowy winter day when we broke someone's window in a block of council flats the other side of Kingswood Road, in Streatham Place. We all felt mischief in the air that particular day. At first someone suggested we play Knock Down Ginger, and we knocked on a couple of doors before immediately running away to avoid being caught. Then one of the boys made a snowball. Whether he intended to break a window I do not know, but he threw it and it did. We scarpered from the scene as fast as we could. I was only six years old but knew right from wrong and realised we must have caused a lot of stress to the resident of this flat. I was too much of a coward to own up to the vandalism and I did not want to split on a friend. Fortunately for us we were not pursued.

One early sexual encounter I definitely did not like was one I experienced around the home of my friend Carol Watson. Carol was a lovely girl who came from what I thought was a loving, caring family. One day when I was in her house playing with her and her younger siblings, I saw a rocking horse. This was a bit of a novelty for me and Carol's father sat me down on it for a ride. While he held me there, he started rubbing his hands up and down my chest area in a fondling manner as the horse rocked. I did not have even the beginnings of a bosom and could not understand what caused him to touch me in this way, but I knew it was inappropriate. I did not know then it was an attempt at sexual stimulation but sensed he was taking advantage of me. I did not tell anyone but made sure I avoided all contact with Carol's father after this. Carol later told me that her father had seen Can-Can Dancers in France when he was in the armed services and they had danced without their knickers on. She thought this was an interesting piece of news to pass on, but distrusting her father as I did I was not amused. I have since wondered if Carol herself might have been sexually exploited by her father. Did he groom her as a child as he tried to do with her friends? Carol's mother was a tubby, jolly woman and I suspect she may have been in denial of her husband's obvious weakness. Carol got pregnant at a very early age, 14 or 15 I believe. She claimed it was by her boyfriend and I hope this was the case, because he stayed loyal to her at least for the first part of the baby's life. I speculated that early exposure to abusive sex may have been the reason for Carol's irresponsibility – becoming an unmarried mother at such a young age – otherwise she was such a sensible person.

My half-brother Philip was born on 17 May 1951. I was really excited about the prospect of having a brother or sister and couldn't stop talking about it during Mum's pregnancy. Even my mother had to admit that the teachers at my school laughed because I kept telling them "I'm going to have a baby". Unfortunately my mother also took delight in telling me how difficult I found it to adjust to Philip's arrival and how jealous I was of him. I now believe this was a deflective psychological move because it was she who was finding it difficult to cope with the situation of having two children by different fathers in such different situations. I suppose I was fortunate in not knowing then that I was illegitimate and a half-orphan by the age of 4 months; at least I grew up thinking I was wanted by both the mum and the dad I knew. My mother had a bad pregnancy with Philip and was laid up for several weeks. She used to tell me about an incident that was supposed to have happened during this time. Apparently I went into her bedroom on my birthday and said to her as she lay on the bed that it was the worst birthday I had ever had. I think it was meant to make me feel utterly hateful and selfish, but I could not recall the occasion and hotly disputed it. Several years later she told exactly the same story, but this time the complaining child was Uncle Cyril when he was seven years old, and the sick pregnant woman was my grandmother who was expecting my mother late 1919. I think this is the more likely story. I know my grandmother miscarried at some point in her pregnancy, only to be shocked on discovering she was still pregnant with a twin. My mother was delivered safely on 27 December 1919. Perhaps, by transferring the story of the complaining child onto me my mother hoped to gain some sort of emotional moral high ground, allowing her to love the new baby more. Philip's birth was probably celebrated more within our family because he was the child of the formal marriage and had all the traditional links and relationships. In addition from an early age Philip showed himself to have an easy-going personality, as my half-sister was to have later. He was not as self-willed and assertive as I tended to be, and must have been easier to love.

I stayed with my father's parents in Anerley while my mother was in hospital for Philip's birth and post-natal monitoring. When my father came to collect me and take me home, I was naturally keen to see the mother who I had not seen for several days and the new baby whose arrival I had so eagerly awaited. I will never forget the scene that greeted me when I was taken by my father into the first-floor front room of our Thornbury Road flat. My mother was sitting with Philip on her lap. The scene was just like a Madonna-and-Child picture in a church, with my mother looking very regal holding Philip with his special baby robes flowing over her in pretty folds. The problem was I couldn't get near them. My mother had two or three friends surrounding her like the adoring magi or shepherds and she hardly noticed me as I entered the room. I do not think I felt jealous – just surplus to requirements. I am sure my mother did not realise how I felt or I am sure she would have organised things differently. Twenty-eight years later I made sure I did not repeat this same mistake with my eldest son when I introduced him to his new baby brother. I gave him all the attention he needed before gradually taking him over to show him the new arrival. The two boys have been great friends ever since. My father seemed to be more aware of my needs than my mother. He had taken the trouble to find me a child's toy typewriter for a special present to commemorate the arrival of my brother. It might have been second-hand but in those early post-war days it was a luxury. I was very proud of my grown-up toy.

Quite surprisingly I think I was allowed to have a say in the naming of my brother. Before his arrival when names were being discussed I suggested Philip if the baby was a boy. There was a boy I knew and liked in Brixton Hill with that name. I thought this boy was very handsome and had a nice personality and so in my mind the name carried these same qualities. I also considered Philip to be quite a posh name. Both my mother and father agreed and accepted it for our new arrival. Philip as a Christian name was not too common in the 1950s, but it was becoming more so with the arrival of Prince Philip, the Duke of Edinburgh, on the national scene. My brother's second Christian name was Leonard, after his and my adopted father. It was a tradition in our family for the first son to have his father's name for his second one. Knowing what I now know I might easily have been jealous of my baby brother. He had all the trappings of a much-wanted member of the Lewis family. The pictures taken of him at his christening show him laid out in a beautiful christening gown made from the taffeta and lace of my mother's wedding dress, and for his christening cake he had the top layer of Mum and Dad's wedding cake. I have no pictures of my christening. My mother could not do the traditional thing of using her wedding-gown material and wedding cake for me for obvious reasons, and personal relationships must have been strained at my ceremony, not joyful as they were for Philip with his natural father, grandparents, aunts and uncles in attendance. Fortunately I did not realise this at the time, and would like to think that I would not have been jealous if I had known the facts – but who can tell?

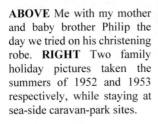

ABOVE Me with my mother and baby brother Philip the day we tried on his christening robe. **RIGHT** Two family holiday pictures taken the summers of 1952 and 1953 respectively, while staying at sea-side caravan-park sites.

Once again while living in Brixton Hill I attended a Sunday school. This time, it was one belonging to the local Baptist church. The children across the road were able to take me and this saved my mother the trouble of making the journey herself. Just as with my previous Sunday school I enjoyed going to that one too. Some years later I met an older girl who had gone to this same Sunday school and we exchanged memories. She told me that when the collection bag was circulated half way through the session, instead of putting the penny in that her parents had given her for that purpose she secretly took one out, and afterwards went to a sweet shop with the two pennies and bought a 2d (i.e. two old pennies) packet of ten Woodbine cigarettes. From early on I think I must have had a prudish streak because I found this revelation quite shocking. I dread to think how old the girl was when she began smoking, and wondered whether the shop assistants believed her when she said she was buying the cigarettes for her father. Perhaps they just did not care!

New Park Road Infants School S.W.2. 1949-1952
(in 1951 Renamed Richard Atkins School.)

My infant school in Brixton Hill was another one of my good childhood experiences. I must have attended it before my parents' actual move to the Thornbury Road flat because for the first week or two I remember being taken there by some boys on a bus. I imagine my mother wanted me to join my new school at the beginning of the academic term, but was finding it difficult to escort me there herself from our Clapham home before our family move.

It must have been the September of 1949 when I was enrolled in New Park Road School, because I remember seeing large trees in full leaf as I travelled with the boys along Brixton Hill Road towards Streatham Place on top of the double-decker bus. (I was pleased to discover some of the trees were still there in 2003.) This would make me four years and eight months old, and so it is a good thing my young companions were

42

responsible and looked after me well on the journey, because if they were in the school's junior boys department, they could not have been much more than ten years old themselves.

The fact that this school succeeded in teaching me to read, where the previous one had failed, has already been recorded. It was certainly a happy school. In particular, I remember the nature table and the nature broadcasts that we heard on the radio. The only bad memory I have at New Park Road School is the time I suffered some minor bullying, detailed on the following Memories Chart, in Appendices 1. Also mentioned on this chart is the time our class was told of the king's death.

School photograph from 1950

In 2003 I met seven other former pupils of the school for a reunion. We were women who had remained at the school into the junior girls department. Together we pooled personal memories of the school, and added them to the ones found on the internet on the Friends Reunited Memory Board. These form the substance of **Appendices 1** to follow, and the later **Appendices 3.** Some of the details recalled may be of interest to educational historians and researchers of London life in the 1950s. Several things are unique to the historical situation of Brixton Hill immediately after the war.

Appendices 1. Chart of Infant Memories (1949-1952)

New Park Road School

I have attempted – not completely successfully – to divide "infant" from "junior" memories that we as former pupils of the school shared at our reunion.

Appendices 1 is a list of what I believe to be mostly "infant" memories

(N.B. I personally have no bad memories of school dinners, or of unhelpful staff, but some of my schoolmates obviously did!)

Susan Bedser

I remember being in the annex, which was the congregational church hall opposite Pride and Clarks Motorcycles, (now demolished) on Brixton Hill. Miss Moore was one of the teachers and Mrs Dalton was the playground supervisor and the dinner lady who also gave us large spoonsful of malt.

Linda Bendy

I remember running betting slips between the headmaster and headmistress of the infant and junior schools. The only other pupils I can remember are a girl called Penelope, a boy Douglas, and another girl called Robina or Roberta Fureash who lived in the flats around the corner. There was also a girl called Margaret who lived in Lyham Road.

Marilyn Church

I remember the school milk they used to put on the radiators to thaw out when it became frozen in winter. It put me off drinking milk for life. I remember the cod-liver oil (or cod-liver oil capsules) we were given and the malt. I hid the capsules under my tongue and then spat them out. My mother said the capsules were the reason I never got a cold! (P.S. I do take them now!)

Wendy Duffy

I hated the smelly loos at school.
I remember the bakers and the one-penny (1d) loaves they sold.

Janet Knight

I was an ink monitor. I remember writing lines "I must not kick boys".
I remember Miss Footit in the infants and Mrs Culverwell (the head of infants before Miss Gee) who was very strict, and had a daughter called Penelope. I remember group violin lessons in the hall when I was six years old plus. I also learned the recorder and played it at an Albert Hall concert. I avoided the school dinners as much as possible. Mrs Chandler and Mrs Tamplin were the dinner ladies and I think they were mother and daughter. I remember the bombs sites near the school and the little corner shops. Bread, milk and coal were sometimes delivered by horse-drawn vehicles. I remember the third of a pint bottle of school milk we were given every day at school. The milk sometimes became frozen in the winter. I remember the toilets out in the playground. The first infants' classes were held in two wooden buildings in the playground.
We used to play kiss-chase in the infants' playground.

Yvette Grove

I used to be force-fed by the dinner ladies Mrs Tamplin and Mrs Chandler. Marilyn McMillan used to cry about half an hour before dinner each day because of these two ladies.

Maureen Lewis

*In the infants, I was podgy, and remember once having to stand with one or two other pupils on the bench under the shelter in the playground, while a few boys hooped around us calling me fatty and another girl four-eyes because she wore spectacles. I remember the nature table in New Park Road infants and also the radio programme we listened to about nature. I remember an infant teacher coming into our class with tears in her eyes, telling us, **"The king has passed away."***

Sylvia Phillips

I remember Miss Gee, the headmistress of the infants. I remember the sweet shop run by Sylvia Pollard's parents.

Carolyn Roll

I remember Mrs Gee, the head of infants. I remember in infants marching around playground on Empire Day waving the union flag. There was also a School Queen ritual just before we left. I loved sports day, but only ever achieved second place in running because Diane Carrell always beat me. I did win the high jump once. I remember the stables opposite in Moorish Road, and also the fish and chips shop and the bakers. They sold gob-stoppers and fizz-balls in the sweet shop next to the Hand in Hand Pub. The other sweet shop in New Park Road was opposite the church (All Saints), and was owned by Sylvia Pollard's parents. She was in our class. There was a bombsite nearby called Chubbs, where a firework party was held on 5 November. I remember lining up in school for a spoonful of cod liver oil and malt, which cost 1d (one penny).

Caroline Skinner

I remember being good at athletics and running against a tall black girl called Norma. I remember the two ladies on playground duty, possibly mother and daughter. The younger one had bleached blond hair, which she wore in a sort of bun or French knot. I once had a burnt foot with blisters through hot tea being spilt over it. I had to go to school with a bandage and a slipper on the injured foot.

Honour Smith

One day a seven-year-old boy called David, who was large for his age, defied Miss Moore to everyone's shock and horror. There were three classes in the infants; the first was in a little room at the front with the alphabet around the walls. The second was at the back of the hall somewhere. The only thing I can really remember about that class was the day we learnt how earthworms mix up the soil. It involved a lot of worms and the boys enjoyed waving them about near the girls to scare them. The top infant's class was held in half the main hall. (The assembly and dinner area was the other end.) I remember a teacher called Miss Power (Powell?) who was Welsh. She taught us England was an island. I told my mother who was not impressed. I joined the infants in the annex. About 1956/57 the bulge of war babies had moved on to secondary school, and the annex was abandoned. Pupils were once again all taught in the main school.

Brenda Stafford

I was in an attic classroom and was ink monitor. I had to fill the white china inkwells from a can that had a long spout and was kept on top of a cupboard. Once I reached up to get it and tipped the ink down the front of my green gingham dress, a teacher tried to sponge it out; first with some milk from the 1/3 pint bottles we were given, then with water. My dress smelt bad for the rest of the day. I was not popular at home for a while, and I had to continue wearing the dress for the rest of summer.

The dress retained the pale blue stripe of the ink stain despite being washed regularly. We couldn't afford to buy a new one.

At our 2003 Reunion we took a walk around the school's surrounding area, pooling personal and general knowledge of the area in the 1950s, and added some historical notes and other information taken from the internet. The result is **Appendices 2.**

Appendices 2. Clapham Park – Brixton Hill Walk

A guided walk for former pupils of New Park Road / Richard Atkins School, at their reunion on 04-10-2003 – with special reference to the 1950s.

Following a brief gathering with refreshments in the HAND IN HAND Public House, we step outside, stop and look at New Park. Road

New Park Road was once an ancient trackway of Streatham, and mentioned in a survey of the Manor of Leigham Court made in 1547/8. It was known as Balams Lane, as it led to Balham (i.e., westwards via the present Emmanuel Road and Tooting Bec Common). It was also once known as Bleak Hall Road, because, in 1650, it led to a farm of that name. The New Park Road Baptist Church, (originally called Salem Chapel) was opened by Rev W Knibb in 1842. He was a well-known advocate in America for the abolition of slavery. Tradition has it that the great man Verdi once stayed at number 138, Gothic Lodge, New Park Road, (now two separate dwellings) on one of his visits to London – and Jimmy Gould, one of the Crazy Gang, lived at 102, New Park Road. Clapham Park-Brixton Hill

The Hand in Hand Public House, seen from the school playground.

Richard Atkins School playground 2003.

The Hand in Hand public house that we knew from our schooldays (visually at least - being sited on the opposite side of the road to the school building) still functions as a pub today. It was built in 1822, and a licence was granted to a Thomas Spreadbury to sell spirits on the spot. On 5 August 1827 he was fined £1 for giving short measure to customers. The present building is Victorian, and was further modernised in the 1930s, when its flat roof was installed.

Just past the pub, in the 1950s, was Beannies, the sweet shop, (mentioned more than once on the Friends Reunited notice board). Customers went up steps before entering the shop. The shop building is still here, but the middle entrance-step is missing. Behind the pub, in Morrish Road, was the stabling yard. You used to smell the horses when you walked past it. Beyond the stables was a fish and chip shop; Janet Knights remembers paying 3d to buy a bag of chips there after attending Brownies, Friday nights. Occasionally she had extra money to buy a pickled onion too. On the opposite corner of New Park Road and Morrish Road was Cloutings the bakery. The firm sometimes delivered goods by horse drawn van, and there was always a lovely smell of baking bread at this spot. The firm Barretts are now (i.e., in 2003) building flats on this site. These will eventually extend down into Morrish Road. The Telephone Exchange still operates in New Park Road.

New Park Road Primary School was opened originally in 1896 by Joseph Rouse for the education of 95 boys. A year later, a larger building was completed for three departments, mixed infants, junior boys and junior girls. It was called Brixton Hill School at its opening, but later renamed New Park Road Primary School, and in 1951 was renamed again; this time to Richard Atkins School. In the early 1950s, there was a school annex in Streatham Hill Congregational Church, because of the additional pupils from the post-war baby-bulge.

Look on the other side of New Park Road, (to the right of the pub and Morrish Road)…

Number 42 used to be Keith's the Greengrocers, and is still a greengrocers' today. (Rumours that Keith had a fondness for young girls led to many avoiding the shop for fear of being molested), 44 was Joseph's the shoe shop (44/46 is now NDC, "New Deals for Communities"). The hairdresser's where Janet used to have her hair cut is still a hairdresser's. Pollards Sweet Shop run by Sylvia Pollard's family was once, (but no longer) in New Park Road. Janet Knights used to go to the shop and its flat to play with Sylvia, and occasionally stayed there for tea. Byng House in New Park Road used to be police flats, but is now McIntyre House and owned by Lambeth Council. Wendy Duffy, who now lives in Sussex, recently met a woman who had lived in these flats as a two-year-old toddler in 1953, the year of the coronation. She remembers being taken by her mother to the window to be shown Richard Atkins pupils marching past their flat, to go up to the cinema to see Sir Edmund Hilary's Conquest of Everest. The outing was a coronation treat for pupils. Diana Knight's Godmother Elsie Fulbrook used to live in Sulina Road.

Cross over the road and begin to walk down Kingswood Road……

This and surrounding roads were built in the 1880s.

Some of the 1950 inhabitants in this street were…number 82 (or 84?) Christine Stone and her family, 51 Valerie Swanborough her parents and brother Michael, (Number?) Eileen Ellis and her family. 48 Rosalina Cooper and family, (Number?) Linda Brown and her family, 30 Pat Abbott and her family, 28 Diana and Janet Knight and their family, 26 Thaddeus, Joan, Hugh and Mary Allen, (Mrs Cole the piano teacher lived opposite, in a downstairs flat), 24 Mr and Mrs Millard, 20 (or 22) Mr and Mrs Aldred and their bulldog, (They were one of the few families to have a television, and several watched the coronation on this set. Children also came to watch Bill and Ben, the Flowerpot Men, and Diana remembers seeing the Magic Roundabout on the set!), 14 Elizabeth and Ann's family, 14a was Oakdene, Theresa Higgins grandma's home. The Quatrini family lived somewhere near here too, 12 Sheila and Margaret Simpson's family.

In the 1950s Saxby Road and Kirby Road was a bomb-site before its development and many New Park Road School children went there to play without parental knowledge. The Rag-and-Bone man used to come to Forster Road and Thornbury Road to give a goldfish in a bag in return for recyclable goods.

Turn right into Thornbury Road

Maureen Lewis lived in Thornbury Road, from 1949 to 1952, in a flat that was then over a Co-op shop. Opposite was Snoswell's, the greengrocers' (owned by Joan Snoswell's family). Theresa Higgins also lived in Thornbury Road. She died as a young teenager.

Pause when you come to Lyham Road

This was once a muddy track leading to a disreputable area until the year 1858, when the residents of Clapham Park funded a road and a church (since rebuilt) on the corner. Kingswood Rd, Chale Rd, Wingford Rd, Thornbury Rd, Rosebury Rd and Thorncliffe Rd were all built in the 1880s. Woodleys Paper Shop sold newspapers, sweets, cigarettes, ice creams etc., in the 1950s. Now in 2003, it only sells newspapers, magazines, travel passes and stamps, but the family business is still run by Paul Woodley. Paul was a pupil at New Park Road Primary School, and remembers the war period when he and other pupils had to have an afternoon sleep to compensate for the air raids that kept them awake at night. Paul sat and won a scholarship for Henry Thornton Boys Grammar School. He transferred there in 1949, when only ten years old. Unfortunately he did not continue to pursue education or an academic career. Maureen remembers going to a local shop near or in Lyham Road to buy Neville's Cut Bread with a boy named Neville. Another point of note in the street is Brixton Prison. The mass murderer Christie was here in the 1950s. The adjacent prison wardens' flats are where Valerie Swanborough as a child had a friend she sometimes visited.

Go past the prison, turn right, walk through the passage by the prison walls to Brixton Hill………………

In the 1950s, the once salubrious and sought-after Brisco Buildings stood here. They remain, but have now been re-named Renton Close, and are far less salubrious. The Methodist Church is still in business on the opposite side of Brixton Hill Road. The building that used to house Biddy Pinchards' Dancing School can still be seen in Brixton Hill, and also the building that was once the Clifton Cinema, with its round turret.

Turn left at Brixton Hill Road, and then left again when you come to Blenheim Gardens, and the WINDMILL…

The Brixton Hill windmill is the only surviving windmill left in Lambeth, and stands in pleasant gardens. This land once belonged to Stockwell Manor, but was purchased in 1802 by a Southwark merchant called Christopher Chrysall Hall. A windmill was constructed here in the year 1816 and the following year it was leased to a miller called John Ashby. It is believed the Ashby family were originally from Ireland and were Quakers by religious persuasion.

Due to loss of the surrounding farmland through intensive building construction, milling was transferred to Mitcham in 1862, and the sails of the windmill were temporarily removed to leave the tower free for use as a storage unit. The sails have since been replaced.

Blenheim Gardens is where there was, and still is today, the Post Office sorting office that we knew as children. Irene Holbourn used to live at 48, Blenheim Gardens. Maureen Lewis remembers going to a party in Irene's house one day, and remembers meeting Irene's mother and father who were hosting the proceedings and looking after guests.

LEFT
Photo of the
Lambeth Windmill
© Robert Cutts – Wikipedia

48

Walk back to Lyham Avenue, through Ramilles Close............

In Lyham Road, there used to be a builders' yard run by Pamela Fawns family, a bootmaker's/repairer's was on the corner of Chale Road and on the opposite corner was Penties the grocer's shop, run by the Pentecost family, (now Phambra, an Asian food store). The Wagon and Horses Pub is still to be found in the road. It used to have a bad reputation, and prisoners were once caught drinking there. All Saints Church still conducts its services in Lyham Road, but in a new building to the one we as pupils knew in the 1950s. Sylvia Phillips lived in the once smart flats opposite the church, Valerie Wimpenny lived in Dumbarton Road, and Carolyn Roll, Penny Brocklebank, Ruth de Souza, Janet Sinclair lived in the flats at Dumbarton Court, considered up-market homes of the time, but no longer so and have since been taken over by Lambeth Council. Gillian Clack lived in Roseberry Avenue, Rosalie Spencer in Wingford Road, and Ann, Eileen and Ron Crawford lived in Chale Road.

Continue on to the left, back to New Park Road...OR – if you wish to see the Richard Atkins Monument – you may want to take a cab, or a bus or do the forty-minute walk to St Paul's Church, Clapham Common, Old Town.

FOR THE CONTINUED WALK........... *turn right into Lyham Road – then left into Crescent Lane, go over Kings Avenue, past the school and then turn immediately right into Park Hill. At the end of Park Hill, continue straight over into Clapham Park Road which will lead you to Clapham Common Station. Cross over the main road and slightly to your left is "The Pavement", follow this around, bearing right and it will lead you into Clapham Old Town, and eventually to Rectory Grove. At the very end of Rectory Grove you will find St Paul's Church, and inside, in an inner room, the monument.*

The present St Paul's Church was built in 18 15, on the site of the old parish church. The church and its surrounding community have had strong links with radical movements such as the suffragettes, anti-slavery and evangelistic movements. Many names such as William Wilberforce are associated with the area, and the Clapham Sect was a significant political force here. The church's most impressive memorial is that of the Atkins family, who were once Lords of the Manor. It contains five marble figures designed by William Stanton. Sir Richard Atkins died in the year 1689, but before this he commissioned a memorial to be made for his three deceased children, Henry, Annabella and Rebecka. After Sir Richard's death his wife Dame Rebecka in 1691 commissioned a chest tomb to be constructed for her and her deceased husband. It was to support two life-sized figures of the pair. Dame Rebecka died in 1711.

When the old parish church was demolished, the Atkins Monument disappeared. It was discovered fifty years later buried deep in a vault. The grand monument was re-instated in the new St Paul's Church, and in 1970 was cleaned and restored. The first member of the Atkins family to buy Clapham for £6,000 - thus becoming Lord of the Manor - was an earlier Henry Atkins. He was physician to King James 1st, and believed to have cured the infant Prince Charles of a dangerous fever. Following several generations, the Atkins line eventually died out; the final heir dying in 1756, unmarried and without offspring."

If you have survived so far, you may wish to hobble over to The Windmill Pub on Clapham Common for a drink or two, or perhaps an evening meal.

I left New Park Road Primary School late 1952, due to another family home-move. By then, the school had been renamed Richard Atkins School. I was however able to return and be a pupil in the school's junior girls department in 1954, for the last part of my primary school education. Needless to say, the reason for this was a further family home-move.

Chapter 4

Greyhound Lane, Streatham Common, S.W.16. 1952-1954

I do not know exactly when we went to live in Greyhound Lane, Streatham, but it must have been during the summer of 1952, because I was no more than seven years old. I distinctly remember that as being the age I was when I had what I considered to be my very first boyfriend. His name was Michael Hall and he was a pupil in my class at the new school, Woodmansterne Road Junior School, Streatham Vale. Michael and I used to walk home together arm in arm along Streatham Vale towards Greyhound Lane, both feeling very grown up. One day my mother came up unexpectedly to meet me with my brother Philip in his pushchair. When she saw me and Michael walking along the pavement, I immediately felt embarrassed. My main aim in life was to make my mother take me seriously and I knew I had now given her a chance to ridicule and laugh at me for my early attempt at romance. I was the tallest girl in my class and Michael was the tallest – and in my opinion the handsomest – boy. Apart from Michael there was another boy I liked, but in a sisterly way. He was a jolly, tubby lad. I was fond of him because he used to do cartwheels around the playground to amuse his classmates. I thought he was very outward-going and brave considering his weight problem. I was a bit fat myself, and knew what an effort it was to remain cheerful and positive in such circumstances.

Woodmansterne Road School S.W.16. 1952-1954

Mr Zoeftig was the headmaster at Woodmansterne Road School (I think this is the correct spelling). I cannot remember the name of my first class teacher there, but I remember his character well. He was a youngish man who did not get overly involved with his pupils as my teachers at New Park Road School had done. The only time I remember him interacting with me in a personal way was when he threw a book at me across the classroom that hit me on my head. He then accused me of bullying one of the other girls in the class. I felt victimised. I could not remember any confrontation. Usually I knew if I had been unkind to someone, like the time I previously recorded in my grandparents' garden in Anerley. The teacher did not describe the bullying incident, and I was given no opportunity to challenge his accusation. I felt particularly hard-done-by because I could not share this incident with my mother. From day to day I never knew what mood she would be in or how she would react. Even if she decided to believe me, she often did not help matters with her impulsive reactions, so I kept the injustice to myself for some time. When I did finally tell her what had happened, she declared that if she had known at the time she would have gone to the school to "sort the teacher out". My mother could punish and belittle members of her family, but woe and betide anyone else who tried.

Class photograph taken at Woodmansterne Road School.

The teacher who threw the book is in the centre. I am the tubby girl sitting on a chair, second from the left. The boy who did the cartwheels is on the far left, second row down, with his shirt tied up at the waist, I think Michael Hall may be the boy standing in the same row behind the teacher – although I do not recall him as being so plump

Another memory I have of Woodmansterne Road School is of the room that we had to go to have our spoonsful of malt and our cod-liver oil capsules – health perks for war and post-war pupils. It was a small room, probably a storeroom, and on a wooden table by the wall was a large jar of malt with a dessertspoon nearby which was dipped into the thick sticky malt mixture and handed to us pupils to be licked clean before being sterilised ready for the next pupil. A further memory I have of the school is of its crab apple tree in the playground. I had never seen a crab apple tree before. Once again, as a phenomenon of nature it seemed to hold some magical significance for me, and the image of it has remained indelible in my mind to this day. This tree gave our playground a real rustic atmosphere, especially with the distinctive smell it emitted in autumn when it shed its fruit.

On the way home from Woodmansterne Road School, I would sometimes cross over the main road in Streatham Vale to buy a penny currant bun from the baker's shop the other side. My pocket money was a penny a day and so I sometimes used it for this purpose. It was a fair distance between my school in Streatham Vale and my home the far end of Greyhound Lane near Streatham Common, but in those days there was little danger in a seven-year-old making the journey alone or with friends and many of us did, and I'm sure the walk was good for our health.

In my second or third term at Woodmansterne Road School, the coronation of the new queen was being celebrated and our school organised a pageant for the occasion. My class was chosen to portray the work of Florence Nightingale and her nurses in the Crimean War. I gather from this event that not all the teachers at this school were in the same frame of mind as my book-throwing class teacher and his dislike of me, because another member of staff chose me to take the leading role in our class's tableau. I was to portray the heroine, Florence Nightingale, and take centre stage. The pageant was the only occasion at Woodmansterne Road School where I remember feeling proud, other experiences were not so positive or memorable. I recall little of my lessons or my learning progress there, although that is not to say it was not a progressive school – perhaps I just did not adjust to my new situation! I think my so-called boyfriend Michael Hall may have left the school by the time of the pageant. At some point I remember him moving with his family to live in Manchester.

The Coronation Pageant held at Woodmansterne Road School

Pupils are dressed as nurses and wounded soldiers in the Crimean War. I am sixth from the left in the back row trying to look like Florence Nightingale despite the fact that I thought my mother hadn't done too good a job on my head-gear, which looked more like a baby's bonnet!

One lasting memory that the school has left me with is of class singing-practices in the school hall. Traditional hymns such as "All People that on Earth do dwell", "He who would Valiant be", "Holy, Holy, Holy, Lord God Almighty", "Let us with a Gladsome Mind", "Immortal, Invisible" were practiced. I can still hear the piano tinkling away and the unusual, multi-syllabic words of a different era resounding through the premises. These words, despite the caution of present-day educationalists, gave us no trouble in pronouncing and eventually understanding. Children in the 1950s were given educational challenges, not watered down so-called play-learn activities that later pupils were to receive. However on the whole I looked on Woodmansterne Road Primary School as more of an endurance than a pleasant learning experience.

Other than the school pageant I have no further recollection of 1953 coronation celebrations at the school or elsewhere in the Streatham area, apart from a special children's party I went to, held at Telferscot Road School, Balham S.W.12. The building of this school bordered Streatham Hill where Aunty Kit and Uncle Harry lived and it was through their link with the Sternhold Avenue Coronation Party Fund that a ticket was obtained for me.

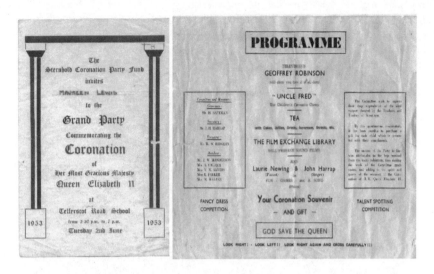

I should have been grateful I suppose. I know Aunty Kit and Uncle Harry had put themselves out to get me the invite. I was not a resident of the area and did not really merit the ticket. The main problem I had was that I did not know any of the other children at the party and so the organisation seemed rather orchestrated and impersonal to me. I played along as best I could – did as I was told – sat where I was placed and joined in with the activities. At one point the leaders wheeled a television-set into the hall for us to watch some of the coronation proceedings, and at the end of the party souvenir gifts were given to each child. The pageant and the party are the only two coronation events I am able to remember. My friends at Richard Atkins School in Brixton Hill seem to have remembered and enjoyed far more. I still have a coronation teaspoon that was given to me either at Woodmansterne Road School or at the Telferscot Road party. It is now old and tatty; some of the red, white and blue enamel around the top inscription has worn off. I believe I may also have received a coronation mug, but this has long since disappeared – unusual in my case with me being a natural hoarder as can be seen from the party programme I kept and still have – shown above.

As with my previous two homes, I continued to attend a Sunday school near my new home. This time the Sunday school was held in a building only a short distance from our flat. To get there I would walk up to Streatham High Road, turn right, go past Immanuel Church and then walk into Factory Square where the Sunday school building was. This building had originally been the church's primary school. Immanuel Church was about to become a prominent part of my childhood and teens, although my early memories of involvement are vague, but I do recall the alleyway we had to walk through to get to the Sunday school building and the first-floor room where our class was held – but little more

It was down this same alleyway into Factory Square that my mother went for her part-time job in Cow's Factory when we lived in Greyhound Lane. She went there a few evenings a week to help make gas masks, although the firm probably was more famous for its production of Cow Gum. After the war some firms continued to make gas masks as a precaution against any possible future chemical attack. My mother brought a gas-mask home one day for us to see, and I remember trying it on.

1972 photo of Immanuel Church School, designed 1861 by Gilbert Scott, and situated in Factory Square, now demolished. (I think my Sunday school class was held in the top first-floor room of the jutting out wing on the left.) All three images © Ideal Homes

The public drinking fountain situated in front of Immanuel Church 1950.

P.B. Cows Rubber Factory, Streatham Common – seen from Immanuel Church tower 1985, during redevelopment.

FACTORY SQUARE, STREATHAM.
In 2002 the book "From Silk Mill to Superstore. 1820-1989" was published.
It was written by Brian Bloice, a member of the Streatham Society, and outlined the history of Factory Square, Streatham, South West London.

Mr Bloice's book utilises some of the research of local historian, John W. Brown, another member of the Streatham Society, who had spent time exploring the background to Factory Square, the site that faces Streatham Common. This site was one of London's oldest and most important industrial areas, and Mr Bloice surmised that many of the present-day shoppers drinking coffee in the coffee shop at Sainsbury's Superstore now adorning the site, would be unaware of this fact and the site's history.

The story begins at the time of the Napoleonic Wars, when Stephen Wilson, a silk merchant from Hoxton, Middlesex (now East London), heard about the new Jacquard Looms operating in France. He decided to visit Paris and investigate the matter further. His enthusiasm was soon frustrated however, when he was arrested by the French authorities who put him under house arrest there for five years. On returning to England Mr Wilson moved to Streatham, near the common, where he found a large house to live in. It stood where Texaco Garage now stands, at the junction of Streatham Common South and the High Road.

It appears Mr Wilson's spirits were not dampened by his French experience because he continued to pursue his interest in the new Jacquard Looms, and subsequently, in 1820, he subversively engaged French agents to obtain some of the revolutionary new machines for him, and set about secretly building a large silk mill opposite his Streatham home to house them in. The position of Streatham was advantageous because it was far enough away from Spitalfields, London, where most of Mr Wilson's English rivals operated, and far enough away from the regulating authorities in Central London who were keen to uncover non-compliance, and whose suspicions might be aroused by his business. Mr Wilson's last act of preparation was to smuggle in a French weaver, who would be able teach local employees how to work the new looms, and produce intricate silks more cheaply and quickly than his English rivals.

In 1831 the Streatham silk mill was flourishing and employing 20 weavers, but misfortune continued to follow Stephen Wilson and the business was comparatively short lived. Fashion trends were changing, and the repeal of the Spitalfield Act in 1826 saw an influx of cheap silk and other fabrics from abroad, lessening the impact of produce from Mr Wilson's Jacquard Looms.

By 1838 the silk mill was no longer viable, and Mr. Wilson rented the site to Thomas Forster for use as a rubber factory. In 1857 Peter Brussey Cow joined Thomas Forster and the two men developed one of the largest India rubber works in the country. In 1893 it was employing 500 people, but after 150 years this too became an impracticable business, and the site was sold on to the Sainsbury's firm for development as a supermarket that opened in 1989.

Another part-time job I remember my mother having when we lived in Greyhound Lane, which may have followed, preceded, or been current with the factory job – I'm not sure which – was ice-cream lady in the Gaumont Cinema, Streatham Hill. Once or twice I went with her and was able to watch the films being shown there. Cinemas in those days usually put on two films per session with an interval between to show newsreels and advertisements. Some of the films I saw were made for an adult audience and so I did not always understand what they were about, but nevertheless I enjoyed going and seeing my mother at work. She looked very important walking up and down the aisle in the intervals in her smart uniform – an overall that covered most of her clothes and a matching headband. She carried a torch and a large tray of ices and drinks suspended in front of her by a band that hung around her neck. I also enjoyed being made a fuss of by her friend, the usherette, who made sure I was sitting in a good position and not bothered by anybody. Another cinema in Streatham, The Odeon, Streatham High Street, was where I went most Saturday mornings for a children's matinee programme. Sometimes I went with Michael Hall and together we would watch Shirley Temple, Charlie Chaplin, Laurel and Hardy, cowboy and other films. We also saw cartoons and children's newsreels. Halfway through a man we called the Master of Ceremonies would organise yo-yo competitions, quizzes and other events for us on the stage in front of the screen, and occasionally there would be a magician to entertain us.

My father also took on a part-time job during this period in Streatham. In addition to being a full-time Cooperative grocery assistant, he became caretaker of the Cooperative Hall which was just over the road from our flat in Greyhound Lane. On occasions I accompanied him there and amused myself while he did his cleaning. It was like having an indoor playground all to myself. I can still smell the wooden chairs, parquet floors and the cleaning liquids my father used on them. Several social activities took place in this hall including Woodcraft Classes, the socialists answer to the Boy Scout and Girl Guide movement I believe. I went along to one or two Woodcraft sessions myself and remember sitting at a long table doing craftwork – nothing too exciting, and certainly not as stimulating and character building as the activities my sons were later to enjoy in the Scout Movement, although I'm sure the Woodcraft organisers were doing their best to keep London youngsters interested and occupied.

At some point during 1952–1953 my father won a television set in a raffle and we really thought we were going up-market. This and few other pieces of good fortune, together with the extra money brought in by the part-time jobs my parents were doing, meant we could have a few more luxuries, and go on family outings together. I remember taking day-trips to Box Hill, Leith Hill and Chipstead Valley, especially in the bluebell season. It was probably at my mother's prompting. Now that we were a family of four, she may have felt the stigma of having a baby out of wedlock had been forgotten and that we were now seen as a proper family. She often reminisced about the days when she was a girl and went on outings with her parents in their Ford car. I suppose she wanted to relive those happy times. Taking public transport to places on the outskirts of London was not quite as glamorous as going by a family car but the next best thing.

As our finances improved Dad began to bring home a few new gadgets and gimmicks, nothing too big, the latest design for a cruet-set dispenser, a new electrical invention, and so on. He loved innovation, but Mum got cross and thought he was wasting money. Dad also enjoyed continuing to experiment making things in his backyard workroom-shed. I suppose this was a habit he acquired from working with his own father in Anerley, making things like my dolls' house. I remember being with my father in his workroom on a few of these occasions. While he was occupied with his carpentry, I would attempt to nail two pieces of wood together or saw a small object in half. If only this innocent father-daughter relationship had continued my father would have made an excellent mentor and role model.

Our flat in Greyhound Lane was quite spacious, and it spread over two upper floors. Once again, the flat belonged to the Cooperative Society, with a Co-op grocery shop operating beneath us, and, similar to Thornbury Road we had a back yard that we shared with the shop. I loved this home. It was in a very convenient location at the bottom of Greyhound Lane, opposite Streatham Common. Over the road to us there was a small bus terminus outside the Greyhound Pub. The number 130 bus to New Addington stopped here in the 1950s, and I think the 118 bus may have paused there too on its semi-circular journey between Mitcham Common and Clapham Common. In fact we were central for much of the local public transport. Several buses went along Streatham High Road, one or two went down Greyhound Lane towards Mitcham and Tooting. We were not far away from three overhead train stations, but there were no trolley buses and trams as in former times, or underground trains.

In addition to good transport links Streatham enjoyed facilities such as a large public library, an ice-rink, a dance hall, a theatre, swimming baths, (with two other open-air lidos not far away at Brockley Park and Tooting Bec Common,) three or four cinemas and a large, posh departmental store called Pratt's. I once bought my mother a pretty embroidered handkerchief in an exclusive presentation box from Pratts. It was to be a special present for her. I made a big effort at times to try and please my mother. I loved her but just could not get on with her.

The departmental store Pratt's of Streatham, circa 1950.

My friend Karen Fagan was a shop assistant here in the early 1960s, by which time the store's frontage had been updated, and in my opinion made less attractive than the one I knew in 1952.

The famous Old Crocks' Race used to pass by at the bottom of Streatham Common on its way to Brighton once a year. We only had to walk about fifty yards or so from our Streatham flat to watch it. At least once my father took me out to see the old cars drive past as we lined up with others on the pavement at the bottom of Streatham Common. Although I do not personally recall it, my friend Karen tells me there were still post-war prefabricated houses situated at the bottom of common in the 1950s.

Our move to Greyhound Lane did not improve my parents' volatile relationship. One evening Mum asked me to look after Philip while he slept in his cot so that she could go out. She wanted to catch a coach that was returning to London from a Co-op works-outing with Dad on board. Companies such as the Cooperative Society made a big effort after the war to provide a good social outlet for their staff. It was quite late when she went and I think she hoped to catch the coach as it turned back into the depot and offloaded its passengers, but she came back home alone. I suspect she had missed the arrival of the coach otherwise, knowing her, she would have confronted my father there and then. Soon after Dad came home and another blazing argument began between them, with my mother claiming she had seen my father get out of the coach in a clinch with another woman.

Somehow, I do not think I helped matters as a child and teenager. I am sure I unforgivably did some occasional social stirring. For instance there was the time when we were on holiday in Climping, Sussex, at a caravan site, and went to nearby Littlehampton for the day. At some point, my father wondered off and I caught him looking at a "What the Butler Saw" machine. These machines were accepted as good harmless fun. They merely showed a few saucy scenes of nude women, but I think I knew what my mother's reaction would be when she heard about it. I intentionally dropped my father's activity into a later conversation and my mother immediately found an excuse to start yet another row with my father. In my view she definitely had some sort of sex fixation. Most of her jokes and innuendos were sex orientated and she always thought she was so extremely clever in what she said, while I just thought she acted like a silly teenager, not the with-it modern woman she imagined herself to be. When I was not much older than twelve years old, she repeated a punch line from a film she had seen that amused her. Someone in the film had said, "She was only an undertaker's daughter, but she loved to lie under the sod." I pretended to be humoured, but didn't think it was particularly funny or a clever pun although I understood the double meaning. When I was older, I shared many sexual jokes, double-meanings and innuendos with friends, but I considered my mother to be sex-obsessed and smug. She seemed completely wrapped up in her own opinions and views of relationships, sex and life, and found it difficult to accept that there might be different points of view. This attitude did not help my father who not long after began to develop some minor perverted sexual behaviour that was to have an impact on the family and me in particular.

For as long as I can remember my mother went to central London once a month to draw money out of the Canadian Bank, and on some of these visits she would take me with her. The money as I later discovered was my pension from the Canadian Government, the one my mother claimed was an endowment she had taken out for me before my birth. When I joined her on these trips I was sometimes allowed to choose and buy a small gift from one of the department stores. In hindsight this may have been her attempt to keep a link between me and my natural father. On one of the last trips I went with her – I must have been about ten or eleven and living in Balham by this time – I begged her to let me buy a toy golliwog. I had not had one before and although I was well past the age for dolls, I felt I had missed out. She allowed me to buy one in a Woolworths' store and for once did not make me feel stupid or childish. The 1950s had not yet reached the age of political correctness and there was no one around to tell me I was being racially insensitive, which is just as well, because I went on to enjoy a full adolescent social life with many friends including ones with black Caribbean and African heritage. Having a golliwog did not make me patronising or prejudiced. To me the toy was just another loveable caricature like Mr Magoo, Popeye, Pinocchio, Dizzy Lizzie and so on. I have grown to hate the politically correct lobby who try to dictate what should be done and said by others. These people usually have no idea what causes real racism and are often unwittingly and subconsciously racist themselves.

I imagine my mother went down "Memory Lane" on these monthly trips. It was on one such outing that she pointed out to me the Stork Club behind Regent Street. She told me she had frequented it during the war, leaving me later, with better knowledge, to wonder whether it might have been one of the haunts she was taken to by my natural father.

Uncle Cyril continued to play an important role in my life at Greyhound Lane. I began to put him on a pedestal, and treat him like a hero. I also developed an innocent romantic crush on him and remember once being alone and singing and dancing around a broom wearing a housework-pinafore over my clothes. I was standing in front of a first-floor living-room window in Greyhound Lane imagining I was Cinderella and that Uncle Cyril was coming to take me away to some wonderful palace beyond the rainbow just like Prince Charming – when to my surprise I suddenly saw him through the window coming through the back gate into our backyard. He was not expected, and it was just a coincidence that I had been thinking of him at that particular moment.

A family picnic in woods behind
the Rookery Gardens, Streatham Common, 1954.

By this time Uncle Cyril was working as a steward on the big ocean passenger liners. When he was on leave at home in England, he would always come to see us and every time brought us along some exotic foreign gifts. I was given items such as a sandalwood-wood fan from the orient, which smelt absolutely divine, a bisque-faced life-size American walky-talky baby-doll and toy koalas. He even sometimes brought back beautiful parrots for us to keep as house-pets. Mum was relieved once on hearing that he had dropped the idea of bringing us back a live monkey for a pet. I probably enjoyed Uncle Cyril's presents more than any others I received, because although Philip and I had lots of gifts to unwrap at Christmas and birthdays from our many real and adopted aunts, uncles and cousins, these occasions were usually very unhappy times for me. They were often marred by family disputes and arguments, many of which seemed to centre on something I had said or done. Perhaps my mother found these times particularly stressful, or perhaps I was especially wilful during the lead-up to these busy celebrations; whatever the reason, we always ended up having rows. The excitement and anticipation of fun, presents and good food was overshadowed, and I would go to bed in floods of tears and remain miserable throughout the festivities. Fortunately Philip was too young to understand the family dynamics in Greyhound Lane, and later in Cavendish Road his placid temperament helped him escape many of the squirmishes. My mother openly admitted she would rather have had ten sons than one daughter. She also continued to claim that I was jealous of my brother whereas I really felt I loved him, if anything I was sorry for him having been born into such a dysfunctional family. I enjoyed mothering Philip and playing with him. Once when he was still a baby, I was allowed to hold him while my mother sat nearby. I felt very privileged. Then the worst possible nightmare happened; I accidentally tripped and dropped him. I felt awful and believed I would never be forgiven. Fortunately Philip was not hurt and my mother did not tell me off or make me feel too guilty on that particular occasion, which came as a great surprise and relief to me.

Chapter 5

192, Cavendish Road, Balham, S.W.12. 1954-1963

We could not have lived in Streatham long before we moved on once again, and I do not know the reason why. Our new flat in Balham was adequate but not nearly as big and spacious as our flat in Greyhound Lane had been with its first and second floors. We also did not have the same convenient surroundings that we had become used to in Streatham. Once more my parents were renting a Co-op flat over a Cooperative grocery shop. I do not know whether my father was working in this Balham shop at the time of our move. I can remember him working there at some point, but as before he continued to move around to other branches as and when required. Moving to be near work was definitely not the reason for our move. The journeys between Streatham and Balham and other South Suburban Cooperative shops in south London were not that excessive anyway, especially for Dad with his bike.

Our new flat had a street door in Yukon Road but the front of the flat faced Cavendish Road. As we went through our front door, we were faced with another door immediately to the right. This led into the Co-op shop but was rarely opened or used. My father had a key to it if access to the shop was urgently required at any time, but I can only remember the door being opened once or twice during our whole stay there. We used the main entrance of the shop to go in and buy things or to see friends who were working there. Inside to the left of our front door was a flight of stairs leading up to our living accommodation. At the top of the stairs, the first room on the right was the kitchen. In addition to Mum cooking and doing other domestic chores here we also ate our meals in the room sitting huddled round a small kitchen table, all that the limited space would allow. The next room along the corridor on the right was a bedroom. This became mine. The room after that was another bedroom and was given to Philip. He was rapidly growing into an active toddler and needed his own space. The door after that, facing you at the end of the passage and stretching across the whole width of the flat opened into a fair-sized front room that had windows looking out onto Cavendish Road at the front and Yukon Road to the right. My parents put a double put-u-up bed for themselves in this room. During the day it was folded up to the wall leaving a comfortable lounge or front room for all the family. I particularly remember the fire grate in this room; it was on the left-hand party-wall. In winter open coal fires were lit there making the room very cosy as we sat in comfortable armchairs reading or watching the television.

On the other side of the flat's corridor, to the left as you walked away from the stairs, was first the toilet. On opening the door, you were faced with the water-closet, to the right of which was a large airing cupboard containing an emersion heater and a couple of shelves to store linen and the vacuum cleaner. On the tiny wall to the left of the WC was a small window that overlooked the shop's backyard. We had our own backyard in Balham, situated just beyond the shop one. The tiny wall to the right of the room was the dividing wall between the toilet and the bathroom, the next room along the corridor on the left. Our bathroom had no windows at all. Its back wall like that of the toilet was the divider or party-wall between our flat and the adjoining property. The small left-hand wall of the bathroom was the divider with the toilet and the small right-hand wall was the divider with the front room. We entered the bathroom through a sliding door which helped save some space. This room was the only one that had access to the roof-loft and so a ladder was kept in it to reach the hatch-door when entrance to the loft was required. There was a bath, sink, linen basket and some small shelves for toiletries in the bathroom, but little space for anything else.

My father made quite a few small home-improvements in our flat to compensate for its compact nature. He built shelves and small cupboards over doors, in alcoves and wherever he could; he customised facilities and decorated each room in turn. My mother had a good eye for colour and design and we tried to be as modern in décor as possible with our limited finances. Strong colour was the fashion of the late fifties and I had black patterned wallpaper in my bedroom with mauve or purple paintwork. This was my choice I believe, and my mother never argued where modern trends were concerned.

A popular flooring material of the 1950s was the hard, industrial-wearing linoleum tiles. I remember a neighbour, Leslie Smith, (Les,) coming in to lay some of these on our kitchen floor. He worked for the Marley Tile Company and I think he was able to get hold of end-of-production tiles, or left-over ones, because our floor looked really stylish when it was finished but he had had to use several different colours and made them into a chequered Harlequin-type pattern. I do not think the job cost us much money despite Les having to spend several days at our flat to do the work. I have since wondered whether he might have been having an affair with my mother at the time. He, his wife and two young sons lived across the road from us in Yukon Road. It was my mother who first befriended them and my suspicion about a relationship was fuelled when I realised my mother was aware of some intimate details concerning Les and his wife – not the sort of details a neighbour, man or woman, normally shares with another neighbour, more like pillow talk between lovers. I also remember my mother being particularly silly, gigglish and girly when Les was around – although having said this she was naturally flirty by nature.

Soon after our arrival in Cavendish Road, at the age of nine or ten I was old enough to go off for reasonable periods of time and for reasonable distances on my own. We were within walking distance of both Clapham Common that I had known as a baby and toddler, which was to the north end of our road, and Tooting Bec Common with its swimming lido at our road's south end. I would sometimes walk to Clapham Common with friends and go fishing. We took jam pots and children's fishing nets hoping to catch a few tiddlers in the ponds there. On my first fishing outing I was not sure what to do, but a passer-by told me to sweep my net close to the side of the pond, around the edge where the plants clung. I did this and immediately caught a very large tiddler. It was beginner's luck, and this success was not repeated too often after that but it was still fun, and on a couple of occasions, I was able to bring back home a few small tiddlers in a jar of water to keep as temporary pets.

I cannot remember my mother having a part-time job outside the house at Cavendish Road, but my father kept his part-time caretaker's job at the Co-op hall in Greyhound Lane. He rode there on his bike when his services were required. Mum wanted him to better himself and get a car, but he seemed quite content with the bike. He would cycle along Cavendish Road to Tooting Bec Common, over the common, through Sternhold Avenue, down Streatham High Road to Streatham Common and Greyhound Lane. Later, as a young teenager, I sometimes did this journey by bike myself. My mother did however take a part-time job within the house. She took on some baby minding to supplement our income and I appear to have made myself the champion of the children that she minded, looking out for their interests. Perhaps I imagined half the problems and may have been over-critical, but I definitely felt she was occasionally being cruel and hurtful to the children in her charge, both emotionally and sometimes physically too. I can remember her false feeding some of them when they were being fussy about their food, and there was one incident concerning a young brother and sister that caused me some heartache.

Philip had been wearing his Red Indian costume and he had tied up the pair with a rope and was unceremoniously dragging them around the flat as he whooped and treated them like victims ready for a lynching. My understanding was that the children were petrified but were trying to look as though they were enjoying the game because they had no other choice. My mother ignored what was going on and made no attempt to show Philip, who was too young to judge for himself, how to incorporate sharing and collaboration into his play. He did not realise he was being dominant and I felt she should have helped him consider the needs of his playmates. I am sure Philip did not mean to be rough with the children and he has since grown into a loving, and thoughtful individual so he could not have been greatly influenced by these early incidents, whether real or imagined on my part.

This brother and sister were from a single-parent family. Their mother went out to work in a desperate attempt to keep herself and her children in the bare necessities of life and was dependant on my mother's support. She thought she was doing the best for her children's future but did not realise how miserable and lost they were from the moment she left them at our flat until her return when they began to smile again. On the few occasions I tried to tell my mother that I did not like what was happening she seemed to turn-the-tables and made it appear as if it was me who was out of touch, and the one who did not understand the welfare of children. It was implied (but not said in so many words) that I should not interfere or my life would not be worth living. There was little I could do anyway. It is just possible that because of my own unhappiness at home I took a biased view of the situation. Unfortunately there is no one to give an objective, balanced observation of these incidents. They were things that happened behind closed doors and I can only give my impression.

Other than Les and his wife we had other family friends in and around Balham. In my view they were mostly people who seemed to be in awe of my mother. In company she was the life and soul of the party, full of joviality and good humour even if her jokes were mostly at someone else's expense. Lillian and John were still very much on the scene and through them my parents were introduced to a crowd who lived in the Walworth area of South East London. As a family we began to go over to Walworth for all-night parties at Christmas-time. The other partygoers were not what I would call my mother's usual choice for companions. Normally she would have considered them "common" and "rough diamonds", being a snob she preferred to mix with a more "refined sort of person" but the Walworth friends seemed to serve a purpose. They were a bit outrageous, full of fun and allowed my mother to let her hair down when she was with them. One or two of the crowd played the guitar, and apart from the availability of food and plenty of drink at these parties there was also lots of bawdy singing accompanied by suggestive actions. A few other children and I would join in enthusiastically singing our hearts out and feeling very grown up, not knowing all the implications to the words and actions we were using, but knowing they were saucy. As children we tried to stay awake as long as possible, but invariably slipped off to the makeshift beds long before the adults did.

One couple my mother befriended in Balham were Edie and Joe. They were not such social creatures as my mother's other friends tended to be but they were easy going, open to suggestion and had the knack of boosting my mother's ego. Sometimes my mother would ridicule the pair behind their backs, especially Edie for her old-fashioned and obsessive ways; for instance Edie possessed two of everything, in case one of the items broke down. Edie and her husband allowed my mother to act out her fantasies of grandeur and so they remained friends for a long time. Like Lillian and John, Edie and Jo too had no children. My mother continued to remind me that children ruin your social life and nobody wants you when you have them.

My mother also kept up regular contact with Jean and Bert Simcock, before they left Acre Lane, Brixton, for Devon. Sometimes Mum used to take me and Philip around to their flat during the day. Mum would talk to Jean, while Philip played with her son Richard who was close to his own age, and I amused myself. Occasionally we visited the Simcocks in the evening, when my father and Uncle Bert had finished work. We also continued to visit Aunty Kit and Uncle Harry at their home in Sternhold Avenue, Streatham Hill. Once when I was older and went there on my own, I met a young man who turned out to be the Deans' estranged son. Aunty Kit was becoming very asthmatic, and I suppose her son was trying to forget wartime family problems and be reconciled.

Holiday photos taken circa 1956, after our family's move to Balham.

Two family snaps taken while staying at a holiday caravan site. In the first I am with Philip on the beach and in the second standing with a friend I had met at the caravan site.

Richard Atkins Junior Girls School. S.W.2. 1954-1956

The move to Balham suited me at least in one very definite way. I was able to return to my old school, New Park Road Primary School since renamed Richard Atkins School. It was some distance from our Balham flat but easy to reach on the number 118 bus. I was nine years old and joined the junior girls' class, penultimate to the one where we as pupils would be taking the eleven-plus examination for secondary school selection. My re-admittance was especially fortunate because the teacher I was given for those two crucial years was a very gifted and talented woman called Mrs Litschi. In addition to having a teacher with expertise, many of my new thirty-nine classmates were to become very good and long-term friends.

By 1954 I was overcoming much of my personal insecurity. My self-esteem was increasing and I was developing good peer relationships and losing the puppy fat that I had been plagued with. Mrs Litschi was a factor in nurturing some of this newfound confidence. She encouraged me and her other pupils individually, but also ensured we gelled together as a mutually supportive body. Perhaps not everyone saw Mrs Litschi in quite the same light as I did, as memories on the following juniors chart in Appendices 3 will show, but the evidence is that most of her pupils developed into happy, self-fulfilled individuals who excelled academically above normal expectation. A high proportion of her class went on to attend grammar schools and many of the remainder took up places in special technical schools.

Lessons at Richard Atkins School were child-centred and activity-driven. Pupils were exposed to community events, celebrations and character-building exercises, alongside what I believe to have been an excellent academic curriculum. The "Three Rs" were taught methodically and thoroughly, alongside a variety of drama, music, sport and art challenges. Several of us kept photographs taken at our drama productions and still have them in old age, including the following one that was taken 1955, during our Christmas pantomime performance. Some of us took it along to the 2003 reunion.

LEFT to RIGHT
Rita Allen=pageboy
Wendy Duffy=chimney sweep
Irene Holbourn=Cinderella
Maureen Lewis= fairy godmother

Class Photo
Centre back=Mrs Litschi
Left of Mrs Litschi=Diane Carrell
Left of Diane=me with my wonky fringe.
Carole Watson is in front of Mrs Litschi slightly to her right.

The only event I came to regret at Richard Atkins School was connected to one of the drama productions, and my remorse was not of the school's making but the situation I found myself in. I had been chosen to be a medieval-lady in a period play, and my mother had gone to the trouble of making me a lovely medieval costume in bright red and green with matching, pointed headdress. Our class rehearsed carefully towards the final performance, then at the last minute, Uncle Cyril wanted to take me on an outing to Whipsnade Zoo to meet Phyllis, his new woman the day of the performance. He had often socialised and paired up with women he had met as a steward on the ocean liners, but Aunty Phyl, a Welsh woman, was becoming a permanent fixture in his life. I am not sure whether there was a special reason why the outing had to be that particular day but I was given no other option. I wanted to go with them but also did not want to miss acting my role in the play. In the end my mother persuaded me to go to the zoo and my medieval dress was lent to a stand-in. After that any public stage performance I took part in seemed to be marred with nervousness and anxiety; I developed feelings of extreme stress whenever I had to do something, or say something before an audience from that time on. I suspect the guilt of having let down my teacher and classmates was too much to come to terms with.

As mentioned in chapter three, eight of us former pupils of Richard Atkins Junior Girls School met up for a reunion in 2003. Appendices 3 is a list of our junior school memories alongside other reminiscences that were added from the internet's Friend's Reunited Memory Board. Members at the reunion admitted the experience gained in Richard Atkins School helped to form our characters and equipped us well for secondary education and our future careers.

Appendices 3. Chart of Junior Memories 1954-1956

Richard Atkins Junior Girls School

To repeat......... I have attempted – not completely successfully – to divide "infant" from "junior" memories.
Appendices 3 *is a list of what I believe to be mostly junior memories*

Linda Bendy

I was suspended for pulling other pupils' hair. I left in 1954/55. I remember having Black Beauty read to us by a teacher every Friday afternoon. I sometimes rang the bell at the end of playtime. I remember running round a big tree in the playground on Empire Day wearing my Girls' Brigade uniform, (others wore Brownie uniforms etc.) On Coronation Day, I had to meet with others at Streatham Hill Station 4 o'clock in the morning, in the rain, and carried the Richard Atkins School placard with the girl called Penelope.

Susan Blow

I left Richard Atkins when I was 8 or 9 years old to go to Fenstanton. I remember Jennifer Tideman, Barbara Connolly and a girl called Pauline.

Wendy Duffy

I was a skinny pupil and possibly bossy. I left in 1956. I remember Linda Greenwood and Mary Rastell, who I think lived at 107, New Park Road. I have recently been in touch with Pamela Tyler and Yvette Grove through Friends Reunited. When at school, I lived near Gloria Young and Sandra Goodfellow. I remember Mrs Litschi and Mrs Holland. My grandmother used to know Mrs Litschi's mother and taught Mrs Litschi's daughter Isolde to play the piano. I remember needlework in particular and geography where we were once taught about Switzerland. I did not go on school journey. I remember a day at Windsor and with other pupils watching the queen and Duke of Edinburgh drive past. I also remember walking up Brixton Hill to the cinema to see the film of Sir Edmund Hilary conquering Everest. I recently met a woman who lived in the police flats, Brixton

Hill, as a two-year-old in 1953. She saw our class walking past her home to see the Everest film.

Yvette Grove

I left in 1956 I remember Carolyn Roll, Sandra Lummis, Pat Coates, Gillian Wright, Sandra (i.e., Sylvia) Pollard, Irene Holbourn, and Maureen Duffy (i.e., Maureen Lewis + Wendy Duffy). Mrs Litschi and Mrs Holland were the best teachers in the world, and I sometimes wonder what happened to Mrs Holland. I have recently been in touch with Mrs Litschi's daughter, Isolde, who like me now lives in Australia.

Irene Holbourn

I was the pupil who always stood in the corner for talking! I left in 1956. I remember Gillian Ball, Eleanor Zemit, Yvette Grove and Dorothy Jarvis. I can't remember much about lessons because I seemed to miss so many, standing in the corner as I did. I remember staying in the Hotel Bonair, Paignton, Devon, on school journey. I remember Blenheim Gardens where I lived, and the bakers. The loaves cost 1penny (1d).

Janet Knight

I remember learning some of the sewing stitches. I remember knitting squares and being a prefect in top juniors. I left in 1957.

I remember Gillian Clack, Theresa Higgins, Daphne Mitchell, Janice Gamgee, Claire Shipman, Ruth De Souza and Sylvia Phillips who lived in the flats at the top of Lyham Road. I also remember Irene Holbourn from Mrs Litschi's class. I remember Miss Davies who played the piano in assembly, Mrs Freeman (did she teach music?), Mrs Litschi, Miss Booth (poetry). I remember Miss Morley the head of juniors quite well. I went to school journey in Paignton Devon. Mrs Litschi was the organiser and she took along her husband to help. We stayed at the Hotel Bonair. I shared a room with Theresa Higgins. We had a trip to Kent's Cavern and one evening we went to a show on the pier. (I remember singing Que Sera Sera.) I remember sports days on Tooting Bec Common, and the Lynham Road Gymnastics display for which I have photos. I remember the Coronation in 1953 and receiving commemorative presents, and also waiting in Christchurch Road for the queen and Prince Philip to drive past. I remember the tests we were given leading up to the Eleven Plus exam, and the children lining up in front of the class according to the marks they got. I remember the skipping-games in the junior girls' playground. Other crazes we had at the time were cats-cradle, hula-hoop, luminous socks, hopscotch, two/three balls and Davy Crocket hats.

Maureen Lewis

I left juniors girls, in 1956. I remember being friends with Lesley Broughton, Geraldine Johnson and also Dianne Carrell who lived in the Poynders Gardens Flats near to me. (I lived in Cavendish Road, Balham when I was in the juniors.) I also remember going to a party in Irene Holbourn's house. I had a love-hate relationship with Colleen More. I remember Carole Watson, and remained friends with her for some time after I left Richard Atkins. Mrs Litschi has always stayed in my memory. I remember her in a stylish black dress that was rouched up in front of the bodice with some embroidery on. I remember her telling us about meeting her husband in Switzerland after the war when she went on a skiing holiday. She said he had come to England with her because it was not easy to find work in Switzerland. I loved the school journey week in Paignton, Devon, and remember going to Cockington, Totnes, Kent's Cavern and travelling to these places by coach. I remember the eleven plus exam and Mrs Litschi walking round and trying to give us encouraging looks.

Sylvia Phillips
I left in 1956 I remember parading in the playground on Commonwealth Day dressed in my Brownies' uniform. Others wore uniforms of the organisations they belonged to.

Carolyn Roll
I left in 1956. I have had contact since with Yvette Grove, Linda Greenwood, Sylvia Phillips, Diane Carrell and Valerie Wimpenny. Brenda Newman was my best friend at school. I remember Mrs Holland and the junior girls' head teacher Miss Morley. I know some of the pupils liked Mrs Litschi but I found her rather fussy and old-fashioned. My happiest memories are of the drama lessons. I was a Brownie, an elf, an old lady and once played Ali Baba in a school show. We did lots of drama and I loved it. We were once asked to memorise a poem or some pros and I memorised "to be or not to be" from Hamlet. I can still recite it today. Mrs Litschi found out my dad had bet me a shilling I wouldn't be able to learn it by heart and she derided me for it. I think bribery is the best form of motivation myself. I use it all the time. I remember "Topics". For this I put together a scrapbook on the queen. Miss Morley wasn't too happy with my effort as we were supposed to choose a more educational subject and include more writing. (Someone even made a rug!) I know I had memorised all my times-tables by the end of infants' school, and I was certainly not alone in this. I remember buying dinner tickets for school dinners. I thought the school dinners were foul, and I hate peas-pudding to this day. The dinners used to arrive in large metal containers and were heated up in the building at the end of the playground. (This had turned into two classrooms by the time I returned there to do an evening class some years later.) Sometimes we found insects in our vegetables, and there was lots of fat on the meat. I remember running to the pig-bins before the dinner ladies could make me eat up the grots. (These are my worst memories of Richard Atkins.) We were allowed out of school to go home at dinnertime if we wanted. During the break-times I sometimes played with a tennis ball in a sock, or two balls against the wall. I remember the yoyo craze and hula-hoops.

I will never forget the school journey to Paignton, and staying at the Hotel Bonair. They had a plague of crane flies at the time. They were everywhere. I shared a room with Yvette and someone else. One day, I locked Yvette out of the room in her pants. I got told off for not taking a proper school shirt with me, and Miss Morley sent a postcard to my mum saying, 'Please send Carolyn a school blouse.' My mum was not well off at the time, and probably had to go without something herself to buy it. I never wore it again after the school journey. I remember a wardrobe falling on top of me in the hotel room. Yvette went outside the room yelling and jumping the stairs three at a time. Mrs Litschi came into the room, and saw I was stuck on the floor under the wardrobe. I remember her saying, 'It's all right! It's only Carolyn.' I remember the Eleven Plus results being read out in class, and the disappointment on one girl's face when she heard she had failed. I remember before the university boat race one year lining up outside the classroom door of 4C – Oxford supporters on left and Cambridge on right. I remember the prefect system in the top juniors. I used to be horse-mad when I was at school. Generally I was very happy in primary school, and Richard Atkins inspired me to enter teaching as a profession. My dad also went to New Park Road School, as it was called in his day. I have a picture of him taken there about 1918. A few years after leaving Richard Atkins, I remember Christine Stone winning The Twist dancing competition at Clapham County School in the sixth form.

Caroline Skinner
I had a friend in the flats in New Park Road. I left Richard Atkins in 1957 to go to Dunraven School.

Honour Smith
I left the junior girls' in 1959. I have a photo of our class taken about 1955, which shows we were in a class of forty pupils.

Valerie Swanborough
I did not always keep to the school rules. I left for grammar school in 1955. I knew Sylvia Pollard in Mrs Litschi's class, and went to her home at the sweet shop in New Park Road for tea, and to play. Mrs Litschi took me for needlework. Her subject report for me said, 'Weak, absolutely lacking in effort. I remember a teacher called Miss Wapalong who became Mrs Leigh.

Valerie Wimpenny
I left in 1956. My mother was friendly with Valerie Swanborough's mother. I have been in contact with Diane Carrell and Carolyn Roll. I remember Christine Stone well and her lovely singing voice. I also remember a girl called Beatrice who was very poorly dressed and looked like a waif. She was unlikeable as a character. Mrs Litschi was still at Richard Atkins when I went back there to do my teaching practice. She was very helpful. I had always got on with her when I was a pupil, but she once hit Beatrice so hard it made her fall over. In Paignton, on school journey, I banged my head in a fall. As a result I caught pneumonia after returning to London, and had to have three months off school. It affected my performance in the Eleven Plus examination.

Most of the class in my last year at Richard Atkins went on school journey to Paignton, Devon with Mrs Litschi and another teacher. (The class that went the year after were accompanied by Mrs Litschi and her husband). The coach came to collect us from the school gate and we drove off down New Park Road. My mother came and stood on the pavement with Philip in the pushchair to wave me goodbye. The day before I had been brave enough to ask her if, on my return, she would make me lemon pancakes – my favourite dessert. I was sufficiently confident to ask for the occasional favour by this time, but still felt as though any request I made to her was an imposition.

The school journey was packed with interesting things to do. I can still picture most of them in my head. We had visits to Kent's Cavern, Cockington, Totnes, Babbacombe and Dartmouth. There was leisure-time on the beach, fun and games at the hotel and a visit to the local theatre. My best friends in the Paignton hotel were Lesley Broughton and Geraldine Johnson. I do not think my other friend, Diane Carrell, went. In my eyes Mrs Litschi was an excellent organiser, allowing pupils sufficient freedom and emotional outlet to explore their surroundings while in the background remaining strongly in charge. As I have said, there were one or two pupils who thought otherwise, and some of their comments are noted on the Junior Memories Chart. Carolyn Roll in particular recalls problems with her school uniform in Paignton, and some messing about in a hotel wardrobe which consequently collapsed.

LEFT-Colleen Moore and Geraldine Johnson at Hotel Bonaire, Paignton, while on school journey, 1956.
ABOVE-Junior Girl school prefects 1956. Back row left to right =Christine Stone – me (with wonky fringe) – Diane Carrell.

Former members of the Richard Atkins Junior Girls School at our reunion in 2003.

Mrs Litschi and me at her home in Sutton Poyntz, Dorset, when I paid her a visit in 2003.

In her role as class teacher Mrs Litschi was not afraid to share some of her personal life with her pupils. On the Memories Chart I have recalled how she told us about meeting her husband in Switzerland. She also sometimes mentioned her daughter Isolde, who was a few years younger than our class – but she never put her family on a pedestal; she merely fed enough information to make us think about our own lives. Perhaps Mrs Litschi's influence and this new period of my assertiveness unwittingly increased the emotional wedge between me and my parents.

About this time my father began to show signs of personal stress. I am convinced that in the beginning he tried to be a good father, but from about the age of seven my mum would often wait for him to come home tired from work and then start complaining about my behaviour. She would tell him how I was becoming more and more uncontrollable, expecting him to take on the role of disciplinarian. He would often end up by hitting me even though he was unaware of all the circumstances leading up to the alleged misbehaviour. It made me very resentful. I began to despise him for being so weak and easy to manipulate, especially as from the age of nine other areas of my life were becoming increasingly happy. I was developing new interests and new hobbies. Mrs Litschi helped with this but I was also encouraged by friends and relatives. I began to build several collections – stamps, miniature dolls-house accessories (plaster casts of cakes, meals on plates, joints of meat etc.), celebrity autographs and so on. I also began to go out more on my own or with friends to markets, swimming pools and fun fairs. One of my friends at Richard Atkins School, Diane Carrell, lived quite near me in Poynders Gardens Flats. It was easy for me to call round and see her at her home. I always felt welcome there. In fact, it surprised me how many of my friends shared their families and homes with me. I usually felt more comfortable in other people's homes than I did in my own. I remember Diane's mum teaching me about mushrooms one day when she was getting some ready for their tea. She told me how to prepare and cook them. Mushrooms were a vegetable my mother avoided for some reason. I was not everyone's best friend however. Colleen Moore was one girl I had several arguments with. Her mum came up to the school one day and told me Colleen had lost her dad in the war and I should be nice to her or she and Colleen's older brothers would come and sort me out. Colleen's mother was a very large lady, unsophisticated with straggly shoulder-length hair and uncensored speech. She was definitely not one to try and cross. Mum seemed uncharacteristically angry when she eventually heard about it a year or two later. When I learnt that my own natural father had been killed in the war, I realised the reason for my mother's reaction.

As said, Dad seemed unsympathetic in what I considered to be my mother's unfair judgement of me, her constant accusations and her ways of putting me down. She would make me feel guilty for anything and everything that went wrong. I would be the death of her she repeatedly said, and she often threatened to come back and haunt me when she was dead. I began to grow a thick skin and didn't let the emotional blackmail hurt, but this only made her more hateful. She would lash out verbally and physically, and I suppose I did wind her up at times. When she lost her temper anything might happen; once a wooden brush was thrown at me causing a deep bruise on my arm. Occasionally when Dad was not around to do it for her she would use a stick or a strap on me herself; once or twice my mother pulled my hair. Looking back as an adult I now know my mother must have become emotionally unbalanced and was letting out her frustrations in the only way she knew how. In my teens I tried to discuss our family problems with Uncle Cyril, and I remember him muttering something to the effect of "I think she may be jealous of you". I could not understand the reason why; I did not have my mother's privileged upbringing or the attractive looks she had had when young. Another time Uncle Cyril hinted my mother was "not quite all there" – and this from a loving brother who was without doubt very fond of his sister. Many times I cried myself to sleep at Cavendish Road. I wanted my mother to come and comfort me, but I can only remember one occasion when she made a weak half-hearted attempt to do this. In the end, I began to retaliate and be hateful myself. I resisted the physical attacks when they came and in my mid-teens began to physically fight back with her and my father. I started looking at my mother with distain; the way she sipped her hot drinks loudly particularly filled me with disgust for some reason. I often recoiled and saw her as an item of contempt. I was too immature to view her as just another unhappy victim of circumstance who could not cope with life.

Philip was no longer a baby, and I wanted so much to be part of his life. Whether it was me being an over-bearing, bossy, older sister, or whether it was my mother in the background stirring up discontent between the two of us and causing problems I do not

71

know, but my mother always seemed to be around interfering, and straightforward games and play would turn into a battlefield. With this tension Philip would often get frustrated and once or twice when he had pencils in his hand lashed out at me. I carried semi-permanent lead-marks under the skin on the palm of my hands for several years after these stabbings. Philip is not an aggressive character, and in my mother's eyes it was always my fault if something went wrong. "You got what you deserved," she would say. She never showed an interest in building a good positive relationship between me and my young brother.

Streatham Junior Red Cross Cadets S.W.16 1956-1960

At some point towards the end of my time at Richard Atkins School, I became a member of the British Junior Red Cross cadets.

I had made up my mind that I was going to take up nursing as a career. The cadet unit I joined met in a public building in Pinfold Road, Streatham, a few yards from the main public library, not far from the Odeon Cinema. Once again, I used the faithful 118 bus to take me from Cavendish Road to the venue. When I transferred to secondary school my fellow Junior Red Cross cadet companion for many of these bus rides was a girl who, like Diane Carrell, lived in the Poynders Gardens Flats; she was my age and a pupil of Rosa Basset Grammar School. She too planned on taking up nursing when she left school. With similar ambitions we soon became friends, although I have since forgotten her name.

My junior cadet group was for girls only. I do not know if there was an equivalent group for boys in Streatham. The uniform we wore was navy skirt and beret, white blouse and socks (or stockings) black shoes, and I think we had a slim red tie. Our leader was a plump, motherly woman who took us through several Junior Red Cross programmes including First Aid, Home Nursing and Mother Care. Each programme culminated in an oral test and a practical test. The first time we were examined in one of the programmes we were presented with a certificate if we passed. The programmes rotated, and so we would eventually return to the same programme again. When tested for a second time in this programme the questions and practical task would be harder, and if we passed this time we were presented with a superior proficiency certificate and a medal to pin on our blouse that we wore with pride on our Junior Red Cross parades. The main Junior Red Cross cadet parade was held annually in Central London. I remember marching past Westminster Abbey with my Streatham group on these occasions; in front of us and behind were cadets from other parts of London and the Home Counties. After the parade we attended a service at St Margaret's Church. Apart from the annual parade, and some smaller more local ones, we also had the option of attending a few public events such as rallies, sports meetings, and fairs where we would help members of the Senior Red Cross cadets give medical aid and attention to those who needed it. Although we were only children, or young teenagers, we treated our Junior Red Cross activities with great respect. We felt privileged to belong to an organisation that had purpose and structure and (if I am honest) we enjoyed being on display to the public.

I am sure the discipline of the Junior Red Cross regime – the parades, drills and study courses – paid off in the improved attitude and approach we had to life in general. We practiced drill every week before our study session. We would stand to attention – at ease – march round the room – right wheel – left wheel and so on. After being a member for some time I was made one of the group's section leaders, and eventually I became the head section leader, in other words top girl of our group. Unfortunately about this time things at home began to deteriorate rapidly and my attendance and effort at the Junior Red Cross cadets dropped. During my more reliable period however the leader asked me if I was interested in becoming a member of the Wandsworth Council of Youth, to represent our association within that body. (Streatham was then part of the borough of Wandsworth, not Lambeth as it is now.) I agreed, and thought it would be a new experience, and another interest for me to chalk up for future reference.

Clapham County Grammar School S.W.4. – Part 1
1956-1962

At school I worked hard, and when I took the eleven plus examination, I was found to be border-line for a grammar school place. This meant I was able to go for interview and sit an additional exam to try and gain one of the retained places that were held in grammar schools and used at the discretion of the school governors. I applied for one such place at La Retraite Roman Catholic Grammar School. This school was on the corner of Atkins Road and Cavendish Road only a few yards away from our flat. It would have been very convenient for me travel-wise, and with my Christian leaning I would have felt at home with its religious ethos. However I was not a Roman Catholic, maybe for this reason or for some other, my application was side-lined. I was then accepted for exam and interview at Clapham County Grammar School and surprised and thrilled on finding out that I had been granted a place there. I knew my handwriting, grammar and spelling were anything but "polished", but I think I probably had a logical approach to educational tasks and showed a bit of a creative flare. My mother was obviously pleased that one of her family had done something noteworthy to boast about for a change. She told Aunt Lizzie, who in turn passed the news on to her friends, one of whom (possibly Aunt Ada) claimed Clapham County was "only an ordinary county council secondary school". Mum indignantly found the papers that stated it was in fact a "grammar school for girls".

My mother and I went to a firm in Victoria, London, called Kinch and Lack to get my new uniform. Miss Willey was the headmistress when I first arrived as a pupil at Clapham County School. (We pronounced her name Will-ee but most people these days prefer to pronounce the name While-ee to avoid jokes and puns.) She was a very conservative person and consequently our uniform was very traditional. My mother had to order a velour hat with brim and hatband for winter, a panama hat with brim and hatband for summer, a winter gymslip in navy-blue and square necked white blouses to go with it, sax-blue gingham dresses for summer, old-fashioned strapped house-shoes to wear inside the school, sensible brogue shoes for journeys to and from school, navy knickers, knee-length navy blue pleated shorts for games, navy blazer and topcoat with the correct school badge on – and so on. It was a new experience for me. I'm not sure how my family afforded this uniform, perhaps we received a council grant or in hindsight my mother may have acquired the money from my Canadian pension fund. As soon as we collected the uniform from Kinch and Lack, I put some of it on and went around to show it off to Diane Carrell and her family. Many in Mrs Litschi's class had managed to gain a place in grammar school, but Diane was not one. She had, however, been offered a place in a good technical (or commercial) school called Ensham in Tooting. Her uniform was to be green and included a sensible beret. I now realise it must have looked as though I was going around to boast and show-off, but this was certainly not my intention; I was just excited. In their usual kind way Diane and her family did everything to make me feel good about myself, my new school and the uniform. I knew that Diane with her gifts and talents – and being the thoughtful intelligent person she was – would succeed wherever she went and whatever she did.

FOOTNOTE – I regained contact with Diane, now married and surnamed Storey, towards the end of 2008. She had indeed had an eventful and very successful life without the asset of a grammar school education.

Personally I believe that a good educational opportunity at that point in my life was crucial for me. It was a much-needed morale booster. I needed something to counteract the negative things that were happening at home. If I had gone to a more regular school, I think I would have sunk socially, emotionally and motivationally. I needed the challenge, though this is not the answer for everyone. The grammar school regime is only useful to pupils who can relate to firm discipline and who have a strong concentrated focus, and of **ALL** my faults in youth, these two were not among them.

In my first couple of years at Clapham County I did well, gaining top marks in French and Latin and very high marks in several other subjects. I loved the novelty of learning in a place that had special science laboratories, customised music rooms, a fully stocked library and so on. I also loved the firm behavioural guidelines and institutionalised rituals, many of which were far more formal and sophisticated than I had been used to before. At dinnertimes we had properly organised dinner tables with two monitors sitting at the head of each table serving out even portions of food from large metal containers to the six surrounding diners. The cutlery on the table was laid out properly, and to my surprise we used a spoon **AND** a fork for dessert. For the curriculum we had special kit for art, sport and science. We went on field trips, had concerts, debating societies, visits to the opera and much more. In the first year, I progressed from the bottom ability form, Class 1B1 where I had originally been placed, to Class 1B, and then in the second year I went up further to Class 2A1. I was awarded several progress prizes that I received on Speech Days, going up onto the assembly hall stage to receive them – and my literacy and language skills improved greatly from having been

74

introduced to Latin that helped me to understand certain structures of the English language. Regrettably this progress slowed down and had almost evaporated by the end of my third year. There was a dramatic increase in the problems at home and I suppose I allowed my teenage social life to distract me from these mounting emotional pressures; my earlier serious approach to studies took a back-seat at this time.

I made many new friends at Clapham County. In the first year, I was friends with a girl called Barbara Ramsay. Barbara and her parents were friendly, jolly, well-built individuals. They lived in Clapham North with Barbara's serious looking older brother who wore forbidding Buddy-Holly style spectacles, and her young sister. Mr Ramsay was a long-distance lorry driver. I do not think the family had a lot of money but they shared what they had, and in the summer of 1957, they took me and a friend of Barbara's brother on holiday with them to Pevensey Bay. They rented a bungalow at the top of the pebbled beech. I enjoyed being away from my own family for a while, but my home situation must have been playing on my mind because I woke up one night screaming my head off in bed, having had a terrible nightmare. Mr and Mrs Ramsay came rushing in to see what was happening and to comfort me.

While at Pevensey Bay our party went on several outings. One was to a large public garden with greenhouses, another time we went to see a Doyle Carte production at a theatre. Holidays with my parents rarely included such a variety of activities. This personal and emotional freedom I was experiencing however was nearly the cause of my undoing. One day I went out swimming in the sea with Barbara and the two boys. I could swim ten yards quite confidently but suddenly I found myself being carried out to sea by the strong current and my feet would not touch the bottom anymore. Barbara was walking back to the bungalow by this time and could not hear me call out. I tried alerting the boys who were still swimming, but unfortunately they too could not hear me. Eventually I managed to get back to safe waters on my own. The incident taught me a powerful life-lesson – moderation and caution at all times.

After the holiday Mum asked the Ramsays if she could contribute in any way towards my keep. They refused saying it had been their pleasure to take me with them. My mother always had a strong compunction not to be beholden to anyone, so in the end she bought them a china vase as a thank-you present. In my usual extremely critical manner I thought it was a bit of a cheap and gaudy object to offer as a gift. I felt that if my mother had to buy something it should have been something of reasonable quality – but then I was not paying and I am sure the Ramsays were happy with it.

In addition to taking me on holiday with them Barbara's parents also took me, Barbara and her sister to play tennis on the public courts at Wimbledon Common once or twice. We went in their family car which for me was a novelty in itself; I travelled to most places by bus. The experience of seeing tennis enthusiasts properly attired and pursuing a sport for its own sake, together with other similar experiences during this period of my life, began to open my eyes to new social dimensions. Not being sporty or athletically inclined I did not continue my visits to the tennis courts, but I was glad I had been introduced to the activity. The limitations in my home background and culture were being severely challenged by my new friends and new experiences.

When I moved to Class 2A1 Sheila Haines became one of my best friends at the school, and we have remained close ever since. Sheila lived with her family in Earlsfield, London, S.W.18. Her father had a good job in the printing industry with considerable responsibility in Fleet Street. He worked with several prominent national newspaper editors and journalists. Having said this he had not developed the arrogant, superior attitude as some do in that position.

To me Sheila's mother appeared a sophisticated woman and an accomplished homemaker. I was probably biased having such a low opinion of my own mother but the Haines house always seemed well maintained and organised, attractively decorated and welcoming. Sheila was an only child. She told me her parents would have liked more children but were unable to for some reason. It was obvious Sheila was much loved and cherished by her parents, but she was definitely not spoilt. She always thought of others and shared her belongings. Once again, I had found a good friend and another home where I could go to relax and forget my troubles.

The chalet in Pevensey Bay where I stayed with the Ramsay family on holiday, in the summer of 1957

Clapham County girls on a channel ferry going to France in 1960, for a pre GCE field trip. I am in front, on the left facing the camera. Sheila Haines is sitting on my right.

Wendy Goodship was a further prominent friend in secondary school. She lived in a large ground floor flat or maisonette the other end of Balham to me. It was, half way up Bedford Hill on the left-hand side as you walked away from Balham Station. Wendy was a trendy individual. She was one of the first to wear black stockings to school. Black stockings were fast becoming the fashion of the time and initially banned by Clapham County and most other schools; I assume because they suggested some sort of rebel statement. In the end school authorities had to relent. They could not argue the ban on the grounds of impracticability or immodesty and more and more girls were ignoring this part of the dress code. In addition to being a fashionable teenager Wendy was popular with the boys. She had natural platinum blond hair and a good figure. This, together with her having an older brother, meant she had no trouble meeting and finding boyfriends.

Once or twice I hung around with Billybum; her proper name was Rosalind Williamson. From recent references on social media I gather Rosalind has since tried to forget her rather unfortunate school nickname. She was a well-built girl with short, blond, curly hair and she had a hoard of friends in the Battersea area where she lived with her parents and older brother. The Williamson home was a smart flat in one of the new council blocks that were built after the war. Mr Williamson was a professional chef and the family never seemed to be short of money or good food, while on the other hand, from what I could see, Billybum's friends tended to come from poorer more humble backgrounds. I went to a coffee-bar-cum-club with her a few times. It was near Battersea Bridge and I met some of the social crowd she mixed with there. These individuals appeared to be mostly older boys, possibly friends of her brother, and some of them looked as though they would be more at home in a borstal rather than in a respectable school or in a proper job and so it was a pleasant surprise when I discovered their appearance did not match their character. I found out that one of the boys regularly went and collected a wheelchair-bound young man from a local institution and integrated him into the coffee-bar crowd. The able-bodied ones at the bar-club helped to feed the young man who had poor coordination. They were not patronising or self-righteous about it – just good friends to a handicapped individual. I thought they showed a real streak of kindness and humanity and it taught me not to judge people by appearance alone. Through Billybum and the Battersea connection, I began to visit Battersea Fairground now and again.

Battersea Funfair opened as the Festival Pleasure Gardens in 1951 as part of the Festival of Britain. Sadly, it closed in the mid-1970s.
LEFT image = © John Barber – creative commons license
RIGHT image = © Estate of Roger Mayne / Mary Evans Picture Library

When I was thirteen years old, I took a Saturday job selling ice cream in one of the kiosks at Battersea Funfair. The kiosk owner knew I was under age for employment and paid me hardly anything. I did not think the money matched the commitment and so I gave the job up after only a couple of weeks. Battersea Fairground was the place to be seen in the late fifties and sixties. It was famous for its Easter Day Parade. Many film stars and celebrities attended this annual event and among others I saw Diana Dors, Terry Dene, and Arthur Askey.

My other recollection of the Battersea area is of the café-kiosk which was then situated south side of Chelsea Bridge. I suppose I must have been a little older when I was taken there because I remember being taken by a boy wearing his full leather riding-gear on the back of his motorbike. He took me to meet his biker friends who were sipping tea and coffee and eating hot-dogs by the stand. It was all good fun, with a little snogging thrown in. In those days we could enjoy being part of a group without having heavy personal relationships to contend with, complicating the social dynamics. Romance was usually of the light-hearted variety and non-serious. It was fun being young in the 1950s. In addition to an atmosphere of brotherhood within the groups of young people there was also little conflict.

A few years ago, following my retirement from teaching, I began to research my family tree and was surprised to discover I have deep family roots in Battersea. One of my great, great, grandfathers, born in the City of London became a businessman-merchant in Battersea, and his son my great grandfather, stayed on in the area and became an influential building contractor and was master of the RAOB Lodge at Battersea Park.

Another great, great grandfather came to Battersea from Dorset with his family. He was a qualified stonemason and came to help in the urban development and construction of the capital city. Had I known of my Battersea family roots as a teenager it would have increased my feeling of affinity with the area.

Returning to my Clapham County friends.........

Medina Johnson is someone else I remember from my Clapham County days. She lived with her mother and brother in a flat above a shop near Balham Market. I came to the conclusion Medina had no known-father. She never mentioned one, I never saw a man in the flat and there were no pictures to indicate a paternal figure. When I was a girl it was not uncommon to be the offspring of a serviceman who had been killed in World War Two, or the result of a short-lived wartime romance, but it was still far more usual to have two parents in the home rather than just one. I never discussed the situation with Medina but admired the way her mother, as a presumed single parent, had an occupation and managed to keep her family and home together so well.

There was also a pupil in my year called Evelyn Cohen. I took note of her because like Billybum she was well built girl with blond hair and blue eyes, but I thought this unusual in Evelyn's case because she was a Jewess, and her features were not those of other Jewish people I knew. She lived with her family in a large, smart detached or semi-detached house near the roundabout at the bottom of Atkins Road, S.W.12., (possibly at the top of Thornton Road.) Unfortunately one day the council decided to build a public toilet-block on this roundabout, greatly devaluing the family's property. This toilet-block has since been removed and when I last passed the roundabout the block had been replaced by vegetation and greenery. For some reason I remember two sisters at the school, Ingrid and Astrid Anderson. They were Scandinavian, at least in part, and had inherited classic Nordic features with pretty fair hair.

There were only a few non-English born girls in Clapham County School when I first arrived, and the first coloured girl I encountered there was Desiree Singh. (Yes – many of my early dark-skinned friends preferred the word coloured to black, the present supposedly politically correct word! You can argue and debate the inferences of these adjectives, but in my view, it is the tone behind the adjective that counts and not the word itself. Many of my Caribbean friends have, and are proud of mixed-race heritage – and so coloured is the description they prefer, not black or white but mixed.) I first noticed Desiree's presence about the middle of the second year, or year 8 as it is now called, but it has since come to my notice that she arrived at the school the same time as I had done. She had no inhibitions about her ethnicity and certainly did not play on the fact that she had a different colour skin to the rest of us. We in turn did not treat her in any special way. We might occasionally ask general questions about her life and circumstances as we did to each other and Desiree did not mind answering and joining in the banter. I personally do not know where Desiree had lived before arriving in Clapham, or the nationality of her parents. These things were not important to us; although I am sure her close friends would have posed such questions at some point. Desiree's physical features were African but her surname was Asian. As far as I can remember she did not have a strong foreign accent except perhaps for the hint of an American one. What was more important to fellow pupils was the attitude, personality and talents of their class mates and Desiree had a surplus of good attributes that helped her make friends easily. Pupils in the 1950s found a natural level of socialising with one another without any social engineering from above. We enjoyed each other's company without worrying about whether we were being politically correct. Later political developments in England with positive discrimination, social engineering and imposed multi-cultural reverence, has in my opinion ruined any chance Britain had of achieving healthy racial and ethnic integration. In the 1950s there was only a small proportion of coloured and black people in London and I experienced no polarisation of the communities. I remember seeing coloured or black people for the first time around the year 1952, when I was walking through Brixton with Uncle Cyril. We saw a group of Caribbean men, some wearing trilby hats, walking along the street and presumably going to work. Someone in our class at Clapham County School (possibly Yvonne Parret) said her aunt lived in the Caribbean and had seen posters on display trying to recruit local people to go and work in the UK to support its public services.

Some other girls I remember, though not close friends, were Do, Jo and Po that is to say Doreen, Josephine and Pauline. I was often linked to them by name because I was called Mo. Classmates loved to talk about Do, Jo, Po and Mo – silly and childish perhaps but it amused our young minds. I began to be known as Mo soon after arriving at Clapham County. I had not heard of this pet name before. It was explained to me that several people named Maureen (Moreen etc.) were called Mo for short, as was the case with Little Mo the famous tennis player.

"In 1953, a young girl named Maureen Connolly won the Grand Slam of tennis. She was the first woman to ever capture this elusive crown by winning the Australian Championships, the French Championships, Wimbledon and the United States Championships. She was only eighteen years old when she accomplished this magnificent feat. From that time on, Maureen was known as the incomparable "Little Mo". In July 1954, Little Mo injured her leg in a horseback riding accident which ended her tennis career, but she continued to be a major influence in the world of tennis."

© Harry Pot – Wikimedia

Our school did its best to try and widen the social horizon of its pupils. In the upper school, it attempted to ensure the shyer and more reserved of its pupils (certainly not me) enjoyed the company of boys in what the school considered a relaxed structured environment without flirtation being an essential factor in the equation. Consequently a periodic dance was held in the school, and boys from the local Henry Thornton Boys' Grammar School and a few others were invited along. These events centred mostly on ballroom dancing with a little rock-and-roll thrown in at the end of the evening. I remember on one such occasion dancing the foxtrot or waltz with Mrs Pinder's son, John. Mrs Pinder was our RE (religious education) teacher and was a very dedicated mentor. She worked hard for the school and her pupils. After her death at her memorial service we learnt that she never once used the excuse of being a wife and a mother to take time off from her teaching commitments and she did not slacken her effort or avoid extra responsibility when it was requested of her. Her son was a serious looking young man, not at all my usual choice of dancing partner, but he proved likeable, friendly and un-opinionated, and I suppose I was secretly flattered that the son of a teacher had asked me to dance with him.

Mrs Pinder knew only too well the single-track mind of teenagers. In class, she tried to give pupils a balanced view of life especially where romance and sex were concerned, and we as her charges frequently found ways to bring personal questions and issues into our RE lessons. We knew these would divert Mrs Pinder from the lesson-topic and lessen the prospect of our being given subject-related homework. Mrs Pinder was keen to reason with us on the necessity for restraint in sexual matters as she responded to questions such as "How far should I go with my boyfriend?", "Is heavy petting really wrong?" and so on, all put to her with dead-pan faces. Most of us already had an opinion on the matter and knew our own minds, but in her innocence Mrs Pinder assumed we were seeking guidance and tried to educate and persuade us into making sensible choices, while the "Journey of the Israelites through the Wilderness", or whatever other topic had been scheduled, was forgotten.

My closest friends at Clapham County were all very different to each other. For a period of time I knew and associated with a Welsh girl called Mary Price. She was different in outlook, interests and personality from those I have mentioned already, such as Barbara Ramsay, Sheila Haines and Wendy Goodship. Mary was the daughter of the Baptist minister at Ramsden Road Baptist Church, Balham. On the couple of occasions I went around to see her at the Baptist manse near the church, where she lived with her father, mother and younger brother, the family always welcomed me but with so much going on, phones ringing, visitors calling, etc., I never really got involved with them. Mary was a fairly modern girl and she had a couple of mild teenage romances but she was primarily dedicated to her studies. In attitude I sometimes felt she was a bit of a snob, especially when my own priorities began to alter in the third year. Mary had big ideas about her future career, the people she hoped to mix with and the type of person she wanted to marry. It probably irritated me because I was beginning to lose focus in my own life. By the end of my fourth year all I wanted to do was survive, while Mary (at least in my view) was anticipating being offered a place at Oxford University (in the end she was content to accept a place at York University) rubbing shoulders with the elite and being courted by a rich young man from a well-established family with good financial and career prospects. Despite our different outlooks on life Mary was an interesting person and I am especially grateful to her for introducing me to the Baptist summer schools that I enjoyed so much as a teenager.

Baptist Summer Schools 1960-1961

The first residential Baptist summer school I attended was in Lytham St Anne's, Lancashire, near Blackpool. The idea of Baptist summer schools was to give young people a good well-organised holiday while at the same time introducing them to, or reinforcing for them, the Christian message of commitment and discipleship. This was done through short morning gatherings and evening epilogues with personal counselling when, where and if required. In 1960, Mary's parents were about to lead one such summer school in Lytham St Anne's, and Mary was to accompany them. She asked me if I wanted to go along and join them for the fortnight. Anything that took me away from home seemed a good idea so I readily agreed. I even somehow persuaded my parents to pay for it. From the beginning I felt free and happy at the summer school. There were lots of interesting things to do including sport-challenges, day-trips to the coast, the Lake District, Blackpool and other places, and there was a general relaxed atmosphere. Everyone seemed to get on with each other and there was lots of laughter and a great deal of fun. In addition to going on outings and participating in group activities, there was a continuous effort by us young people, to try and harmlessly outwit those in authority as teenagers do.

Members of Lytham St Anne's Baptist Summer School 1960

Mary Price's father, who led the party, is sitting centre of front row in line with a pillar of the pavilion. Mrs Price is on his right. Mary is in the back row, extreme right and I am to her left, leaning on her shoulder.

The following year, 1961, saw me going for a fortnight to a second summer school with Mary. This time it was held in a large house called Cilgwyn, in Newcastle Emlyn, Carmarthenshire, Wales. Mary went independent of her parents this time; they were leading a Baptist summer school elsewhere. Helen Hodges another friend from Clapham County School was persuaded to go along with us. I think I enjoyed being at Cilgwyn even more than I had done at Lytham St Anne's, probably because I knew what to expect this time and was less inhibited.

Although sixteen years old I was still young enough to enjoy childish pranks, and one night at Cilgwyn when the leaders and adults were in bed and asleep, I and Mary joined a few others at an impromptu party in one of the downstairs lounges. Towards the end of it we decided to move some furniture around. Unfortunately one of the boys tried carrying a large Edwardian clock up the stairs when it suddenly began to chime, arousing the other residents. We scarpered back to our rooms as fast as we possibly could like naughty little children, jumping into our beds with our clothes on as we were pursued by some of the adults. Next day it was not difficult for the leaders to work out who had caused the commotion and the eight or so of us responsible had to go and explain ourselves and apologise. During the discussion it was implied that Mary Price should have known better. I was a bit put out that the leaders should think that just because Mary was the daughter of a Baptist minister, she should have higher standards than the rest of us.

Andy Strutt was the young person at Cilgwyn who discovered my GCE O-Level exam results had arrived in the post. They had been sent on to me by my mother from Balham. Andy came bounding into our girls' bedroom and jumped on top of me as I opened the crucial envelope. I suppose I wished he was interested in more than the contents of the envelope, but I knew he was spoken-for; his girlfriend Marion was also at the summer school. The boy at Cilgwyn with whom I had a light-hearted holiday romance was Grub. He had been given this nickname when it was discovered his job was assistant trainee chef at the Dorchester Hotel in London. He was not particularly good-looking but great fun and a very nice person. Mary's teenage romance at Cilgwyn was with a boy who came along with a group of young people from Chatsworth Baptist Church, in West Norwood, London, S.E.27. This church had a very lively youth club, and some of its gregarious members played a prominent role in the fun, games and leisure activities of our summer school.

On leaving Cilgwyn and returning to London, the West Norwood group invited Mary and me to a special youth service at their church. We went along and met the group outside the church building before entering. It was a large, modern, stylish church unlike any other I had seen before. Mary and I were taken inside and upstairs into the gallery that over-looked the auditorium. Here we had a good view of the proceedings and the rest of the congregation, many of whom were young like us. The service that followed was well structured and everyone sang the hymns, (which were partly traditional and partly modern,) loudly and enthusiastically. All felt part of something important, especially with the ceremony of adult baptism that was incorporated into the service. Afterwards a large reception was held in the church-hall, and this too proved to be well organised with a good atmosphere. There was light-hearted fun and banter balanced with the more serious elements of the occasion. Later I attended a few more events at this church, enjoying every one.

Lesley Knill who I met at Cilgwyn was to become a lifelong friend. She, her friend Julia Foster, Andy Strutt and Marion, had all come along to the Baptist summer school with a party of young people from Southampton. In 1965 Lesley married David Osman and I went to their wedding. Soon after they immigrated to Australia, and forty-three years later I visited Lesley and David with my husband at their home in Brisbane, New South Wales. Julia Foster went on to marry John Barfoot and stayed in the Southampton area. I have kept in touch with this couple too.

Members of Cilgwyn Baptist Summer School 1961.

I am sitting in the front row, third from the right. Lesley Knill is on my right. Lesley's friend, Julia Foster, is standing in the second row from the back – seventh from the right – on her left is Helen Hodges with Marion (Andy's girlfriend) on her right. Among the boys in the very back row is "Grub", fifth from the left, turned and facing the pavilion. The tall, fair-headed boy third from the left in the back row is Andy Strutt.

Clapham County Grammar School S.W. 4. – Part 2
1956-1962

The relationship between myself and fellow pupil, Yvonne Parret, at Clapham County School was a love-hate one. One minute we were sharing things with each other and the next fighting. As time went by a definite personality clash began to develop between us. In my case I began to see Yvonne as representing everything I detested. She was over-confident and full of herself, always boasting and name-dropping. One day she delighted in telling me and some friends that when her mother saw her standing naked in front of a mirror, she commented what a lovely figure and beautiful ankles Yvonne had. I imagine Mrs Parret may have been trying to encourage her daughter whose ankles were in fact quite thick-set. The distorted image Yvonne had of herself made me squirm. I suppose once again jealousy was my main problem. Yvonne had many things, material and social, that I lacked. Alongside doting parents she had a lovely head of blond hair that was always stylishly set and she was usually dressed fashionably in good-quality clothes. She was the only child of a young father and an older but very sophisticated Jewish mother who was not common and brash as I considered mine to be. Yvonne's father had met his wife in Germany where he had gone to study or work in the late 1930s, before the war. When I visited Yvonne Parret's home in 1957 her family were living in a council flat on the Clapham-Balham border. I have already hinted that council flats had no stigma in the early post-war years; everyone was trying to re-establish their lives and re-gain some sort of social grounding after the traumatic six years of war. With so many houses not yet rebuilt, house ownership was not a priority for many people. The Parrets council flat was well positioned in a smart complex and filled with good-quality furniture. Eventually the Parrets bought their own property in a smart area of Upper Norwood, and following our O-Level exams at Clapham County School Yvonne was sent to a private finishing school.

During one of Yvonne and my hate-phases we actually had a physical fight. I'm not sure what the provocation had been or the lead-up to it, but I do remember the shameful scene that took place in our classroom. A few of my friends had been goading me on and telling me to "sort Yvonne out". I was easily led and eventually snapped grabbing Yvonne by her hair while she bit and kicked me. Fortunately Miss Franklin, our form tutor at the time, came into the room before we could do much damage to each other and we were suitably reprimanded. Another incident I am ashamed to recall happened in the gymnasium. Yvonne appeared smug and arrogant as she held her head high and went to volt over the exercise-horse. She ran to the jumping position, sprang up and fell flat on her face the other side. I couldn't help but smirk – so much for select young grammar school girls. Some of us were more like yobs.

Strange to say after we had both left Clapham County School Yvonne suddenly appeared on my doorstep in Yukon Road one day. If you saw the way we related to each other on this occasion you would have thought we were blood-sisters. She told me all about her life, and I told her about my studies at Camberwell Art School. I especially remember and enjoy the account Yvonne gave me of an incident that happened at a cocktail party in her private finishing school. She told me students, family members and other guests at this evening function began to circulate and socialise. One of the mothers approached Yvonne and started talking about the public school her daughter had previously attended, (Roedean School, Sussex if I remember correctly, or perhaps it was Cheltenham Ladies College). She then went on to ask Yvonne where she had previously studied. According to Yvonne she did not batter an eye-lid but replied in a very matter-of-fact way, "Oh, I went to the CCS." The mother was confounded, feeling she ought to know of this prestigious institution and asked no further questions. The person I was sharing these anecdotes with was certainly not the Yvonne I had known in our last years at Clapham County School. She was realistic and entertaining. I hoped I might have changed for the better too.

There were many other pupils at Clapham County School who were my friends, but I will end this section by mentioning Janet Harris. She was a serious, conventional, predictable sort of character, not loud, vocal and assertive as I was, but we appeared to hit-it-off for a time. Her family were Jewish business people and her mother ran a hairdressing salon (or salons). They lived in a large house in Nightingale Lane not far from our school. Apart from Janet and her mother there was also an aunt and I think a cousin living in the home. If there was also a father and uncle at the house, I never met them. It is possible the men were off the premises and working late when I visited. I did however meet the domestic hired-help of the family. The routine of the house was very formal. When I was invited around there for tea, I assumed I would be offered the substantial after-school snack or meal that I was accustomed to at home – the main meal of the day for my mother and father. Instead, at about five o'clock, small sandwiches, a cake and a pot of tea were presented to us on a tray by the helper. After nibbling at the refreshments Janet and I returned to whatever recreational activity we had been involved in. Then about seven o'clock in the evening I was ushered home. Apparently this was when the family sat down to their proper meal of the evening. It was a bit of a culture shock for me coming as I did from a London working-class family. When Janet came around to our flat for tea, we had our usual hot snack with "afters" on our little table in the kitchen-diner.

Some of the pupils at Clapham County were difficult for me to relate to. One such group centred on two girls, Anita Batty and Cluny Gillies. These two were very worldly-wise and sophisticated both in appearance and outer-school activities. By the fourth form (year 10 in today's educational language), they had become quite self-contained and content with each other's company, while at the same time revelling in the small train of admirers and devotees who were beginning to follow them. One of these devotees was a girl whose name I am not sure about, but may have been Jennifer Craven-Griffiths. Her appearance was the complete opposite of her two heroines. To my mind, she was old-fashioned, short, plump, plain looking with bulging eyes and hair styled in out-dated plaits. I imagined she must have had little social experience before latching on to Anita and Cluny, who appeared to enjoy her idol-worship. My assumption was that the girl was enjoying the credibility she gained from being associated with the pair. Before the fourth form, and before Anita, Cluny and their train of followers were too exclusive, I was invited to one of the parties held in Cluny's home, a large, smart house in Clapham Park. During the party Cluny's mother made an appearance. I was told she was a social worker and she looked every bit the stereotype of one – professional and eccentric. She wore dark shaded spectacles and fashionable clothes, and had a designer basket draped over her arm. For a while she sat in a dramatic pose on the sofa for all to see before disappearing once more.

With their increasing isolation from the majority of their peers, Anita and Cluny started to hold loud conversations with each other about their sexual exploits, details of which became more and more explicit as time went by. These accounts and tales of sexual practices were unknown to the majority of us and were obviously meant to create awe and wonder in a captive audience. We assumed much of their experience and knowledge had been acquired with boys they had met at the jazz club on Eel-Pie Island in the River Thames that they frequented. Despite Anita and Cluny's reputation for knowing "the ways of the world", and having everything in control, Cluny found herself pregnant while still at school, and had to take a break from her studies. After giving birth, she returned to Clapham County School and completed her secondary education. She may have been one of the first girls in British state education system to do so. Our head mistress, Miss Viner, would have been a prime facilitator in this happening. Her modern and compassionate views ensured Cluny's studies were not disrupted more than necessary on account of the unplanned pregnancy.

Miss Viner had taken over headship of Clapham County School in January 1957. Miss Willey was head mistress at the school for only my first term there and then she retired. Miss Viner was one of the youngest (if not **the** youngest) head of the time to take up such an important role in a grammar school. She went on to modernise the school, both its uniform and practices. One of the things she did was to scrap segregation by ability in the pastoral forms. Under the new system it was only in academic subject-lessons that pupils found themselves selected according to ability. It has already been explained how I had progressed from the bottom pastoral set, 1B1 to IB then 2A1. It was at this point that Miss Viner's new policy kicked in and I suddenly found myself with new classmates in a new mixed-ability pastoral form called 2F. My class teacher was Miss Franklin the PE teacher, hence the title 2F, but for most of my lessons I still had to go to traditional ability-set groups. With other pupils I moved around rooms between the lesson-bells to find my particular set for that particular subject lesson. Not many of us felt victimised by this setting method; it was an incentive to try harder, and aim to be promoted the following term or year. It also meant we could be placed in different subject settings according to our various strengths; we did not have to be in the same ability set for all subject lessons. Unfortunately not long after this change of policy my marks and progress began to fall.

Miss Viner's discipline was quite firm, but she approached pupils in a far more personal way than Miss Willey had done before. When I was in the third or fourth year, and emotionally at a very low ebb, I was summoned to Miss Viner's office one day. I was anticipating and was not disappointed to witness the characteristics for which she had become renowned, namely her repeating several times "You do see, dear?" as she tried to reason with you, and seeing her sitting absolutely upright, or leaning towards you by her desk in perfect posture. We assumed she was supported by a very large, firm corset. As pupils we laughed at her for these things, but in hindsight, I realise she was trying to be professional. Her verbal expression was an attempt to connect with her pupils and her posture was meant to be a visual example of correctness as she attempted to make herself a good role model.

Miss Viner wanted to know what my problems were. At first, I was not very responsive, and so she tried a different tactic asking about my ambitions and dreams. Although my progress was deteriorating, I still seemed to have grand ideas. Originally I had wanted to be a nurse but now I thought it would be wonderful if I could be a medical doctor and told her so. She could have sneered and pointed out my inappropriate attitude, background, marks and lack of recent achievements but she did not. Instead she said she would be willing to help me try and fulfil my ambition if I did my part by being more directed and motivated and organise my study-schedule better. That was just what I needed, to feel that there was hope at the end of the tunnel.

In the late 1970s when I became a member of Quondam, a society for former pupils of Clapham County School, I was able to renew my acquaintance with Miss Viner who had recently retired as head teacher. She became a friend and confidante of mine from that time on until her death in 2005. I did not always agree with her thinking and philosophy. I for example felt there was no harm in selective labels as long as everyone was valued for one reason or another. I was proud that I had been granted a place at grammar school; it counteracted my low self-esteem, while Miss Viner rarely used the word grammar school believing it placed a stigma on other pupils. I had several friends who went to a secondary modern school, and they received a good education and managed to find fulfilment in their lives in many different ways; I do not believe they were greatly penalised. Miss Viner also continually tried to keep abreast of the times by experimenting with up-to-date uniform and school practices, while I preferred the stability of tradition and age-old customs. Miss Viner was certainly a woman for change and improvement but was sincere in motive and in her unquestionable care for young people.

Although Miss Viner continually offered praise and encouragement to others, she rarely broadcast her own achievements, many of which were only discovered at her memorial service, after her death. We heard that she had been head-girl at Clarendon House Grammar School for Girls in Ramsgate, Kent, at the same time former Prime Minister, Sir Edward Heath, was head-boy at the brother school, Chatham House Grammar School for Boys in Ramsgate. I believe this brought the two of them in regular contact, and was the beginning of a mutual respect and friendship they had for each other. Surprisingly this piece of news did not surprise me. From the beginning, Miss Viner had reminded me of Sir Edward Heath both in looks and mannerisms. Perhaps existence in the same educational environment for seven years had helped the pair acquire similar physical attributes. Following formal education Miss Viner was offered a prestigious post in Creative Productions with the BBC, but the war and its associated traumas prevented this materialising and she found herself working in state education. We also found out at the memorial service that Miss Viner had endured several personal tragedies. Her fiancé and only brother had been killed within a short time of each other while on active service in WW2. Later, in 1945, she lost a sister to TB and after that, for a substantial period of time, in addition to her full-time teaching career she helped look after her parents and the four children of her dead sister.

Early photograph of Miss Willey, the headmistress who retired from Clapham County School December 1956.

A 1992 "reunion" photograph of Miss Viner, who succeeded Miss Willey, taken 16 years after her retirement from the school.

Another photograph taken at the 1992 school reunion, my close friend Sheila Banks nee Haines.

I will forever be grateful for the opportunity I had of knowing my old headmistress in a more personal way in her last years. She became a true friend, and before my own retirement from the education system assisted me whenever and however she could, offering advice and giving professional references – despite the fact that her official responsibility for me had ceased decades before. I will keep and treasure the last note she wrote and sent me not long before her death. Characteristically she began the note by encouraging me in my latest ventures and then uncharacteristically she hinted that she was running out of stamina; this from someone who was not far off ninety years old and who not many months before had been doing voluntary work, "helping the old folk".

| Clapham County School, Broomwood Road, S.W.4 | Old classmates attending the 100th anniversary celebration of our school building in 2009 | The hall of the school with the supporting gallery-cherubs |

In addition to my headmistress there were other members of staff at Clapham County who made a lasting impression on me; Mrs Pell was one. She helped to develop my artistic interests. I had enjoyed my art lessons with her predecessor, the former head of the art department Miss Fleischmann, but Miss Fleischmann was much older and not used to tough London pupils who tested her patience. We did not get much work done in Miss Fleischmann's lessons. With hindsight, I have wondered if Miss Fleischmann might have been from one of those pre-war refugee families who, having come from a good established background back in their home-country, found it difficult to adjust to a new, less privileged existence in England.

LEFT
The first school badge I wore as a pupil of Clapham County School
RIGHT
The new school badge designed by Mrs Pell in 1959 for our school's Jubilee Year. It shows our school's motto "discendo veritas" – "truth in leaning", and an image of some broomwood to reflect the school's address in Broomwood Road.

Miss Stamps was another memorable teacher. She was head of the music department the whole time I was at Clapham County. We assumed she was middle-aged but her appearance may have made her look older than she actually was. Her hair was wound round in plaits at the back of her head, and being on the stout side her clothes tended to look frumpish. Miss Stamps was very strict about posture and correct pronunciation when she was teaching us. She was especially pedantic about the four and five syllable words we came across in the old hymns and songs that we had to practise and sing for formal school gatherings. Miss Stamps taught us how to sing traditional Church of England chants such as the Te Deum and Nunc Dimitis for matins and evensong. These left us, her pupils, with a rich legacy of meaningful language. My feeling is that traditional songs and chants are far superior to the weak, insipid, repetitive church music and secular songs we have around us today. When still at school many of us thought we were undergoing educational torture with our old-fashioned musical diet but most of us have since agreed the diet has been of huge benefit to us in our later years, with the words and tunes returning to inspire. Miss Stamp's rigid attention to such things as timing and the decoding of musical scores, proved to be an asset in other areas of our learning too; it helped in our general concentration and orderly discipline around the school.

Once when Miss Stamps was leading and talking to several classes in the hall, for some reason since forgotten, she began to talk about and promote the school choirs. She then strolled to the back of the hall while we sang to the accompaniment of another teacher on the piano. To my surprise she stopped where I was standing halfway down the hall and said something about my voice having potential. I was flattered, especially as my mother usually made very negative comments about my voice when she heard me sing. Even I accepted my singing voice came and went and more often than not it was quite ropey. I was not very confident with my singing at all, and did not want to take up Miss Stamps' offer of joining a school choir, but when I hear a full-blooded professional choir I love trying to sing along with them – but this is not the same as getting anywhere near the notes required for joining a proper choir.

We seem to have had an odd set of Latin teachers at Clapham County School. First there was a woman who reminded me of Miss Haversham in Great Expectations. She would waft through the school corridors and up the school stairs, leaving in her wake a trail of strong-smelling, cheap, unattractive scent from the face powder she used, and which made her face look white and ghostly. Apart from being old she looked as though she was stuck in a time warp from a different era and appeared to relate little to people and things around her. Then there was the Latin master who did over and above his duty to try and get his pupils successfully through their GCE O-Level examination. I remember him going backwards and forwards to Foyle's Bookshop in the West End trying to sort out a mix-up over a set of Latin textbooks the shop had wrongly sent to our school. Unfortunately he suffered from a war wound of some kind, causing him to emit body fluids that (not to put it too vaguely) made him stink. At times we were very unkind to him. I remember members of our class opening all the windows before he entered the room even when it was the height of winter and freezing cold; the implication was obvious. Another time one Christmas someone left him a decoratively wrapped present on his desk. When he un-wrapped it in front of us it turned out to be a bar of soap. Our only defence for this mischief was that we were too young and ill-informed to realise his sad predicament.

A few women teachers at our school continued to wear the engagement ring their wartime fiancés had given them before being killed in action. Miss Alford, the geography teacher, and Miss Bowers the French teacher, were two such individuals. I think they stayed faithful to their deceased partners for the rest of their lives. Now and again rumours circulated about the sexual orientation (as it is called these days) of a few unmarried lady-teachers on the staff, in particular Miss Franklin and Miss Thwaites the P.E. (physical education) teachers. Stories would be told of how these two had been caught ogling girls in the changing rooms and even sometimes brushing up against them. Whether there was any substance in these rumours, or whether it was just malicious gossip, I do not know.

There was one teacher for whom there was no doubt about his sexual orientation. He was a science teacher, and one of the first male teachers to be appointed to the staff of Clapham County by Miss Viner. Miss Viner wanted to break the gender taboo because previously our school had been an all-female enclave. This young science teacher was extremely laid back and overtly uncommitted to a vocation in education, a rare thing for teachers in grammar schools in the late 1950s. He openly admitted his first love was acting and that he was just waiting for a chance to go on the stage. He was trendy, womanising and full of himself. He had no qualms about mixing socially with some fifth-year pupils, including Anita Batty and Cluny Gillies, who I believe he met on his visits to the jazz dens on Eel-Pie Island. Another male teacher appointed by Miss Viner, also for the science department, was completely the opposite. He lacked confidence and could not control his classes or keep the interest of his pupils. Once he became really frustrated, lost his temper and threw a blackboard rubber (one of the old-fashioned ones with a hard, wooden handgrip at the back) across to the room to the back row of laboratory desks where Wendy Goodship and I sat gossiping and paying little attention to his lesson. Wendy and I were certainly out-of-order and knew we deserved a reprimand but a better method should have been applied. I suppose that in those days of post war regeneration it was difficult to find and appoint appropriate teaching staff. (I wonder what the excuse is today.)

Former pupils usually love to reminisce over the times they managed to get the upper hand on teachers at their school. We at Clapham County were no different. Among other things we were prone to playing April fool's jokes on staff; nothing too serious, just immature childish pranks such as the time we put butter on the handle of a classroom door. Miss Bowers was the intended victim and on entering the room to take our French lesson she found her hand in a sticky mess. Her response surprised us. Instead of looking angry as we expected her to, she demurely took a linen handkerchief from her pocket, wiped the grease off her hand, threw a half smile in our direction and carried on. Our image of her as a stern, avenging Victorian character changed after this and we saw her in a softer, gentler light. To add to this new image we had of her, in the fourth year Miss Bowers took our year group on school journey to Paris, in the hope of improving our spoken French ready for the not-too-distant O-level exam that included an oral element. Here she surprised us again when she turned a blind eye to a few girls who had made friends with some French boys and started walking with them hand in hand along the Champs Elysees. In Miss Willey's days this would have been an unthinkable act, possibly ending in school expulsion, but probably remembering her own sad curtailed wartime romance Miss Bowers allowed this mild flirtation.

Some teachers did not fare as well as Miss Bowers where our humour was concerned. In fact, we must have been quite horrible and obnoxious at times. I have already described the Latin master and our reactions to his hygiene problem, another incident occurred one lunchtime. It involved reducing a young female probationary teacher to tears. She had come along to the lunchtime music club to sing some classical pieces for us. She had taken the trouble to dress formally in a proper evening dress and her voice proved to be wonderful, but she lacked confidence. On a particularly high note she hesitated and warbled a little. We burst into laughter which made her flee from the room in tears. Fortunately the other staff present knew what to do. Without going over-board with recrimination they threw a look of disappointment at club members and then one of them went out of the room and encouraged the probationary teacher to return and finish her repertoire.

Among the teachers who appeared to have no problems with school life was Miss Knowles, an English and religious education teacher. She appeared to be on top of every situation and could cope with any unexpected challenge that came her way. She was not the youngest on the staff but dressed stylishly and was quite sophisticated. We learnt her father had been an artist. He was Horace Knowles who designed illustrations for the New English Bible that was becoming popular at the time with its more modern approach and updated script. Our school enthusiastically bought and used a large quantity of these Bibles.

Three illustrations for the New English Bible designed by Horace Knowles

Mrs Swell was one of the geography teachers at Clapham County School, and although not that young, being married with two daughters, must have attended a modern progressive post-graduate teacher training college, because her teaching methods were quite innovative. To help us understand latitude and longitude she brought along an orange and dissected it in front of our class, and to show us the tilt of the earth's axis she skewered another orange and held it up at an angle for all to see. When talking of important air currents and prevailing winds she would whoosh herself around the classroom with her arms flayed out. We dare not laugh. Secretly we thought she was a bit eccentric but she must have known what she was doing because these lessons have stayed vivid in my mind, and most of us passed our GCE in geography.

A week or two after my joining Clapham County School, and having had only one or two French lessons, our class was given a short-cut path to French pronunciation. We were taught how to say and spell, Miss Labouchiardiere. This was the name of a French woman who was coming to teach at our school. An established member of staff practised the name with us, making us repeat it several times so we would not embarrass the newcomer or ourselves when we addressed her.

It would take too long to mention all the teachers so I will end with my reminiscences of Miss Rayner who I greatly admired. She was efficient, caring and a thinker. Once again in many ways she was very different to me. She was old-fashioned, manly and an atheist. I considered myself to be modern, feminine and a Christian, but I couldn't help but feel a strong affinity with her. I saw her as a genuine person. "What you saw was what you got!"

Many subjects were taught at our school, and some of these were divided into modules so that more than one member of staff from that department might be involved in delivering the subject to us. The diversity of topic and teaching personnel widened our interests, as did being exposed to new relationships, new ideas and new experiences. Even as new 11-year-old pupils, we began to feel the world belonged to us now, and not to adults any more. Certain incidents intrigued us, especially in the lower school where we were sometimes known to manipulate them to our advantage. While still fairly new to the school some friends and I came across someone we considered a "dirty old man". He was exposing himself, showing his manhood to us as we walked home across Clapham Common, heading towards Cavendish Road one day. Immediately we ran back to Broomwood Road and the school to tell staff what had happened, and then we sat down and enjoyed the pursuing fuss. Our headmistress phoned the police who soon arrived to interview her and us as the witnesses. We felt very important. The safety of children was paramount in those days. Fortunately, as far as I am aware, none of us experienced anything more serious than that on future journeys to and from school, except perhaps for a few minor physical assaults that we received in squirmishes with girls from the Marianne Thornton School.

For a long time our school had been known locally by some disrespectful people as "Clapham Cow Sheds" because of the CCS letters on our school badge. (I have since learnt that Walthamstow County Grammar School suffered the same fate and indignity, being called Walthamstow Cow Sheds.) We didn't mind a certain amount of leg pulling but the girls from Marianne Thornton began to use the name with aggression and distain. The government of the day knew they were moving towards comprehensive education and decided to plant a girls' secondary modern school on our doorstep in preparation for future amalgamation. Right from the beginning there was a lot of resentment between the two sets of pupils. Marianne Thornton girls made fun of the Clapham County uniform and the arrogant ways they assumed we as grammar school pupils had, while we felt we had to prove we were just as tough as they were – proper Londoners from ordinary homes. Several times there were clashes of words and sometimes flying satchels, pushes and shoves. As I have said I had many friends in secondary modern and commercial schools, and we all got along well together out of school, but the Marianne Thornton pupils seemed to carry a special chip-on-their-shoulder. They had been indoctrinated to think they were the heirs to a brave new world and had been told by some in the media that they were missing out in the education stakes, when in fact they had far better vocational resources on their premises than we had at Clapham County. Their school had brand new technical rooms and ample sports and study facilities; pupils received a far more personally tailored and customised education than those of us at Clapham County. This was a better situation than was to follow in later years when the fully instituted comprehensive system took over. In my opinion education then became prescribed, stereotyped, watered-down, and executed in large impersonal buildings. Learning at grammar schools involves a lot of theory, rote learning and personal discipline, which is only appropriate for some. Others learn better with more tactile and psycho-linguistic methods. If only the pupils from Marianne Thornton School had realised this, and had allowed themselves to enjoy their privileged facilities and curriculum without envy and resentment.

Private Piano Lessons 1956-1959

Piano lessons were an additional study I took alongside my normal school education. I studied piano playing and theory from about the age of 11 until I was about 14 years old. My mother had kept the old piano from her childhood home in Penrith Street, Streatham and it stood proudly in our front room. Mum frequently referred back to her childhood when she claimed her family and friends enjoyed happy gatherings and parties around this piano, playing it and singing the old music-hall songs of the day. She constantly complained that things were not half as good as they had been when she was a child. According to her in the 1920s and 1930s everyone in her street had a large Christmas tree lit up in their front window at Christmas-time and neighbours would circulate around each other's homes partying and generally having a good time. Whether this image was true or exaggerated I cannot be sure, but I think my mother hoped that one day I might be able to play the piano competently enough for us to have similar parties. She paid out three shillings and sixpence per week for me to have an hour's private piano lesson with Miss Ellis, a musician who lived in one of the large old Edwardian terrace-houses across the road from us in Cavendish Road.

Miss Ellis was a stout person, physically and character-wise. She had un-styled straight hair, thick rimmed glasses and her clothes were unfashionable but always clean and presentable. Her house was quaint and furnished with antiques. I learnt later that her parents had travelled widely and brought these artefacts back from the countries they had visited. Miss Ellis's Christian name was Audrey, and she had a sister named Janet. (I believe there was also a brother, and possibly another sister.) Janet's career had been in nursing and in that capacity, like her parents, she had travelled widely but eventually returned to Balham to live with Audrey. I remember vividly the smell of kippers cooking in the Ellis kitchen as I arrived at their house for my weekly Thursday evening piano lesson, about six o'clock in the evening. It was Audrey and Janet's supper for that day of the week. Audrey and Janet were very friendly, and often used to show me things of interest in parts of their home. In later life Janet gave me a few keepsakes, a pair of pearl earrings, a small Dolton jug and a turquoise tie-pin for my husband. Janet was much more feminine than Audrey. She wore flowing dresses and had her hair swept up in a classic style. Like Audrey she too was a very proud Miss.

Miss Ellis with two of her pupils.

The photograph was given to me by Audrey's sister Janet, after Audrey's death.

My piano lessons consisted of scales, arpeggios and pieces of sheet music. At the beginning, I tried to practice regularly at home between my Thursday lessons, but my mother frequently moaned about the inconvenience of it; it never seemed to be the right time for her. Apart from this discouragement it was not long before I found other more interesting distractions in my life – and to be honest I do not think I had much musical talent anyway. I made little progress with my set pieces, and found it difficult to gain the necessary dextrous agility I needed. Nonetheless Miss Ellis continued trying her best to instil me with a love of music. As a teacher she found novel ways of passing knowledge on to her students, especially in relation to rhythm and timing. One method was to mark out the notes and beats in a dance-like routine across the room. She would hold her students around their waist and waltz or step out with them and do other bendy movements as she chanted the appropriate beats of the tunes they were studying. In fact she was generally quite a tactile sort of person but thankfully not too familiar because later she told me she was "not like other women". "Janet and I have a special relationship," she said, "Janet is the feminine side of our relationship and I am the masculine side." I think she thought I was more worldly-wise than I actually was – I was really quite naïve and it took time and reflection for me to realise she was talking about lesbianism.

By this time I had more or less weaned myself off of my weekly piano lesson. I felt very guilty towards the end because I had become a very unreliable pupil and was finding weak excuses to explain why I had to miss some of the lessons. I realised my three shillings and sixpence must have been a part of Miss Ellis's income, but she never complained or asked for money to compensate for the missed lessons. It is possible Miss Ellis gave me a special tuition-fee rate anyway, because she and Janet got on quite well with my mother. I know for a fact that some time after my lessons had terminated my mother confided some of her personal problems to these two sisters. Mum was more confident sharing troubles with people she knew would remain passive and sympathetic, rather than with people who might be more objective and possibly offer constructive advice. The Ellis sisters were the former, caring, well-meaning individuals who rarely judged a situation.

While still in my first year at Clapham County School my mother announced she was going to have another baby. I loved young children and was thrilled at the prospect. The new baby was expected November 1957, when I would be in my second year at Clapham County School.

Three family photographs taken on summer outings in 1957. I assume Dad was the photographer

ABOVE Philip, me and our pregnant mother.

Knowledge of the prospective birth became a topic of conversation for me and my school friends on our way to school in the mornings. For the first two years of my education at Clapham County my usual route to school was – once I had left home – to walk along Cavendish Road till I reached Clapham Common. Here I met Christine Stone, Carolyn Roll and Valerie Swanborough, who like me had transferred to Clapham County from Richard Atkins Junior Girls School. Together we would cross the main road at South Side, walk over the common, go along The Avenue and down Broomwood Road till we reached our school building. Christine Stone had recently had a baby brother herself and so we had mutual interest, but in any case, babies are an easy topic of conversation for young girls. At the beginning of my mother's pregnancy things did not go well and she was laid up for days at a time. When I found out the reason, I told Aunty Kit who said she suspected my mother might be pregnant because the discomfort and symptoms she was experiencing were similar to those she had when expecting Philip.

Our new baby sister, Jill Elizabeth, was safely delivered on 9 November 1957. She was born in the now dismantled Clapham Women's Hospital, which was situated at the bottom of the Clapham Common not far from our home. The hospitals position was convenient for my mother and also for my father who took her there when her labour began and waited in the hospital's reception till Jill was born.

South London Hospital for Women, Clapham © Veronika Chambers

The hospital was founded in 1912, and opened by Queen Mary on 4 July 1916. It was entirely staffed by women, and enlarged in the 1930s. It closed in 1984.

Less fuss was made over Jill's arrival than had been the case when Philip was born and brought home to Brixton Hill. Relatives were not so much in evidence. Aunt Lizzie had died the December before, and Dad's parents were elderly, with his mother suffering the early stages of dementia. Generally speaking we had become more isolated since our move to Balham. We were further away from Mum's older brother Jack and his family, who a few years earlier had bought a grocer's shop with accommodation in Norwood where they went to live. (Like Dad, Uncle Jack had worked for the Co-operative Society before the war and used his experience to set up his own small business.) Dad's brother and his family also continued to reside in the Norwood area – and so with work, school and other family commitments Balham was not an easy journey for these relatives to make. Although Jill did not have many visitors following her birth, there were plenty of cards and presents and Dad was absolutely pleased and delighted. Immediately after her arrival he rushed back to our Cavendish Road flat to relate the good news to Philip and me who were sitting waiting excitedly by the open coal fire in the front room.

I loved my brother dearly but was thrilled that at last I had a sister. I imagined all the girlie things I would be able to do and share with her, and the information both practical and emotional I could pass on. When Jill was a few months old she was christened at Immanuel Church, Streatham, near to our previous home. I had continued to be a member of the Girls' Bible Class there and this link with the church probably made it easy for my mother to organise the christening. She must have run out of ideas for god-parents though, because at my suggestion she allowed me to be one of the traditional three god-parents, (two women and a man for a baby girl, two men and a woman for a baby boy), the names of Jill's other godparents I have since forgotten.

Something that happened soon after my mother returned home from the hospital with our new addition surprised me. I remember saying jokingly and quite light-heartedly in an exaggerated voice, "What a shame! I won't be nanny's only granddaughter anymore!" It was meant to be a tongue-in-cheek bit of irony. Other than me, Dad's parents only had grandsons, Philip my brother and Uncle Ken's sons Michael and Trevor. My mother's reaction was sharp and negative. She did not take the comment in the spirit it was intended and told me off for being so selfish. Many years later of course I realised I was not a proper blood granddaughter of Mr and Mrs Lewis senior, only Jill might possibly be able to claim this. It must have been my mother's knowledge of the truth that made her so negative and deflect her guilt onto me. In recent years the incident has made me wonder whether Jill herself might possibly not be a natural child of Dad's. Not long after Jill's birth my mother repeated a few times that women could conceive even if sperm only touched the top of their vagina. She said this was the case with Jill's conception. In her usual uncensored manner that spared no blushes, she claimed that my father could not keep an erection and so they were overjoyed to discover she was once more, for the third time, pregnant. I suppose I was meant to feel sorry for her but I did not. I knew there were often two sides to a story, especially where my mother was concerned. She was good at extracting sympathy with her highly selective information. I could sense my father's humiliation at the attacks on his masculinity and saw my mother as a self-centred woman who did not care who she hurt if it was for her advantage. It was nothing for her to joke or make light of my father's sexual inadequacy while in company.

As I had done with Philip, so I did with Jill; I tried to take an active part in her life. I remember taking her out in her pram now and again. Once I walked with her to the far end of Balham High Road, and into the Woolworths Store there. Here I met a middle-aged woman who stopped to admire the baby. She commented how lovely Jill was, then looked at me and said, "I hope she isn't yours, dear!" I suppose I had made myself look older than my recently acquired 13 years, and was trying to act like a mother, but I was put out by the woman's speculation.

While Jill was still a baby my mother had to go into hospital to have her appendix out, and while she was there, I helped my father look after Philip and my new baby sister. I thought I was doing well but sometime later, at a point when my mother wanted me to feel bad about myself, she recalled something Aunty Kit was supposed to have said. Apparently during my mother's hospitalisation Aunty Kit claimed she had seen me smack Jill as she sat in her pram. Once again it is an incident I could not recall. I suppose it is just possible and I may have thought that was what mothers did if a baby was being stubborn, never having been shown how to care for a baby. (The Mother Care course I took with the Red Cross cadets centred on practical things such as feeding babies and changing their nappies.) I wouldn't have meant any harm and would be surprised if the smack was anything more than a light tap – if one at all. I only have my mother's second-hand account about the incident – and if there had been any substance to the allegation it is a pity I was not told about it sooner; then I would have been able to learn from my mistake.

Our first family holiday with Jill in 1958. Once again Dad must have been taking most of the photos because there are few of him

I began to grow even further away from my parents at this point in my life. I suppose I was never that close anyway, but with teenage hormones taking over I was becoming more and more rebellious and independent. I felt I had little in common with my parents and I was fed up with what I considered to be the emotional and physical abuse I was receiving. Even in my mid-teens I was being hit with objects when tempers flared, but it was the emotional sniping that hurt me most. My mother seemed to enjoy making me look small and stupid in front of friends, implying I was jealous, unthinking and self-centred. After a time, as I have already noted, I began to give as good as I got in physical confrontations. Following these incidents I would spend days not speaking a word to either parent, staying much of the time in my bedroom and sobbing myself to sleep. Somehow throughout all this I managed to retain some personal confidence. Fortunately I had very good friends and continued to enjoy life outside the home. Others compensated for the support I felt I should have received from my parents.

Early Leisure Pursuits 1956-1960

I enjoyed being at a girls' school and having lots of girlfriends but I was becoming more and more boy-conscious. Soon after joining secondary school a boy called Tony from Honeybrook Road the other side of Cavendish Road took a fancy to me. He was good looking and seemed an interesting individual and so I agreed to go out with him on a date. He took me to see a film at a local cinema. The film was either Rock around the Clock with Bill Hayley, or more likely Jailhouse Rock with Elvis Presley, both being shown around that time. The cinema he took me to was the Odeon in Balham. I made an effort to wear my most modern clothes and persuaded my mother to buy me a new pair of the latest casual shoes – basically pumps made of a white canvas mesh-like material with flat heels and round toes – the rage of the day. I enjoyed the film but did not continue to warm to Tony, possibly because my mother was so enthusiastic about him and seemed to be encouraging the romance. It was always a worry when my mother was "for" something. I didn't trust her or her intentions and I lost interest in Tony after our first and only date. He asked me out several times more, but I always had an excuse ready as to why I could not go out with him and in the end I just refused his invitations outright, much to his and my mother's disappointment.

The Odeon Cinema, Balham Hill. Image by © Historic England license.

In my first few years at secondary school parties were the main means of meeting boys. I remember one party I went to at Barbara Ramsay's house in Clapham North, and recall exactly what I wore. My outfit included my first real pair of stockings held up with a suspender belt. Apart from dancers using them, women's tights were not in general circulation at this point in time. I also wore the new white casual shoes I had worn on my first date with Tony, a crisp short-sleeved blouse and a knee-length full-circle skirt made from a royal-blue felt material. It billowed out when I danced – a real rock and roll accessory. This skirt was divided into two across its diameter, with a hole in the middle for my waist; the two halves were then joined together with large black buttons that proved too much of a temptation for one of Barbara's brother's friends. When I was sitting down and not looking, he started to undo them. Luckily I realised what was happening before I stood up and lost my skirt completely, much to everyone's amusement. It was all good fun and I joined in the laughter. During the party, we danced and sang along to the popular tunes of the day such as Buddy Holly's "Peggy Sue" and "That'll Be the Day". Only one incident caused me stress. One of the boys who was dancing in the middle of the room had his hands hidden up his sleeves. It was fashionable then to dance in a hunched, rolled up manner. Being a bit merry I called out, "You look as though you have lost your hands." He did not answer and I soon realised why. He actually had lost one hand and arm below his elbow. I wanted to crawl under a chair and die when I realised.

Another party I attended while still in my first couple of years at Clapham County School was at Sheila Haines house in Earlsfield. This one was an all-girl event, but towards the end a shy boy appeared on the scene and sat down with us. He was David Banks a local boy who later became Sheila's husband. Another party I remember going to a year or two later, I recall with some misgiving. One of the boys brought along his recently acquired tape-recorder. This gadget was a new invention then and everyone at the party was curious as to what it could do. The boy passed it around for all to say something into the microphone and have their voices recorded. When it came to me, I froze and could not utter a word despite encouragement from the others. This emotional reaction may have been a side effect of the since partially forgotten event at Richard Atkins School where I was withdrawn from a drama production at the last moment; whatever the reason I was all but paralysed. Thankfully I did not have problems interacting with individuals in face-to-face situations.

The open-air lidos in South West London have previously been mentioned. These were yet further places to meet other young people and make new friends in the 1950s and 1960s. A small fee was paid on entering the lido. Once inside we were confronted with a large swimming pool surrounded by changing cubicles – boys' and men's to one side and girls' and women's to the other. These booths or cubicles usually stank of chlorine and were not very pleasant, but it did not take long to change into our swimming costumes and come out to the pool area. Here a different world was waiting to greet us. Tooting Bec Open Air Lido had a sunbathing area in front of the canteen at the far end of the pool. Weather permitting, young people used this spot to lie out on towels and rest between swimming sessions, some using the opportunity to catch the eye of a member of the opposite sex as they rubbed sun-lotion on their bodies, or combed their wet hair. Not all experiences at the lidos were pleasant however. I remember one occasion when I decided to try the slide at Brockley Park Open Air Swimming Pool. I was not a very good swimmer and could only float or swim a few yards, but everyone else seemed to use the slide without a problem and it did not look very big to me so I went on it and shot down into the water. When I opened my eyes all I could see was murky, swirling water all around me. I did not know which way was up and which way was down. I began waving my arms around, but this only made matters worse. Eventually – I do not know how – I managed to arrive at the surface just in time to gain the essential breath of air I needed. Another bad experience at the lidos was when we girls occasionally came across individuals trying their luck in the water, usually older men who used the opportunity to grope or brush up against young girls, and sometimes young boys too. Usually we dealt with this menace ourselves. It was difficult to prove to adults that the incidents had not been just an unfortunate accident, so we depended on each other to sort out our would-be abusers.

The Locarno Ballroom Streatham became a permanent feature of my youth, as it had been for my mother as a young woman. I began to go there for entertainment from about the age of twelve because the Locarno held a Saturday afternoon dance specifically for young teenagers. Sometimes, when on good terms with Yvonne Parret, I would go along with her. We would meet each other outside the building and join a long line of teenagers waiting for the doors to be opened. When they were opened, we would enter. pay a small fee and go on into a smartly decorated ballroom with tables and chairs surrounding the dance-floor. Modern popular music was played on the stage and we spent the next few hours socialising, sipping Pepsi-Cola at the tables, jiving, rock and rolling and taking fashion notes from the older, more worldly-wise dancers.

Beehive hairdos were all the rage for women then. Some of the girls at the Locarno had hairstyles twice the size of their head. Winkle picker shoes were also in fashion for both sexes, and some competed to see who was wearing the longest toed shoes. The boys wore thin ties and sometimes instead of winkle-pickers had crepe-soled shoes, and they sported slick hair-does. Young girls like me usually danced with another girl but sometimes we would be asked by a boy to dance with him. When older I went to the evening events organised at the Locarno Ballroom, or go with a friend to another local dancehall such as the Wimbledon Palais. My first choice though was always the Streatham Locarno!

It was a real treat for me when I was invited to go and see the singer Jerry Lee Lewis in the flesh. He had come over from the United States of America and was booked to make an appearance at the Granada Cinema in Tooting. I was thirteen when I went to see his performance on 26 May 1958. My friend Penny Smith from Mitcham, who I had met at the church Bible Class in Streatham, had found out about the concert and asked me if I wanted to go along with her. Being a year or two older than me Penny was quite happy to sort out the organisation and book our tickets.

Another old photograph of the Locarno
Ballroom, Streatham Hill.
© heartstreatham

Publicity photo of Jerry Lee
Lewis. © discography-Wikimedia

On the day of the concert, Penny and I swung to the live music being played on stage. We especially loved it when Jerry Lee Lewis sang his chart topper "Great Balls of Fire". On reaching the crescendo, he jumped up on the keys of the piano and played the notes between his feet as we sang along. We looked at him with admiration, if a little bemused by the fact that we had learned he had just married a thirteen-year-old girl. Apparently this was permitted in his part of the USA, but it seemed very alien to us and the newspapers had been having a field-day with the story. I have gathered from the internet that some of the audience at the Granada, Tooting, were heckling him about his young bride, but Penny and I did not notice it; to us the audience seemed to be as awe-struck as we were.

OUTLINE OF JERRY LEE LEWIS'S BRITISH TOUR:

In trying to research the background of Jerry Lee Lewis and his visit to England, I have resorted to articles found on the internet, and therefore cannot guarantee complete authenticity of detail as I would have been be able to do had I used official public records. However, I believe most of the following is correct. Much was lifted from an article published in Penthouse by Nick Tosche in 1982.
Jerry Lee was the son of a tenant farmer from Louisiana. He was born in 1935. Mr Tosche believes his upbringing was a real contrast between "the Devil and the Holy Ghost". Apparently most of Jerry Lee's family were members of the Assembly of God, a Pentecostal Church that practices prophesying, interpreting visions, speaking in unknown tongues, spiritual healing of body and mind, and other supernatural phenomena. This encouraged Jerry Lee to think about entering the church ministry himself, and for a short time he attended the Pentecostal Bible

Institute in Texas, but he was also influenced by his love of self-indulgence and his strong sexual appetite.

Before old enough to officially buy a drink, Jerry Lee could be found with abandonment and little self-discipline in the saloon bars of Natchez across the Mississippi River to his home, and his sexual needs led him to be married at the early age of 16 to a girl called Dorothy Barton. This marriage did not last long and within two years he had married again, this time to Jane Mitchum. Incredibly the second marriage took place before his divorce from Dorothy had come through. The second marriage produced two sons, Jerry Lee Junior and Ronnie Guy. Jerry Lee never accepted the second son, claiming Ronnie was the result of his wife's adultery, and the child was not his, (detail of which he communicated in less than kind language to any who would listen). The next sexual attraction on the horizon for Jerry Lee was his 13-year-old cousin, Myra Gale Brown. He began divorce proceedings from Jane and went to live with Myra Gale at her parent's home in Memphis. Jerry Lee had been married to Jane for four years, and their divorce was granted by a Memphis judge on the 13th May 1958, but once again Jerry Lee had already married Myra Gale Brown in an official ceremony some months earlier.

Jerry Lee Lewis's record "Great Balls of Fire" was released in 1957. It became the biggest hit in the history of Sun Records, and brought him extensive fame and fortune, enlarging some claimed, his already inflated ego. His growing arrogance led him to refuse to precede any other act or artist on the stage.

On 22nd May 1958, Jerry Lee Lewis arrived in Great Britain to begin a thirty-seven-day concert tour. He ignored the advice of his management to leave Myra Gale at home and took her with him. Most of the British public were unaware of Jerry Lee's complicated personal life until they heard the questions that were hurled at him by reporters and photographers waiting for him at London Airport. The couple came down the steps of their plane arm in arm, and seemed to enjoy the attention and publicity they were receiving. In answer to the press's questions Jerry Lee claimed Myra Gale was 15 years old and that they had married two months ago. Myra Gale commented that young people could marry at ten if they wanted to where she lived, and said she did not think she was too young to be married. The couple then escaped the media, and were driven away in limousines to Westbury Hotel, Mayfair, where they checked in to room 127.

The next day, 23rd May, someone showed Jerry Lee a copy of The London Daily Herald newspaper. It had a large photograph of him and Myra Gale at the airport in a clinch, large black print stating Myra's age was 15, (the incorrect age the reporters had received from Jerry Lee,) and other information revealing Jerry Lee was into his third marriage. The article was obviously meant as a critical observation of the singer or at least a whimsical one. Someone else who had picked up the negative vibes, and growing public disapproval, was Sam Phillips, the president of Sun Records. He picked up a copy of the Memphis-Scimitar in the USA a newspaper that had also taken up a questioning stance on Jerry Lee's life-style. The press in Britain and the USA did some digging and discovered the truth of Myra Gale's age – she had been born 11th July 1944. They also learnt that Jerry Lee married Myra Gale before being properly divorced from Jane Mitchum.

On the evening of the 24th May, Jerry Lee and Myra were taken to the Regal, Edmonton in London, a large entertainment complex. This was where Jerry Lee was to perform his first show of the tour. It was later estimated that there had been two thousand– mostly teenagers – in the audience. Jerry Lee entered the stage wearing a shocking pink suit with sequined lapels and a black ribbon-tie. The enthusiasm of his admirers encouraged Jerry Lee to go full pelt into the energetic playing and singing of his repertoire, but it lasted little more than ten minutes and one British newspaper reported that when the curtain was lowered the admiration of the audience began to disappear, with some hissing and jeering. One member there started to sing the British national anthem and others joined in suggesting there was now some disillusionment with the American rock and roll scene. The curtain at the Regal, Edmonton, rose once more, and Jerry Lee Lewis shared a little more of his frenzied musical talent before finally leaving the stage. On Sunday 25th May, the Daily Sketch newspaper wrote a critical article on Jerry Lee's contribution to the music scene, describing in detail the artist's inappropriate body language, facial and vocal expressions and general poor attitude. The article said his performance was "everything that was bad in rock and roll". Another article in the People Newspaper wanted all teenagers to boycott Jerry Lee Lewis's concerts, and called for the Home Secretary to deport him. On Sunday, Jerry Lee and Myra Gale were taken to Kilburn State Theatre for the second show of the tour. The day after the Herald Newspaper reported that there were only 1000 in an auditorium that could hold 4000, and the London Evening Star on Monday also continued with some negative reporting.

Jerry Lee continued with the tour and appeared at the Granada Theatre in Tooting that evening. Here it was reported that he met with cries of "Cradle Robber" to reflect the age of his young bride **(though as said, Penny and I were unaware of this)**. The next show should have taken place the following evening at the Odeon, Birmingham, but Leslie Grade, Jerry Lee's British agent, who had booked the tour, had earlier in the day met with the President of Rank, who owned the tour's venues. At this meeting it was decided to cancel the rest of the tour, and at 2:15 p.m. Jerry Lee and Myra Gale left the Westbury Hotel through a side door, got into their limousine, and went back to the airport where photographers and reporters had assembled, some of whom heard Jerry Lee say "Who's this De Gaulle guy? He seems to have gone bigger than us." This followed Jerry Lee picking up a newspaper that reported on its front page that Charles De Gaulle had averted a civil war in his country, blazing his name in large letters.

Saturday and Holiday Jobs 1958-1964

I began taking paid part-time casual work long before I should have done legally. The Saturday job at Battersea Funfair has already been referred to. Another time I was employed painting novelty Santa Claus Christmas soaps in a small factory that functioned in a shed behind a building in Abbeville Road, Clapham. Yet a further job was collecting money for the coalman. I went around to the clients who had been out when he had had delivered their coal and so still owed him money. My mother knew this coalman and I think it must have been she who negotiated the job for me. In one of my summer holidays I worked at the Sunlight Laundry, Stockwell. Most of the workers in this laundry were middle-aged women and had what I considered coarse manners and a vulgar way of communicating with each other, but as I was to learn they also had hearts of gold. They may have talked and acted crudely, especially with the young delivery boys who they loved to tease and embarrass, and may have shrieked with laughter at the misfortunes of their bosses, but when they saw me – who might have been thought of as a stuck-up grammar school snob – sorting out dirty linen they had a serious talk with the supervisor and pointed out that a young girl "like me" should not be doing such dirty work. They made him change my task to checking the clean sheets and sorting them out according to their invisible number-codes. I was very grateful for their concern, and greatly humbled.

Once I had a Saturday job working in a ladies and babies' clothes shop at Clapham Junction. It was run by a middle-aged Jewish couple who knew how to make and save money. Both of them were short and plump and they used to sit at the back of the shop drinking foul smelling tea as they watched their young assistants serve customers and sort out the stock. Apart from the funny-smelling tea there was generally an unattractive odour about the place. I was never quite sure where it came from. It was not bad enough to be blocked drains, more like stale milk, but I couldn't trace it to any particular source. It didn't make for a very pleasant working environment. It was at this shop that I learnt how to fold blouses the professional way, replacing them neatly back into the plastic bags from which they had been taken to show prospective customers. I also learnt how to arrange baby layettes to their best effect and how to encourage clients to buy more than they intended. Originally I had been told my starting wage would be seventeen shillings and six pence, and this would rise to one pound after a probationary period. I could then earn even more, as much as one pound two shillings and sixpence for a Saturday if I proved really competent. There were two or three other Saturday girls in the shop, one of whom was older and had a full-time job during the week working at the Meteorological Office in Dunstable. She was paid the full one pound two shillings and sixpence for coming in on Saturdays, and was obviously the favourite much valued by the shop owners. I on the other hand was a clumsy under-age teenager lacking confidence. My wage remained at 17 shillings and 6 pence with no prospects of any increase despite my attempts to clarify the length of the probationary period. While at the shop we were paid a visit by the newly hired children's nanny of the famous film star, Diana Dors. The woman bought some baby clothes in the shop which she said was to be her present for Miss Dors' new baby son. This visit gave the establishment a lot of prestige, and we assistants something to gossip about.

My mother standing on my right at my wedding, wearing the pink fake pearl necklace I had bought her as a teenager with earnings from my Saturday jobs.

Photograph of Diana Dors in her heyday. © The Unholy Wife – Wikimedia

With some of the money I earned from my Saturday and holiday jobs I tried to please my mother and would now and again buy her a present that I thought she would like. One of these gifts was a long, double-string of pale-pink fake pearls, once again the fashion of the day. Shortly after I had given my mother the necklace, we had yet another of our almighty rows. Impulsively and childishly I blurted out "I wish I hadn't bought you that necklace now!" Her response was to unceremoniously return it to me, and she would not accept it back again despite my desperate pleas for her to do so. She knew how much this rejection would hurt me and she eventually put the necklace in the rubbish bin. At some point however, unknown to me, she must have relented and retrieved the necklace from the bin because she wore it on my wedding day many years later. Perhaps I was over-sensitive as a teenager, but at the time it seemed my efforts were never appreciated.

For a few months I worked Saturdays in a baker's shop in Streatham High Road, not far from Streatham Hill Station. The manageress of this shop seemed to warm to me. When I made mistakes she did not pile on the guilt, although she could be quite short tempered with another assistant. This other person was careless and didn't seem to make much of an effort. I think the manageress realised that at least I was trying to do my best. Another short-lived Saturday job was working on a stall in Balham Market. This small market was in Hildreth Street, with about five or six stalls down each side of the road. My job was to assist the owner of a small textile business. He had a stall and small shop on the right-hand side of the road as you looked up the street away from Balham High Road. I remember helping him take large rolls of material backwards and forwards between the stall and the adjacent shop at opening and closing times. In this job I learnt how to unroll and measure material, and cut it in a straight line.

The casual work I did most in my school holidays towards the end of my education at Clapham County, and the beginning of my studies at Camberwell Art School was catering. I joined a firm providing casual workers for catering businesses in the City and the West End of London, covering staff shortages brought about by sickness, holidays and unfilled posts. (I think the firm I worked for may have been called Mark Davies – or something similar.) My work involved preparing and serving food in works-canteens, taking tea and refreshments around to the offices on a trolley and once or twice helping with silver service in the prestigious restaurants set aside for managers and directors. I worked in places such as the Bank of England – Old Change and New Change – and some of the commercial establishments located in the old Barbican. In the late fifties and early sixties the Barbican was still more or less a bombsite after WW2, but the bulldozers were busy, and construction of new developments was underway. A few of the original buildings remained, and these continued business as best they could.

Through my catering work (unofficially and not very "health and safety wise") I learnt how to make an overheated dinner look appetising once more, and how to whiten stained teacups with bleach. I also learnt what Smorrebrod was, the fashionable Scandinavian snack of the day, and where to place items of cutlery in silver service, together with a few other tricks of the trade. Another skill I learnt from catering was how to distinguish true professionals from amateur social climbers, the ambitious nouveau riche with inflated egos. This knowledge came about through my experience with the staff I met in the offices where I took my tea trolley. The latter group tended to be mainly young women who had managed through luck or personal scheming to obtain a prestigious post such as personal assistant to a top executive. Many of these individuals showed me little respect; some even treated me like the dirt on their shoes. They had presumably progressed rapidly in their career and now assumed they were superior, not realising they lacked the social skills necessary to go with their new position. It was the first group of individuals, the ones who I suspected came from well-established stable families that knew how to relate to me as I served them their refreshments. This has led me to value the good manners and high standards that appear to be linked to good breeding – attributes that cannot be achieved "over-night". In my opinion leadership, dealing well with responsibilities, and having good social awareness is instilled over more than one generation. Rome was not built in a day, and good attitudes are best achieved slowly and thoroughly.

FOOTNOTE – Swiftly promoted former cabinet minister John Prescott in 2001 punched a provocateur on the nose in public. In my mind he did not have the necessary background to provide him with sufficient patience, tolerance and dignity to meet the needs of his position.

After this diversion, I will try to return to my memoires.............!

While still studying at Clapham County School Wendy Goodship would sometimes join me for the catering jobs up town, and we would travel together on the Northern Line underground trains from Balham or Clapham South Stations into Central London. A few times we tried to avoid payment of our fares, and on the last of these occasions we were caught by an inspector and instructed to go to Transport Headquarters in Central London where we were told we would, with our mothers present, be interviewed by an official. Wendy and I had separate interviews but on the same day and in the same building. When we compared notes in the corridor afterwards, we realised both our mothers had acted similarly; both had stood up for their daughters and said we were usually good girls but were desperately trying to save money and had made an error of judgement etc. etc. Wickedly Wendy and I laughed at the way our mothers had crawled to the officials, but fortunately for us their effort paid off and we were let off our crime with a caution. I suppose I should give my mother far more credit for the times she has bailed me out of trouble, but my instinct at the time was to think she did it more to save her own face rather than mine.

Early '60s Fashion 1958-1965

Teenage obsession in the late 1950s and early 1960s with the latest dress code has been alluded to in connection with the Locarno Ballroom. Like my mother I loved fashion. Whenever I had some money to spend, or it was my birthday and I could choose a present, I would go and buy a new dress or pair of shoes in the latest style, colour and material. My mother never prevented me from doing this. One birthday I was able to kit myself out in all the latest teddy-girl gear. I had a three-quarter length duffle coat (only mine was cream, while most were dark grey) black drainpipe trousers, luminous socks and a new pair of casual shoes. For a change I really felt I was on a par with other fashionable young people of the day. The only problem was I had to step out into the street in my new attire and as noted I was gaining a phobia about drawing attention to myself. I was petrified of being on show. After a while I did manage to venture out in these clothes, but only for short periods of time at the beginning. Somehow the anticipation of being out and about in the latest gear was marred by my extreme self-consciousness.

I was thirteen or fourteen years old when gingham returned to fashion. I attempted to make myself a new summer dress from large-pattered pink gingham material which I bought from Tooting Market. My mother had an old Singer sewing hand-machine at home with which she occasionally made items of clothing and some home furnishings. If she was in a good mood, she would allow me to use it, and so with the help of a pattern and skills learnt in my domestic science lessons at school I set about making the dress.

Apart from gingham being the height of fashion, so were large leg-of-mutton sleeves, square broderie-anglaise edged necklines and knee-length fully gathered skirts – all of which I incorporated into my dress. Under the skirt I wore a hooped crinoline petticoat. Full skirts were very popular in the rock and roll era and we kept them billowing out with either hooped petticoats, or petticoats made from yards of gathered nylon netting.

Often when I had money to spend on new shoes, I would go to Tooting Market, where there were several shoe stalls selling the latest designs which changed from year to year. For my gingham dress I bought a pair of flat, white, lace-up shoes with long winkle-picker toes. These shoes were made of cheap plastic and so after a while the extremely long toes began to curl up despite wads of cotton wool being pushed down into the empty cavity. Winkle picker shoes gave way in fashion to chisel-toe shoes with stiletto heels. I remember buying a pair of low stiletto heeled shoes, not chisel-toed but slightly pointed, in the latest colour – a wonderful, soft moss-green. Unfortunately I could not afford the matching bag to go with them. Friends and I enjoyed bargaining with the stallholders in markets such as Tooting and Brixton. I grew quite expert at it but confess my method was not entirely honest. I would tell the stallholder some sob story as to how I only had a certain amount of money and desperately needed the shoes or other item for some special occasion. Unfortunately this method of emotional blackmail has remained with me. Even today my conscious needs a lot of prodding before I put forward realistic arguments to negotiate a price. Marion, Aunty Phyl's eldest daughter by her first marriage lived with her mother and Uncle Cyril for a while in their Yukon Road flat. She considered herself to be a modern woman and often helped me where fashion was concerned. When big floppy jumpers came in, I wanted to have the biggest and floppiest ever. Marion agreed to make me one and knitted it to my stipulation in lavender coloured wool. (I think it was more of a cardigan than a jumper, because it had a huge zip up the front.) I asked her to make it even longer than the pattern dictated, and when I eventually wore it, it stretched and pulled down further with the weight of the wool. I had to put elastic around the bottom to keep it in place and stop it swaying about too much. Nevertheless, I loved my fashion statement jumper. When I began studying at Camberwell School of Art and Crafts it became my favourite garment-of-choice to wear.

Poor quality photograph taken in a caravan where I am wearing the gingham dress I made on my mother's old sewing machine.

Sketch of my gingham dress and my plastic winkle-picker shoes, with my hair done up in mini-beehive fashion.

-dancing in the moss green shoes I bought in Tooting Market and wearing a mock-silk green blouse to match.

At some point, I began experimenting with my hair and used a few colour rinses on it. The one I liked most was called Black Tulip, a dark brunette colour with a hint or burgundy. I even slightly bleached my hair on a couple of occasions. As to earrings, my mother had always let it be known she thought having your ears pierced for earrings was common, but it was becoming the in-thing and very trendy. I waited till I was 16 before I had my ears pierced, using some birthday money I had been given. Soon after this, to my surprise, my mother followed suit and had her ears pierced too. Other fashions I recall from my teens involved candy-pink lipstick, sack dresses, wide elasticised waist-belts, mohair skirts and jumpers, seer-sucker dresses and three-quarter jeans.

After the Teddy boy era of the mid 1950s two other youth cultures emerged for us teenagers – namely the Mods and the Rockers, and they played a part in influencing the fashion of the day. The Mods tried to be sophisticated and followers hung around dance halls, smart shops and fashionable places of entertainment. They dressed in the latest prescribed styles for their culture, namely shoe-string ties, uni-sex trilby hats, fancy-cut suits for men and the latest line in dresses for women. Many owned a Vespa or Lambretta scooter and you could often see groups of Mods sitting on their scooters and socialising with each other on street corners. Their contemporaries the Rockers were more practical. They usually rode motorbikes and their clothes were often leather, durable, comfortable and less fashionable. Sometimes they sported way-out hairstyles. Rockers liked to meet at transport cafés and seaside resorts, especially on bank holidays, and occasionally found themselves caught up in minor disputes. There were one or two clashes between rival Rocker gangs, but nothing too serious that I can remember. There were however some more serious clashes between Mods and Rockers. I personally encountered none but the media picked up and reported on bank holiday rioting at some seaside towns between the two cultures. On the whole though young people lived and let live. I did not fit completely into either the Mods or Rockers culture, and mixed with both, but on the whole, I suppose Wendy and I associated more with Mods in the way we dressed and in what we did.

I am not sure when stockings and suspender-belts were replaced by ladies tights. It may have been about the year 1963 that woman other than dancers took to the new garment. I know I was one of the first to wear them in my part of London. Mini-skirts were getting shorter and shorter and when women bent over, especially the fatter girls, flabby flesh could be seen between the stocking tops and the elasticised suspender-belt straps, which were often old and stretched out of shape. It was all very unsightly. I hope I was not one of the offenders but I decided it was about time I found out about the tights that were worn in the theatre. They proved to be very expensive, but somehow I managed to invest in a couple of pairs. Although I plead to having been poor in my youth, I somehow always mysteriously managed to provide myself with the odd luxury now and again! After my first purchase I began to wear tights whenever I had the money and opportunity. Other friends followed suit and it was not long before manufacturers were mass-producing them quite cheaply as their popularity increased.

As a teenager I believed my mother was keeping me short of money on purpose, especially when I needed to buy some new clothes. She appeared reluctant to help but when I think back, I can recall her compromising herself where fashion was concerned. Once, before Jill was born, she attempted to copy a fashionable hair-do of the time. It consisted of short tight curls either side of the face, with short straight-cut hair at the back. She managed to perm the sides of her hair herself, and then had Dad or a friend cut it around the back. It looked very severe and amateurish; anyone could tell it was a cheap copy of the real thing. My mother must have attempted this style for some special event because, at the same time she made a glamorous evening dress on her old sewing hand-machine. It was a sleeveless black dress with a straight skirt, overlaid with a fully gathered net overskirt decorated with black velvet polka dots. A plain black velvet sash completed the outfit which altogether looked quite stunning.

Jewellery was important to my mother. She chose items I thought were garish and cheap. Before she converted to earrings for pierced-ear she had accumulated masses of cheap clip-on earrings in every colour under the sun decorated with plastic or other artificial trimmings. She also loved her make-up that I considered she applied too harshly. I suppose as the dislike of my mother grew, so did my criticism of anything related to her. Any love there might have been between us certainly disappeared during my adolescent push for self-assertion, and her growing inability to cope.

Sketch of the evening dress my mother made for herself.

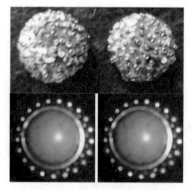

1950s-60s retro-vintage earrings

First Boyfriends 1957-1961

After my primary school attempt at romance with Michael Hall at Woodmansterne Road School, and my first date with a boy called Tony from Honeybrook Road, I began to take an active interest in attracting the attention of the opposite sex, especially the boys from the Balham area where I lived. Before my eleven plus examination my mother had promised she would buy me a bicycle if I succeeded in gaining a grammar school place. Having achieved this I could not understand why the bike did not materialise and began to remind her of the promise. When this did not result in a positive response, I began to badger her more assertively, and a year later my father found a second-hand bike that he renovated and passed on to me. It did not have gears and it was definitely not top of the range, but it was a bike, and I was able to venture out on it and make new friends. A group of us with bikes began to congregate regularly in Atkins Road, near a small park called Agnes Riley Gardens. One of the boys in the group became what I considered to be my special boyfriend. Intimacy was limited to holding arms round each other and a few pecks on the cheek, but the rest of the group considered us to be a pair and at least I liked this boy and enjoyed his company. He compared favourably with the non-starter Tony from Honeybrook Road, who had my mother's approval and consequently not mine.

Nearly everyone remembers their first proper kiss. Mine came one day when I took my bike over Streatham Common with Helen Hodges my friend from Clapham County School who also happened to have a bike. (Helen was the friend who joined Mary and me at Cilgwyn Baptist summer school.) Helen lived in Barrow Road, Streatham, not far from my old home in Cavendish Road, and so I knew her home-area well and I especially liked Streatham Common.

On this particular day we rode our bikes up to The Rookery at the top of the common. I remember exactly what I was wearing; I had on a second-hand but stylish dress with full skirt gathered in three horizontal sections, and my hair was arranged in the fashionable French plait or chignon style of the time. This had been styled for me earlier in the day by Aunty Phyl's daughter, Marion. Marion was a clerk for L'Oréal, one of the top hairdressing chains, and so she was quite knowledgeable about the art of hair dressing. I was feeling very trendy and enjoying a lovely sunny day out with a school friend. As Helen and I were about to leave the Rookery and ride back down the common to Barrow Road we met two boys. They too had been out riding on their bikes. We stopped and talked to them for a while, but as we mounted our bikes to ride off one of the boys pulled me down to the ground and gave me my first proper grown-up kiss. If I am honest, I was not greatly impressed. I didn't know quite what to do and I would have preferred to have been asked about it first. I also didn't think much of his attempt, but at least I was pleased that the boy liked me and I did not complain.

Agnes Riley Gardens, Atkins Road, Clapham © openplay

The Rookery, Streatham Common. © Nicky Johns-Wikimedia

As was the case with most London teenagers of the time a large part of my life was spent with girlfriends attracting suitable boys. On the whole we avoided serious relationships and concentrated on flirting with a little snogging thrown in. On one occasion in my mid-teens Wendy Goodship and I were invited by two boys to go with them to Brands Hatch and watch some banger racing. We did not particularly fancy the boys but one owned a car, and teenagers with cars in the early 1960s was a rarity. The boys picked us up and drove us down to Kent and the Brands Hatch circuit. On the return journey it became clear these boys thought the car gave them the right to seduce girls who accepted lifts in it. The car was even equipped with a mechanism that turned the seats into a bed. Wendy and I tactfully side-lined the sexual advances coming our way and avoided seeing the boys again after that outing.

I did have a few setbacks in flirting. From about the age of twelve, I began to suffer from acne, and would often have a cluster of nasty spots on my chin, back, chest, forehead and face. There was one that nearly always appeared between my eyebrows, and another right in the middle of my chin. I agonised over them for hours and they took away some of the self-confidence I had been gaining. Once when travelling alone on the number 118 bus, and sitting at the front, I began to look at my reflection in the glass panel between me and the driver's cabin and started fiddling with my hair trying to make it cover some of the spots. I felt extremely ugly. When the bus approached my stop at the top of Poynders Road for me to get off, before it turned right into the north half of Cavendish Road, I stood up and saw Uncle Cyril. Unknown to me he had been on the same bus sitting a few seats behind me and was a preparing to get off himself. He had seen what I had been doing and reported it back to my mother when he saw her. I think he was just reflecting on how I was growing up and taking an interest in my appearance, but I believe my mother saw it differently. I cannot remember her exact words but her tone of voice was mocking with the implication that I probably needed some adjustments where my appearance was concerned. Old photographs confirm that my mother had been extremely attractive as a young woman. Wherever possible my attention was drawn to this fact; I am convinced she wanted me to feel inferior and unglamorous in comparison.

At some point, Uncle Cyril had moved into a self-contained ground floor flat or maisonette in Yukon Road with Aunty Phyl, and Marion her daughter who later married and moved on. Uncle Cyril and Aunty Phyl were good homemakers. Aunty Phyl chose décor that made the flat really homely and Uncle Cyril used their small back yard to plant flower tubs and grow strawberries that climbed up a trellis. They did not have a proper bathroom but used a bath in the kitchen which was cleverly disguised with a worktop when not in use. Uncle Cyril was no longer working on the great ocean liners; he did factory jobs instead, once working for the Schweppes soft-drinks company from which he would sometimes bring back crates of soft drinks at cost price for family parties.

FOOTNOTE – I have now found evidence to suggest Uncle Cyril served in a special army unit in the Far East before World War Two, but by the late 1950s he seemed quite content to be in a less challenging job.

In addition to my spots, I acquired a dark hair-shadow on my upper lip in my teens. Most times I managed to disguise it, but obviously not well enough on one occasion. Peter Cox my boyfriend of the time who I had met through the Wandsworth Council of Youth, had taken me home one evening from a council meeting. As we kissed in the Cooperative shop doorway underneath my flat, he looked at me and said, "I didn't know you had a moustache!" He didn't mean any harm. He thought we could be open with each other about such things, but with my over-sensitivity the damage had been done, and after that comment I could not think of him in the same way anymore. I needed to have my morale boosted not deflated. I had enjoyed his company; we had had lots of fun together at parties, dances and the cinema – but not anymore. In some ways it was a pity because he was a reliable person, and serious about our relationship. Although I personally was not thinking long-term, he would occasionally throw out comments such as "when we are married…" "When I am in the army and we are stationed abroad…" – but I was just living for the moment. Now he could dream on. How could he have been so thoughtless?

Other than personal boyfriends I enjoyed several platonic male friendships. As a teenager, I belonged to a group who congregated in Tony's Café at the bottom of Bedford Hill near Balham Market and the High Road. We were all around the same age and met at the café to drink frothy coffee, a recent American import, and to play the jukebox, another American import. When the windows steamed up, we would jive to the music on the jukebox. Tony, the café owner, was a pleasant Italian man who did not have a licence for dancing but he turned a blind eye if we were discrete. The boys of our group became quite protective of us girls, and treated us like honorary sisters. They would not allow boys outside the group to mistreat us – while we knew for a fact that they were capable of treating other girls quite shabbily at times. More than once they let slip how they had managed to escape the consequences of some insincere sexual advances they had made, believing the girls in question deserved what they got.

One of the boys in this group had a minor disability, a malformed spine which left him with a slight hump in his back. We considered him an equal but this turned out to be to his detriment on one occasion at least. A few of us had been sitting around a table in the café when our conversation began to get a little boisterous. During the horseplay that followed I suddenly stood up and this boy who had been sitting next to me lost his balance and went flying across the floor. I had forgotten about his weak physical constitution. Luckily he was not hurt and his pride was soon mended.

The incident I recall that emphasises the fraternal nature of our group happened when I was about fifteen or sixteen. I had met one of the gang members while out very late one evening, and he took me home. I was feeling very low with all the bad things that were going on indoors. When we arrived at my flat, I invited him in; my parents, brother and young sister were already in bed and asleep and I encouraged him to stay. I was yearning for some physical comfort and am sure I would not have minded if he had used the opportunity to seduce me, but we remained sitting at the bottom of the stairs in the entrance hallway just talking, holding on to each other and occasionally kissing. He left early next morning, and must have realised my vulnerability and predicament because he did not taken advantage of the situation – for which I was later grateful. This experience has led me to admire individuals who are single-minded with the strength of character to remain focussed. When my family did eventually wake up that morning, my mother had not even realised I had been missing from my bed. I might have been abducted or attacked for all she cared. Incidents like this hurt me and added to my resentment. I hated my mother more and more for her weak resolve and lack of parental responsibility. Following my earlier years as a pupil of church Sunday schools, I had gone on to be a member of the church Bible Class for older girls at Immanuel Church, Streatham, but I was beginning to have a real problem in believing and practising the Christian faith. I could feel no love or forgiveness for my parents. How could life be so damned confusing and unjust? There was a part of me that wanted to do the right thing, but so many aspects of my life seemed to demand the opposite, and I felt handicapped by the domestic circumstances that surrounded me.

The only advice my mother ever gave me as a teenager was to "be careful when plied with drink, because it lowers your resolve". She also said that if I became pregnant, she would not chuck me out onto the streets as some mothers did. Unfairly I interpreted this to mean she would not mind if in fact I did get pregnant, because I imagined it would give her the excuse she needed to be superior and say "I told you so!" I hope this was not the case, and once again with hindsight I realise she may conceivably have been holding out an olive branch to me, letting me know that she had suffered from having an illegitimate child and would do her best to help me if I found myself in the same predicament. Whatever the reason, it made me all the more determined to keep control of my life and rule my hormones rather than let my hormones rule me.

Wandsworth Council of Youth 1958-1963

Through the Junior Red Cross I became a member of the Wandsworth Council of Youth (WCY). It met regularly once a month in a room at Wandsworth Town Hall, and proved a good social experience. I was able to meet representatives of other youth organisations and groups within the borough and we all got along well together. I believe I was only about thirteen when I first joined, younger than I should have been, but the Junior Red Cross Cadets in Streatham, (then part of Wandsworth,) had no one more suitable to represent them at WCY meetings. Being a bit of a sentimental hoarder I have kept a copy of WCY minutes sent to me following my absence from one of its meetings.

In them the formal structure of WCY can be seen balanced against some light-hearted topics raised.

LONDON COUNTY COUNCIL
WANDSWORTH COUCIL OF YOUTH
Minutes of meeting of the Wandsworth Council of Youth,
held at the Town Hall on Monday, 9 April 1962 at 8:15 pm.

PRESENT
Chairman: Mr Toomey
Youth Officer: Mr J Paton
14 members

MINUTES
The Minutes of the meeting of the Wandsworth Council of Youth held at the Town Hall on Monday, 12 March 1962 at 8:15 pm were taken as read and were signed by the Chairman, Mr Toomey. There were no matters arising.

CORRESPONDENCE
Apologies for absence were received from
Miss A Coysh and Miss M Lewis.

ROAD SAFETY
A brief report was given by the Sub-Committee showing how plans for a Road Safety Competition were progressing. A shop window has been secured at
The Royal Arsenal Co-op Ltd, Tooting.
A meeting of the Sub-Committee is to be held at The George, Balham Hill, on Monday, 16 April at 8 pm.

CLUB PROBLEMS
Suggestions as to what girls might like to do when attending a Youth Club were discussed and Ballroom dancing and visits to other clubs proved to be the most popular activities.

DATE OF NEXT MEETING
The next meeting will be held at the Town Hall on Monday, 14 May at 8:15 pm.

After completion of the business, Inspector Stangroom of the Putney Police gave an interesting and enlightening talk on Adolescent Delinquency.

A HOLDSWORTH SECRETARY

I enjoyed the whole WCY set-up and must have stayed a member for several years according to the date of my saved set of minutes. I particularly remember the time we attended a weekend residential conference in the early days of my membership. We stayed in accommodation near the Devil's Punch Bowl, Hindhead, Surrey, and Saturday lunchtime after the morning session some of us went along to a local pub to relax. I was the youngest by several years and was not the legal age for being in a pub but I was bought and drank an alcoholic drink – albeit only a half pint of lemonade-shandy! I felt I had well and truly arrived in the adult world. The publican never questioned my age, probably because I had made myself look older than I actually was. When we returned to the conference and the on-going debate, one of the boys who had been with us was supposed to give a short speech to second a motion within the debate. Unfortunately he could hardly string two words together. I had not seen him "tanking himself up" in the pub, but guessed he must have drunk more than he should have being nervous and seeking courage for his forthcoming task. After the first few words of his speech he dashed out of the room to the toilets to be sick, much to the disappointment of the leaders.

During my membership of WCY it was led by a fatherly figure who tried to focus the thoughts of self-willed and self-centred teenagers onto more serious issues. He showed us how to plan, think and develop discussion skills. At one of the monthly meetings while trying to do this, he suddenly turned to me and asked "What is your view on this Maureen?" I had not been listening and was lost for words. I blurted out something like, "Well it is the same as men wearing ties, isn't it? What is purpose of that?" hoping this might bear some relevance to the question. He looked stunned and carried on bewildered. It goes without saying my social circle was widened by my membership. Several of us became firm friends and started meeting outside the constraints of the official meetings. One such social event I can recall was a dance held in a building opposite Wandsworth Town Hall. I, together with Peter Cox, (still my boyfriend at the time,) and several others, enjoyed ourselves chatting and dancing to ballroom and rock and roll music. Among the songs we danced to were those of Cliff Richard, Elvis Presley, Buddy Holly and Tommy Steel. Another time a group of us from WCY went to see a horror film together; these films were the fashionable entertainment of the time. We really felt the world was ours. Being a teenager in the late fifties and early sixties was a wonderful experience for most of us.

Home Problems

I am not sure when my father began to show signs of perversion. I think it may have been soon after Jill's birth. First there were a few occasions when I caught him wandering down the hallway naked – not our usual family practice by any means – then there was the spying. At first, I was not sure whether I was imagining it, but eventually I knew for certain that he was spying on me through the keyhole in my bedroom door when I undressed and no one else was around. Bath times too were becoming a problem. As has been mentioned the loft in Cavendish Road was entered through a hatch-door in the bathroom ceiling. First you had to climb the ladder kept in the bathroom, then clamber through into the roof-space which was as big as a small room. My father used the loft-space as his workroom and kept his tools there. He had made a workbench in it and installed electric lighting. I began to notice he was using this workroom most times I was having a bath. He would go up the ladder and close the hatch-door before I ran the bathwater, saying he would stay there until I had finished having my bath, but I started to feel uneasy, especially when I heard disconcerting shuffling noises as I bathed. Eventually one day when I was in the bath, I caught sight of a small beam of light coming through what could have been a spy-hole, so when he was out of the flat one day, I went up to see the situation for myself. I discovered a hole in the wood-partition that had full view of the bath and it even had a swing-cover over it. Confirmation of my suspicion shocked me and I found it difficult to communicate with my father in any meaningful way after this. We were already having regular screaming and physical fights, many provoked by my mother, and it was not difficult to go one step further and break off all communication with the man I had grown up knowing as my dad.

My father and I did not speak, send birthday cards or recognise each other's presence in the room from then on until sometime after I had left home. I did not challenge my father about my discovery, and at the beginning I did not tell my mother either. Quite rightly I knew her reactions would not help matters. When I did eventually break down in tears and blurt the news out to her she pretended not to believe me. I have since wondered if secretly she hoped something like this might happen to give her an excuse to rid herself of the husband she seemed to despise, or at least to have moral high ground over him. She was certainly finding more and more opportunities to humiliate him in public for his lack of sex-drive and lack of general ambition. Several years later, my mother told me she did in fact confront my father with the allegation soon after she knew about it herself, but if she did, I was not involved in the following discussion and certainly did not know the outcome. Whatever she did or did not do was not for my benefit.

I have already described the earlier childhood physical punishments I received from my father, and blamed many of them on my mother as the provocateur. I explained how on his return home from work she would goad him by telling him how difficult and unmanageable I had been, until he finally snapped. Sometimes he would use a strap or cane on me as she did herself from time to time. I had the feeling my mother gained some sort of sick pleasure from seeing my father lash out at me, although once or twice when things got out of hand, she did make a weak unconvincing attempt to intervene. A scene I cannot forget was when my mother was out of the house one day. For some reason I was in the front room and still in my nightdress despite it being mid or late morning. It may have been a Saturday morning, with me staying in my room and in my bed as long as possible to avoid yet more family arguments. Something caused my father and me to begin another physical fight. He tussled me to the ground causing my nightdress to fly up. I felt humiliated and ashamed because I was not wearing any underwear. Instinctively I scratched his arms making him bleed. Thankfully there was a knock on the door at this point. It was the insurance man calling for his money. My father decided he had to answer the knock and while he did so I grabbed some clothes and dashed down the stairs. As I passed him and the insurance man on the door-step I shouted out "sex maniac" to my father. This was unfair, because my father had not sexually assaulted me. It must have looked extremely bad to the visitor with me being half dressed, and my father with blood streaming down his arm. I ran across Yukon Road to Uncle Cyril and Aunty Phyl's flat. Aunty Phyl was there; tearfully I told her about the troubles I was having with my father. She was sympathetic, and I assume in order to try and help me put things in perspective told me about an uncle who had sexually molested her as a young girl. I am so grateful my stepfather had not actually touched me inappropriately. I do not think I was strong enough psychologically to have weathered that sort of situation.

Since reflecting on that unfortunate incident, another earlier occasion comes to mind that shows my father in a more positive light. It happened when my mother was in hospital giving birth to my sister. With her knowledge, and for some unknown odd reason, I shared my parents' put-u-up bed in the front room with my father. Our relationship was still good at this point and I remember him coiling up around me but there was no sexual touching or abuse. This leads me to think that on the whole my father must have been a very controlled man.

Years later after I had left home but still unaware of my true paternity my father openly apologised to me and my mother for his weak moral standing. It followed one of his mental breakdowns and residential stays in Tooting Bec Mental Hospital. To try and show us his remorse he bought and presented us both with a pendant. These two pendantnecklets were identical except for the colour; mine was blue and my mother's mauve. I know he fully intended to try and put things right.

The blue pendant that my father gave me.   The mauve pendant given to my mother.

Immanuel Church, S.W. 16. 1956-1964 – Part 1

The Bible class I attended from about the age of eleven at Immanuel Church, Streatham Common, was the place where I met Penny Smith and another long-term friend, Karen Fagan. Our Bible class group was led by two unmarried ladies, Miss Downing who led the session with Bible readings, short talks and prayer and Miss Locke who played the piano for our hymn singing and choruses. The choruses we sung came out of the Crusader Chorus Book. There was no heavy religious indoctrination in these classes but all the songs and talks were Bible-based and intended to show the relevance of following Christ. Immanuel and many other British churches of the time were benefiting from the work, dedication and leadership of Christians recently converted or inspired by the American evangelist Billy Graham. Our leaders were two such ladies; both proved sincere and caring individuals. After a while, Miss Locke became engaged to a divorcé – with children if I remember correctly. No one in the church criticised her for this despite divorce and remarriage being considered a poor option for Christians in most religious circles of the day. All wished her well and meant it, but there was an undercurrent of feeling that perhaps it was not an ideal situation. Apart from her choosing someone who had already promised to remain faithful to another, whatever problems there might be, there was also the notion that she might be taking panic action because of her fading youth.

I enjoyed going to Immanuel Church for my Bible class each Sunday but as stressed my faith took a battering during this period. I was questioning my childhood beliefs and the central truth of Christianity. Nevertheless I decided to be confirmed as a believing Christian in the Church of England. That was what I wanted. At the age of fourteen towards the end of my time in Bible Class, and before going onto the church's youth group, I with others from the Bible Class were approached to see if we wanted to be confirmed as Christians. Those who did took a short course of instruction culminating in an interview with the vicar, the Rev Donald Whitaker. He made sure we understood the implications of what we were about to do. Rev Whitaker portrayed a fatherly figure, although I felt he was not very interactive with young people. Some years later a younger friend at Immanuel, (who also happened to be the daughter of one of my teachers at Clapham County School,) confided in me that a year or two earlier the Rev Whitaker had made sexual advances to her when she found herself alone with him in a room. The incident had left her emotionally scarred. I believe the matter came to the attention of the church authorities and action, however inadequate, was taken. It was not long after this that the church appointed a new vicar, the Rev John Collie.

Karen, Penny and I took the confirmation course, and were confirmed together at the Church of the Holy Redeemer, in Streatham Vale. Three Anglican churches in Streatham joined forces for this annual event, and the confirmation service rotated between the three church buildings; our year it happened to be the turn of the Holy Redeemer Church to be host. My mother made me a special dress for the occasion in sailcloth, the fashion material of the year. It was white with long sleeves, a high waistline under the bust, a straight skirt to the knees and a rolled yoke-collar – all very stylish. Most of the girls and women wore white for the ceremony and the boys and men wore white shirts with dark trousers. It was 1959 and traditional practices were still respected. Before the ceremony began females were issued with large white nun-style headgear to wear in the church. My mother came to the service with Uncle Cyril, my godfather. He was quite respectful but I know he secretly thought I was getting a bit weird with my religion. Aunty Kit my godmother was not able to attend but sent me a small white-bound prayer book as a present. My two other godparents, with the Canadian connection, had been "off-radar" since my christening and obviously not in attendance. Over the decades that have succeeded our confirmation, Penny, Karen and I have remained very close friends. We have led completely different lives and our personalities, strengths and weaknesses are far from being similar, but the three of us have kept our Christian faith one way or another and we have remained in touch, sharing the good things and bad things that happen to us along the way. We know we can depend on each other for help should the need arise, and we are grateful for the faith that was passed on to us in our youth.

FOOTNOTE – Penny died early 2017, and Karen in 2018. I miss them both dreadfully.

Not long after my confirmation, with some excitement, I joined the church's mixed youth group, the Young People's Fellowship, or YP as it was affectionately known. I was a regular member from 1959 till 1964. The club meetings were initially held in the Beehive Rooms, a building not far from the church. This building has quite a history of which I was totally unaware at the time.

The Beehive Rooms, Streatham – © Stephen Richards.

Members of Immanuel youth club met every Thursday evening in a first-floor room, which because of its shape was called the L-shaped Room. On entering at the bottom of the L shape, you were faced with a table-tennis table and a record player in the far corner. Walking through, and turning right to the back part of the L shape, you arrived at a catering area. The windows on the left-hand wall looked out onto the main road and in the central space there were tables and chairs for consuming refreshments; the sectioned off area against the right-hand wall had kitchen facilities that functioned behind a counter. The furniture in the centre was sometimes cleared, or rearranged, to make way for the more formal gatherings of the club. I have recently seen references on the internet concerning the Beehive Rooms that suggest the L-shaped room must have been the Billiard Room of the original Temperance Coffee Tavern.

HISTORY OF THE BEEHIVE ROOMS
information from details found on the internet

The Beehive Rooms in Streatham is a Grade Two listed building, and is a prominent red brick structure standing opposite Streatham Common. It was built as a coffee tavern in 1878, and was designed by Ernest George. It had been sponsored by the then vicar of nearby Immanuel Church, the Rev Stenton Eardley, and by other members of the Temperance Movement who wanted a local centre where working class men could go for a decent meal and non-alcoholic drinks away from the temptation of the public houses and other hostelries. Land for the tavern was donated by Ebenezer Cow, the inventor of Cow Gum.

On the first floor of the building there was originally a billiard's room, and a reading room, and on the second floor, dormitories for some of the apprentices of the adjacent factory; at the rear was the lecture hall where speakers came to give "improving talks" to the workmen. Unfortunately it was sited close to the Pied Bull Public House, which proved a greater attraction for the tavern's intended customers, and the tavern did not prosper.

The Beehive Coffee Tavern continued to run an eating house on its ground floor into the early twentieth century, but the rest of the building had been taken over by the PB Cow and Co factory by then, and in the 1930s the firm took over the ground floor too. For a while Immanuel Church retained a minor interest in the building and groups such as the church's youth fellowship met there, but little maintenance was done on the structure of the building and in the 1980s it was only the campaign of local people who saved it from demolition.

The building and adjacent Factory Square was then sold to the Sainsbury's firm, and as part of the sale agreement the Beehive Rooms were refurbished by Sainsbury's at their cost. In 1990, Sainsbury's sold the Beehive Coffee Tavern to the solicitor's firm Henry Hughes and Hughes.

The friends I met at the youth club were a positive blessing to me, and played a big part in the next few years of my life. They were my emotional corner stone and stability. As individuals we were very diverse. Some members were medical students, training to be doctors, nurses and therapists, others secretaries, some were shop-workers, students, accountants, factory workers, cleaners and yet others apprentices of one kind or another, some had gone (or were still going) to state school, others to public school, but we were one big family. I remember once talking to a club member who was a trainee medical doctor. I kept stumbling over my words because I think I was trying to impress him. I felt such a fool and apologised. He immediately made me feel at ease by saying, "It's not how you speak that matters, but what you say." I've since forgotten his name but I do remember the name of another trainee doctor at the club. He was Arnold Smith and lived with his parents on the Balham-Clapham Park border not far from where I lived in Cavendish Road. His home was a large house in Clarence Avenue almost opposite Agnes Riley Gardens and his father was involved with the Knights Christian Youth Movement, which had a centre in Streatham Place. (I'm not sure if his father held an official post there or was a volunteer helper.)

Despite Arnold's old-fashioned name, he was a very modern person and was reading medicine at Kings College Hospital, Dulwich – the hospital where I had been born. Once he invited me and a few others to go with him to a medical charity hop in Chislehurst Caves. It was quite an experience. I felt privileged to go but was a little surprised and perhaps disgusted at the things I saw there. I witnessed middle-aged professionals, who I assumed were doctors, surgeons and consultants, slumped in corners of the cave looking very drunk, and younger medical students appearing rather "high", dancing with few inhibitions. This was not the behaviour I imagined from such professionals. Thankfully not all partygoers abandoned propriety. Some, like Arnold, managed to meet friends, enjoy themselves and share laughs without losing self-respect.

FOOTNOTE. As late as 2019 the internet continued to list Arnold as being an active and practising professional i.e. "Dr. Arnold Graham Smith is a Jacksonville, Florida-based male orthopaedic surgeon who is specialized in Orthopaedic Surgery of the Spine." (The background attached with this posting confirmed it was the same Arnold Smith.)

The youth club sessions on Thursday evenings consisted of a main social activity with a short Christian epilogue at its conclusion. Sometimes the social activity would be a competition, quiz or debate, but when all else failed we just chatted to friends, played table-tennis and listened to records on the gramophone with a few of us jigging, jiving and rock and rolling to the music. Occasionally, following the Thursday evening gathering, a few of us would wonder down to the Rumbling Tum Coffee Bar in Streatham High Road, near Streatham Station.

Extra activities arranged by Immanuel youth club included country rambles, one of which was the traditional Boxing Day ramble, and some events held Saturday evenings such as squashes (i.e. parties), and theme evenings including Tramps Suppers and Wild West evenings. My special love was the Boxing Day ramble. On that day two or three leaders would accompany about twenty to thirty club-members into the Kent or Surrey countryside. We would travel by train or coach. Often it would be a cold, frosty, bitter day, and once or twice there was snow on the ground. We wrapped ourselves up in warm clothes and some members took the trouble to decorate their scarves, boots, gloves, coats and hats with festive items. Many of us had over-indulged the day before with our Christmas dinner, and so were looking forward to meeting friends and walking off our excess calories. The routes we took for these rambles frequently went through unspoilt countryside and could be a little strenuous at times but they were never over-challenging. Those who were physically stronger helped those who were less fit. The hoots of laughter that could be heard when we found ourselves stuck in mud, caught in hedges or awkwardly trying to negotiate stiles and fences, confirmed the fun we were having. Somehow the jokes that were told on the Boxing Day ramble always seemed extra comical. Roughly halfway through the ramble we would stop for a picnic and sometimes we found a friendly country pub where we could stop for a festive beverage (non-alcoholic for those under-aged, who sat outside with their orange juice or lemonade!). On the return journey by public transport we would enthusiastically sing aloud the well-known songs of the day, plus a few that were rather risqué for a church youth-club outing, much to the amusement of the other passengers.

I got to know some club members really well; Adele Pentony was one. She was an unusual character, a bit of a hare-brain, which suited me; I never was one for boring, conventional friends. Apparently Adele had been adopted after the war. She lived with her stepparents and stepsister, Marianne, in a smart house in Belltrees Grove beside Streatham Common. Her adopted family came across as generous, caring, friendly and open-minded, but whereas I saw them as sophisticated and suave I saw Adele as the opposite – a bit way-out, trendy and extremely casual. I believe Adele had the same pocket money for clothes and teenage accessories as did her stepsister, but she never managed to look quite as polished; she seemed to enjoy acting the wild-child of the family. As a loving unit everyone was equally valued and Adele's parents did not mind her bringing back her friends to their home. I and other friends enjoyed going around to Belltrees Grove to listen to Adele's music in her bedroom, or look at her latest acquisitions. I believe Adele said her adopted father owned or ran a car-sales showroom near Balham Station.

FOOTNOTE – On 29 October 2008 I had a surprise email from Adele in response to my earlier attempts to contact her. She too had been making an effort to try and find me, and was living in New Zealand. She seemed just as full of life and interests as she ever was, but told me she was NOT in fact adopted, and Marianne was a full-blood sister. The misinformation I had been given earlier probably came about as the result of Adele's mischievous joking. Being the imaginative sort she was she was probably trying to see the reaction of friends to her make-believe tales. I also learnt that her father was some sort of a lawyer working for the Moss and Lawson Company, a car-specialist firm in Balham and Thornton Heath.

Another friend I met at Immanuel, whose name I have since forgotten, was also adopted after the war. She lived in Westwell Road just behind Immanuel Church with her stepparents and stepsister. Unlike Adele this girl was the sophisticated one of her family. She always had her hair groomed stylishly and had perfectly manicured and painted nails. Her clothes looked as though they had come straight off the back of a mannequin. Her adopted family were kind, caring and loving, just as Adele's was, but they lived in a more modest home. It was by no means drab or old-fashioned, but it could not boast all the latest personal and domestic trimmings and facilities that Adele's home had. In her late teens this friend surprised us all be leaving the good secretarial position she held in London, together with the good social life that went with it, and went to work on a farm in the countryside. She forfeited her long fingernails, coiffured hair, stiletto shoes and trendy gear for Wellington boots and dungarees. I am sure it was down to the love and care of her adopted family that gave her the confidence to experiment with her identity, and take on new challenges.

I remember quite clearly one particular boy at the club, although he is another whose name I have since forgotten. Like many families after the war he lived with his parents and older sister in a council owned flat. His one was at the bottom, north-side of Streatham Common. There was a bit of an age gap between him and his sister and I imagined she may have been born before or at the beginning of the war, and he at the end. On leaving school this boy joined a firm to study accountancy. His sister also held a good job in London. In my usual opinionated way I summed the sister up as being a staid, prim and proper individual, so unlike her brother who appeared far more modern, lively and outgoing. This assessment was soon dispelled when I attended a party the boy held at his home one evening. There were about sixteen of us at the gathering, mostly members of Immanuel YP. The boy's parents diplomatically disappeared for the evening and the sister was left behind to keep a discrete eye on the proceedings. There was food,

118

music, dancing and some alcohol. Through the evening I must have eaten and drunk more than I should have done because eventually I disgraced myself and had to rush out of the room to be sick in the bathroom. Unfortunately I missed the toilet and soiled the floor. I felt really terrible. I saw it as a privilege that I had been invited to the party and now I had shown how irresponsible I could be. I expected to be cold-shouldered and sent home, but instead the incident was taken as a matter of course and the boy's sister was particularly kind. She helped me clean up the mess and did not pile on the guilt. I apologised to her profusely but all she said was, "It's just one of those things that many of us experience at one time or another."

Another friend at YP lived in a council flat not far from the one where I had gone to the party. This was Susan Barnes affectionately known as Bunny. Her home proved another where I felt very welcome whenever I went around to it. Susan's parents were young-at-heart and very friendly. I think her father may have been a local councillor. He and his wife had strong political affiliations which I came to realise were Socialist or strong left wing, but they never tried to influence me or sign me up to any of their good causes. I only discovered about their political leanings and involvements through overhearing some of the comments they made to each other. Susan's home was bright, well decorated and maintained, and was a further haven where I could relax from my volatile surroundings in Balham.

Jane and Robert were Susan's much younger sister and brother, possibly twelve or more years younger than she was. Susan told me her parents had only intended to have one child but when they discovered a second unplanned baby was on the way they decided to welcome him or her and go one step further by having a third child so that the two younger children would be company for each other. Once again everyone in that home was loved, valued and cared for. It showed in the way they looked out for each other and regularly talked about each other's interests and achievements. This love extended to those the family came into contact with, and when Susan came to my twenty first birthday party, she not only gave me a present from herself but also one from Jane and Robert, a Churchill Medallion, a gesture no doubt inspired by Mr and Mrs Barnes, one I very much appreciated.

I continued to be close friends with Bunny until well into my career and my thirties. When I acquired a camper van the two of us went on a couple of camping holidays together. I cannot remember the exact career she pursued, I think it was linked to banking or secretarial work, but I do recall the flat she rented with two or three of her friends after leaving school and beginning her first job. It was in Croydon, near the Fairfield Halls. (Later I describe a party I went to at this flat.) Susan eventually married and went with her husband to live and work in Ndola, Zambia, on an expat's contract. Michael, Susan's husband, had strong left-wing political convictions like her parents, but in my opinion, he was more obvious in the way he promoted and advertised this. For instance he was proud to let people know that the Zambian house-boy he and Susan hired in Ndola was not only paid a proper wage but was also given adequate time off and finances by them to further his education and gain qualifications. The young Zambian man was not treated like a servant but as a valued member of a team. I agreed with this totally but felt Michael was a little self-righteous in the way he talked about it. One summer when I was on vacation from my teaching job I went to stay with Susan and Michael in Ndola for the month of August. It was a great experience, one I haven't forgotten because with Susan and Michael I was not just another tourist, but I was able to experience aspects of Zambian life, culture and politics that are not usually encountered by the average British traveller.

There were two boys at Immanuel Church youth club who proved to be very good platonic boyfriends. They were Brian Turtle and Peter Drew. Brian lived with his family in one of the newly erected town houses in Streatham. Town houses were becoming the residential fashion of the day. I think Brian's father may have been a builder and, if so, was probably involved in the house's construction. Brian owned a mini-car which, as has been mentioned, was quite an asset for a young person in the early 1960s. Adele and I would sometimes make up a foursome and go out with the two boys for trips and outings. In hindsight I hope I was not just using the boys because of the car. Brian and Peter were good companions but in my view definitely not romantic boyfriend material. Brian was tall, fair and had a nice personality, but was not what I would call especially good-looking, and Peter had a terrific sense of humour but to me he also was not that physically attractive, although I believe to Adele he may have been because she considered him to have been her first boyfriend. It was Brian's mini that took him, Peter, me and another girl (I cannot be sure it was Adele), to Lee Abbey Youth Camp, in Devon, one year. Brian did all the driving, and towards the end when he was feeling tired swerved the car up on two wheels at an awkward bend on a minor road. If the car had tilted over completely, we would have crashed through a gate and down a steep bank. Fortunately Brian's quick thinking and good manoeuvring meant no harm came to us or his car.

Lee Abbey Youth Camp, Lynton, North Devon. 1963-1964

Lee Abbey Youth Camp was a further great experience I had as a teenager. It was organised by the Church of England primarily as an evangelistic outreach to young people, and was held every year during the month of August. Most campers stayed for a whole fortnight during this time, while a few stayed for just one week. I stayed for a full fortnight the summers, of 1963 and 1964. Many teenagers in the 1960s tended to stay in their childhood home till marriage and the camp was a chance to enjoy a degree of independence, with opportunities to socialise without family interference. This was especially true for students who could not afford the more exotic summer holidays enjoyed by their working friends. The present Gap-Year experience enjoyed by many students these days was a little-known entity in the 1960s. Lee Abbey was a proper well-organised camp with leaders and campers under canvas. There were about eight campers to a tent. Girls slept in tents one end of the field and boys the other. There was a large communal marquee for eating meals and for meetings, a small marquee which acted as the kitchen where volunteers did the cooking, and a further area in the field for the girls' chemical toilets and washing facilities with another for the boys.

On the whole campers were able to organise themselves during the day, choosing which activities to join in and which friends to mix with. Romance was definitely on the agenda for many campers, with several hoping to find a potential boyfriend or girlfriend at camp if they hadn't one already. It was all good innocent fun but there were a few incidents that caused the leaders a headache or two. Although campers wouldn't admit it the leaders were still in the background unobtrusively supervising. Even in our tents we had one older, more responsible person keeping an eye on our general welfare and I suppose our behaviour too. One such incident centred on a girl who was particularly attractive. She had long dark curly hair, a good figure, wore stylish modern clothes and had a gregarious personality. She was also disabled, having only one proper arm; the other was missing from the elbow down. One night she and a boy went "AWOL". The couple were eventually found by the leaders at the Victorian folly, an assimilated ruined tower which stood at the top of the hill the other side of Lee Bay to our camp. This couple had taken alcohol with them and obviously intended getting to know each other a lot better. It was the type of liaison discouraged at the camp and I suspect the leaders felt the girl being handicapped was emotionally more vulnerable than most. Her family would certainly not have approved of her actions. Personal discipline was still expected in church youth groups despite the advancing onslaught of sixties permissiveness.

Lee Abbey House
Lee Abbey is not, and never was a real abbey. The large building was erected by a former architectural romancer. It and its land now belong to a Christian community.

One of the activities I enjoyed most at camp was the challenging ramble down and around Doone Valley, on Exmoor. The route we took was about twenty miles long. I loved the unspoilt countryside we passed and the farm where we stopped for our cream tea. Some of the campers were well equipped and had proper walking shoes, but all I could find to wear on my feet was a pair of old Wellington Boots. Believe it or not I found these quite comfortable and throughout the walk I did not gain one blister which was often the case when I wore heavier shoes. At a later date a reunion was held for Lee Abbey campers in London, and a leader played a cine-film showing scenes from this Doone Valley walk. He made everyone laugh with his comments about me and my boots. That was what I liked about Lee Abbey people laughed with you and not at you. Nobody was belittled or made to feel stupid; everyone was a valuable part of a community.

We had so much fun at camp and made friendships that lasted years. Those who were musically inclined brought along guitars or other instruments, and there were several impromptu sing-along sessions as we sat on the grass outside our tents or on the beach. Other campers were gifted at telling jokes or recalling hilarious incidents and others were just funny in themselves, making us double up with laughter every time they spoke. One rather childish but hilarious prank I remember involved the chemical toilets. We were leaving a camp get-together in the marquee one evening when I joined the usual line of girls going down to the female toilets before turning into our tents. It was very dark and we only had a few torches between us. As we neared the cubicles, we could hear sounds of disgust and dismay from those already in the cubicles. It took some time for it to be realised that the mess around the toilet seats inside the cubicles was marmalade, and not the substance feared. Some joker had taken marmalade from the stores and spread it over the seats while we were at the meeting.

Time at the camp was structured and well organised, but as I have said we could choose whether or not we joined in the activities. Mornings began with breakfast in the marquee. For a prank on one of these occasions the friends of a boy who had decided to

121

skip breakfast to sleep in a little longer dragged him into the centre of the marquee in his sleeping bag as the rest of us were eating. He was obviously sleeping naked and could not escape and keep his dignity intact at the same time. There was a lot of laughter until eventually someone offered him a pair of shorts that he pushed down inside the bag and put on before getting out of the sleeping bag and escaping. The incident was taken in good spirit by victim and audience.

Lee Abbey youth camp looking down to Lee Bay.

Camp tents with chemical loos behind.

The camp with Lee Abbey House just visible on the horizon above.

After breakfast, there was a morning briefing and a small Christian service with a hymn or two and a couple of prayers. Most of us attended this although it was not compulsory. Afterwards, we had the option of joining in the day's activity, which might be a ramble, fun-challenge, sporting event, outing, competition – or spending personal time in the camp or on the beach. Arrangements were made for lunch. Then in the evening after the main meal, there was another gathering in the marquee. Like the morning session this too included a religious service, but a slightly longer one this time with a short Christian talk. Once again most of us attended though it was not obligatory.

Campers relaxing with the camp marquees in sight.

Lee Abbey folly.

The camp with the hill behind that has the Victorian folly at its peak.

Two young people entertaining fellow campers in the camp marquee.

I am on the left of three friends in this picture. We are standing in front of Lee Abbey House.

The talks were often interesting and relevant and seemed to sum up the mood and atmosphere of the camp and were even quite enjoyable at times. At one of the evening sessions, towards the end of each camp holiday, a challenge was put out for campers to become whole-hearted followers of Christ, and many responded and did just that. It was a natural request; there was no mass hysteria or undue pressure. We were all sad to leave when our week or fortnight was up and would spend ages saying goodbye to our new found friends.

One incident I witnessed at Lee Abbey that I originally thought happened when I was a camper there, but recent research reveals it happened in the late 1960s, probably in 1967 when I returned to Lee Abbey as a houseguest one August, was featured in a television documentary about belief in angels, and has also been described and discussed elsewhere in the media. My personal recollection of this incident is of my wandering down to the youth camp field and standing talking to some of its members. Someone near me shouted out "Stop and pray" and pointed across the ravine. This ravine or gully is created by a small stream that runs down to the sea – Lee Abbey House and its adjacent fields one side, and the camp field the other. We all looked and I could see an unmanned tractor rolling down the sloping field the other side of the gully. It was gaining momentum and moving rapidly towards the cliff that overlooks the mouth of the gully. I remember this gully mouth as being wide enough for a few holidaymakers and day-trippers to park their cars in. I realised that if the tractor went over the edge of this cliff, as it surely would, it would crush the cars and far worse possibly some of the holiday makers and day-trippers who were collecting beach things ready to go down to the sea. There was nothing anybody could do. In my mind's eye I can clearly see the person who called out. I knew she was a camp leader and the wife of one of the camp clergy, and I now believe she was the Pam Fardon of the article to follow. I recall her as being slightly stocky with shoulder length dark hair and wearing a light summer top with dark blue shorts. It's funny how certain scenes are etched in our minds like the times we hear of some great international event and can recall exactly where we were and what we were doing.

Luckily the tractor fell on top of just one car, and no one was badly hurt. I think there was a group of children nearby with their buckets and spades waiting for their parents to take them to the beach. I later learned that a worker at Lee Abbey had forgotten to put the hand brake on in the tractor when he left it for a moment. When the vehicle began to move, he was too far away to jump back on and pull the brake back up. The Fardons and some others say they saw a person at the steering wheel of the tractor manoeuvring it to a reasonably safe outcome, when in fact there was no human being in it. They believe divine intervention had taken place and the person they saw at the wheel was an angel. I did not have this same vision but I do believe that prayer is not wasted in dangerous situations.

AN ACCOUNT OF THE LEE ABBEY TRACTOR INCIDENT:

On surfing the internet, I found an article by John Woolner that outlines the tractor incident that I remember. It is a second hand account, but nonetheless confirms my memory. The following is a summary of his account…….

In the late 1960s, Ray Fardon, a clergyman, and his wife, Pam, were helping to lead a youth camp at Lee Abbey near Lynton in North Devon. Pam was outside enjoying the beauty of the countryside and the coastline when she was distracted by the sound of a noisy engine. On looking up she saw a tractor out of control, careering haphazardly down the steep field opposite. The driver steered it through a gate but it accelerated as it rolled down the second sloping field. By this time guests at Lee Abbey House and some of the youth from the camp had come out to watch in horror. Some began praying for the driver who was trying to gain control of his machine racing down towards the car park below, where holiday makers were picnicking. Pam prayed "Lord, please change its direction". Shortly after this it veered to the side, somersaulting over a cliff but missing the car park.

Ray raced down the cliff pathway with a few other men, telling all around to pray. The tractor was found upside down on a car that had been parked by a chalet on the beach. The owner of this car was a widowed mother of a large family, who had just left her car to wander back to the chalet, wondering why she had done so. Her car was completely crushed, but thankfully no one was seriously hurt. Ray and colleagues unsuccessfully searched for the driver of the tractor. Soon after a man appeared on the scene admitting he was the driver but said he had not been in the tractor when it rolled down the fields. He had left it with engine running at the top of the field while he got out opening a gate. It then began moving off on its own.

Ray and Pam Fardon with others are certain they saw someone driving the tractor as it descended, eventually avoiding disaster. Pam described the man as being dressed in brown and leaning right over the steering wheel with his hands crossed over. She and others are convinced it was an angel.

This friend of the Fardons who wrote this internet account believes the only alternative to accepting angel intervention is to believe that a number of people all suffered hallucinations at the same time, and that the convenient diverted route of the tractor was merely a coincidence.

Immanuel Church, SW16. 1956-1964 – Part 2

Leaders at YP changed from time to time but members tended to remain as long as they possibly could, some from fourteen years old until their late 20s. The bonds that were formed between club individuals were even stronger than those I had known at Tony's Café in Balham. One member, Brian Snellgrove was like a brother to me and helped me immensely. When I realised I had to make a clean break from my family in 1963, he found me half-board and lodging, and later when that proved untenable canvassed his landlady on my behalf for a room that had just become vacant in his lodging house. (Further on this is more fully detailed.) Brian was the son of a high church vicar; Immanuel was low church and evangelical, the opposite of the Anglo-Catholic and other high churches that Brian had been accustomed to as a child. Apparently Brian was even designated his own guardian-angel at birth, and was brought up with all the pomp and ceremony of high church culture. When older and an independent thinker Brian seemed more at home with the simple low-church traditions of Immanuel.

FOOTNOTE – Some years later I saw Brian's name in the newspaper. He and his wife were allowing a homeless person to use their garden shed as a shelter, and it was causing controversy with neighbours. This was typical of the acts of compassion I had come to expect from Brian. He took his faith literally, and responded sympathetically and practically to most situations.

MORE RECENT FOOTNOTE – Later still I came across some websites that indicated Brian has since rejected his apostolic Christian faith for mystic practices, psychic-powers and New Age culture – which in my opinion is a great pity!

MOST RECENT FOOTNOTE – The most recent statements I have seen posted suggest Brian has recognised his involvement with psychic activities was a diversion from his Christian faith to which he has returned.

As a 14-year-old at the beginning of my youth club membership in 1959 I was obviously among the youngest, but even among members close to my own age I appeared less emotionally prepared than the majority, many of whom soon embarked on complicated adult relationships. Their liaisons made me aware of some of the problems that can accompany adolescence. One relationship that made me sit back and think centred on Carol Lewis, (no relation of mine despite the same surname). Carole lived with her mother, Welsh father and young sister Christine in a flat near the Beehive Rooms where our club met before the new church hall was built. All the Lewis family were involved with the church one way or another, but they were not pious or over-religious, just ordinary, friendly people with whom I got on really well. Their personalities and interests were similar to mine, and again I had friends I considered to be part of my substitute family providing another home where I could go to be at ease. At the time I did not realise that Mr Lewis had a drink problem. Years later I discovered he and his wife had separated because of his unresolved addiction.

Immanuel YP collecting for Charity in 1962

Six members of Immanuel Church youth club outside the new church hall that was built in 1960 beside the old Victorian church. I am fourth from the left, Brian Snellgrove is on the far right; the young man second from the left has been identified as Kelvin Boorer. Although I can remember the others, I have since forgotten their names.

Carol was very pretty and admired and fancied by all the boys at the club, particularly Jimmy Donald. At first Carole liked Jimmy, but did not see him in the same romantic light that he saw her in; instead, she dated and romanced with other boys. Then to everyone's surprise, including Carol herself in those days of pre-marital restraint, she found herself pregnant. The father of the unborn baby turned out to be a fairly new member of Immanuel YP. He was a charismatic individual, extremely good-looking – and to us girls a real "dreamboat". The unexpected development shook Carol and her family and Carol became confused and self-questioning. She decided that although the father of her unborn baby was prepared to marry her it was not what she wanted. She had been extremely attracted to him but did not love him enough to marry, and chose to go-it-alone and have the baby with the help of her parents. Jimmy remained a close and constant friend throughout. His non-condemnation and faithfulness eventually paid off and Carol began to see him in a new light. After a period of time they married.

I attended their wedding service at Immanuel Church and the following reception in the new church hall with some of our other Immanuel friends. It was a very happy occasion. Carole and Jimmy went on to add at least two more children to their family. The last time I saw them, they were buying a house in Addiscombe, Surrey. Unfortunately Jimmy was bedridden with a back problem when I visited them, which meant he was on long-term sick-leave from work. (If I remember correctly, he was a long-distance lorry driver.) Although not affluent the pair appeared happy and content and all the children were being loved and brought up in a caring home.

Another friend at YP was Janet Jefferies. (I believe she was registered at birth as Sonia Janet Earley.) She joined YP with one of her girlfriends a few months after I had done. To begin with the two girls appeared shy and reserved and were on the fringe of all the fun and activities. Realising this I and my group of friends took the pair under our wing to help them integrate. This having been accomplished Janet began to date Richard Owen another club member. Richard had his own circle of immediate friends, but had no trouble mixing and sharing laughs with our group too. When Janet's romance with Richard fizzled out, she started going out with David Shepherd who had recently joined (or re-joined) YP with his young brother Peter. David had not long finished doing his National Service, and gave the appearance of being very confident and self-composed. This was no surprise to our generation because in the 1950s and early 1960s we could usually spot the difference between those boys who had done their National Service with the Armed Forces, from those who had not. The former were much more resourceful and mature. Two years of disciplined training away from home did much to teach these young men independence and good collaborative skills. At first, we did not notice a change in Janet but gradually it became apparent that she was ignoring old friends and completely immersing herself in David's social circle. For some reason this incensed me. It was to be expected a new romance meant distractions, additional interests and other involvements, but loyalty to old friends had always been important to me. This feeling of indignation may have been a sign of my own insecurity, but as I saw it at the time if it had not been for our group's early intervention Janet would probably have left the club prematurely and forfeited any chance of meeting and going out with David. Why should she cold-shoulder her old friends now I began to ask myself?

When Janet and David eventually announced their engagement and future wedding plans I was once again disappointed to discover none of Janet's original YP friends had been included on the guest list. Again I was aggrieved and sent her a strongly worded letter explaining my views on the subject, saying exactly what I thought of her oversight. This letter must have had an impact because of what followed. One day soon after, I saw David on the platform at Clapham South Underground Station.

Carol and Jimmy Donald's wedding at Immanuel Church in 1964. The best man, standing to the left of the groom is David Shepherd. The bridesmaid on the far right is Carol's sister, Christine.

Carol and Jimmy's wedding reception in the new Immanuel Church Hall.
LEFT to **RIGHT** – Bob Oakley, John MacGregor, David Shepherd, Janet Jefferies, Mr Lewis (Carol's dad) and me.

I immediately felt awkward and guilty realising he would know about my letter to Janet. I tried to avoid him but he saw me and came straight over to tell me how much my letter had hurt his fiancée and had made her unhappy. He said I should have considered her feelings and been kinder and more thoughtful in what I had written. He may have been right, but at the time his intervention only confirmed my suspicion that Janet was losing her personal identity and being managed by her fiancé. Speaking or documenting uncensored thoughts has become my trademark over the years. I only hope that I have become wiser and more temperate in doing so. On occasions, I have excused myself for being offensively blunt by believing my poor communication is the result of an unhappy childhood, but this does not take into account how exceptionally fortunate I have been in so many ways. I have relatives, friends and others who have given me ample time, support and attention, and I have probably received more love than most throughout my life. In theory, I should be more understanding than the majority when considering the needs of others.

Janet and David did eventually marry but as I was to learn not as originally planned. The wedding had to be brought forward because of an unexpected development, namely Janet's pregnancy. This pregnancy proved a complication for David's career plans. He had hoped to become a full-time church youth worker, and had already begun to investigate courses and qualifications in order to reach this end. On learning of the couple's change of circumstance the church authorities advised David to wait before going any further with his ambition. They wanted him to have time to reassess his priorities and ensure his new situation with its extra commitments was compatible with his chosen career at that point in time. Later when I was on more friendly terms with the pair Janet confided in me how she and David had come to find themselves in that position. She said an unexpected death in the family had caused them to be over-emotional and seek physical comfort with each other, throwing caution to the wind. I do not think I really wanted to know the details; it was their lives not mine, but at least she was making an effort to talk to me. The couple married in 1965, and I lost touch with them after that, apart from seeing them at the YP reunion in 2011.

A special friend at YP was Hilary Payne. Her circumstance and family background was very different to mine. She lived in a luxurious five-bedroom house in Baldry Gardens, the south side of Streatham Common. Her father was a professional in the world of commerce. Unfortunately when I knew him, he was wheelchair-bound, possibly the result of a war injury. Hilary's mother appeared several years younger than her husband and I surmised she may have been his secretary or personal assistant before marriage. Hilary's brother lived in the Baldry Gardens house with them.

For some reason Mrs Payne seemed to encourage Hilary and my friendship. It was a situation that bemused me. I assumed my poor elocution, lack of etiquette and weak social skills would be a hindrance to my being accepted into a more middle-class environment. To my understanding individuals mixed with their own kind, those with similar backgrounds and standards; however this theory has proved wrong on several occasions. Maybe my more extrovert nature was seen as an asset by Mrs Payne, because although Hilary had a great character, she was a little on the quiet and reserved side, having a friend with a more outgoing personality might have been seen as an advantage. Whatever the reason, Hilary and I shared a lot of interests and hobbies and enjoyed each other's company. At my 21st birthday party, as was the case with Bunny and her family, in addition to receiving a present from Hilary I also received one from Mr and Mrs Payne, a beautiful designer headscarf with a modern silk-screen print on it.

When Hilary achieved a place at Oxford University I was almost as thrilled as she was on finding out. I even changed my loyalty from Cambridge to Oxford for the annual Oxford and Cambridge boat race. Originally I had championed the Cambridge crew because Uncle Cyril was a Cambridge supporter and I suppose I admired and loved him and wanted to please him. In addition I liked the light blue colour that represents Cambridge. Knowing what I now know, that my great grandmother, Uncle Cyril's grandmother, was born in Fen Ditton, Cambridgeshire, and that we have a long line of Gilson ancestors going back to at least the sixteenth century who worked and lived in the villages around Cambridge City, perhaps I should have remained loyal to Cambridge.

Once I went to stay with Hilary for a weekend in her student digs at Oxford. I felt privileged and found the ancient city of spires with its studious intellectual atmosphere a real inspiration. While studying in Oxford Hilary met her future husband, Peter Cross, a brilliant young musician. I met him at her 21st birthday party. Hilary's coming-of-age celebration was fairly formal but thoroughly enjoyable do. It was held in a smart London hotel and Peter wore a tuxedo, bright red cumber-band, with bow tie and so on, and Hilary wore a classic evening dress that really suited her. I thought they looked a really dashing couple together.

On graduating from Oxford Hilary and Peter married, and after the wedding, in order to boost their income, Peter took up the post of church organist and choir master in the old parish church of St Mary and St Lawrence, Great Waltham, Essex – a village near Chelmsford. I believe this was in addition to the couple's other career involvements. It was fortunate for Hilary and Peter that village accommodation went with the post of organist, and they were given a home in Church Housen, the village's heritage alms houses. (I was told the spelling is Flemish.) I went to stay with Hilary and Peter at their cottage one weekend.

As a young person, I had my childhood definition of success greatly challenged by the people I met through the church – Christian friends, church families, Sunday school teachers, youth leaders, confidants, and so on. They helped me reshape my thinking and understanding of achievement. I began to realise that rating people according to their wealth and social status is not relevant, as is valuing them according to what they can offer me in terms of social prestige and personal advancement. Many of the advantaged and wealthy people I met in the church were totally unaffected by their wealth and possessions.

LEFT
"Church Housen", in Great Waltham, Almshouses, that were built in 1896.

RIGHT
The church of St Mary and St Lawrence, Great Waltham, Essex

Hilary and Peter's first home was in one of these cottages.

Peter Cross was organist at this church © Peter Stack-Wikimedia

They were often humble, unbiased individuals wanting to share what they had; increasing their wealth and position further was not their aim, especially if it was at the expense of someone else. I suspect my earlier class-centred attitude may have been inherited from my mother. Most of her conversation seemed to be about the possessions and good connections of the people she knew. Occasionally she showed a compassionate side to her nature, helping those in need, but more often than not when I was a child, she was just envious of or trying to curry favour with those more privileged than herself. She became very dissatisfied at times, feeling she deserved better in life than was meted out to her, and that others less worthy than her were enjoying the fame and luxuries she should have had.

During my membership of YP in 1962 Jeanne Hinton was appointed as the first salaried youth leader of Immanuel Church's youth fellowship. Jeanne had connections with a Christian community in Lytchette Minster, Dorset. This community operated out of an old manor house which at the time belonged to Lord and Lady Lees – or Tom and Faith as they preferred to be called. I visited the manor house more than once and on at least one of these occasions stayed overnight. The snobbish streak I had inherited was aroused by this. I revelled in the fact that I could claim to have been with aristocrats, eating at their table. One day while on a local outing with Immanuel Church, I saw an older member of the church who I mistook for Tom Lees. It was not unusual for the Lees family to come up to London or the Home Counties to join in church events, and with me being not one to miss an opportunity I went over and started up a conversation with this person. I mentioned the last time I had seen him, when he was walking across a field with Faith on the Lytchette Minster estate, and I went on to say what his and Faith's friendship meant to me. He looked at me mystified. As a church member and friend of Jeanne he obviously must have known Tom and Faith quite well; he had probably even visited them in Lytchette Minster, but he must have wondered why I linked him so firmly to Faith, a married woman – and why I made such a fuss about our acquaintance seeing he only knew me vaguely. Hopefully he did not realise it was my attempt at social grovelling.

On another occasion in 1962 I went with a party from Immanuel Church for the reopening of Coventry Cathedral in the West Midlands. This followed the Cathedral's renovation after the devastating damage caused to it in the war. It was in the month of May, and although I did not realise it then it was to be my last year at grammar school. Churches from all over the country had been organising it so that members of their congregation who wanted to participate in the celebrations could be billeted out for the weekend with church families living in or around Coventry City. I was billeted with another older, single woman from Immanuel Church, in the house of a young doctor and his family. The family lived in a smart suburb of the city and this was to prove yet another situation that went to my head, making me feel my station in life was improving. With this attitude I tried to impress my hosts with pseudo-intellectual and semi-studious banter of no particular relevance at the expense of my unassuming fellow-guest. This inappropriate behaviour seemed to be tolerated by my hosts but on reflection I realise they did not encourage extended dialogue on the topics I tried to focus on; instead they attempted as much as possible to bring the other lady into the conversation. Perhaps they realised I was just an immature individual with an inbuilt inferiority complex, lacking in confidence.

A photograph of a Y.P. outing, taken 1962.

This photo shows one of the many Immanuel Youth Club outings that we as members enjoyed. Jean Hinton, the recently appointed and ever patient and persevering youth leader, is seen climbing down from the coach step, Brian Snellgrove is squatting in the front row holding a paper or map, squatting second from the right is Richard Owen, I am fifth from the right in the back row with my face half hidden by my brother, Philip; (he must have been about eleven at the time and a guest – not old enough to be a YP member,) Hilary Payne, the friend I was so proud of for being so intelligent and yet unassuming, and for gaining a place at Oxford University is to the left of Philip, Adele Pentony is in the back row wearing a light coloured coat. Looking at the many faces in this photograph I have mental flashbacks of happy times, great friends and good, worry-free teenage fun. Being a would-be leader I believe I may have been the one who suggested, and helped to organise this outing. We were going to a quarry in Godstone, Surrey, to celebrate the traditional November bomb-fire night.

At some point while at Immanuel Church, I believe I was involved in Sunday school teaching because I still have my licensing certificate supplied by Southwark Cathedral. Unfortunately I do not remember this involvement although I clearly remember the Sunday school teaching I did a year or two later when living in Walthamstow.

General Socialising

Several times I have referred to the increasing problems I was having at home, and the fact that my education began to suffer around the age of thirteen and was being replaced by a growing interest and involvement in socialising. Wendy Goodship was my most constant companion during this time as suggested by my account of our trip to Brands Hatch – and it was Wendy who I mostly went with to Tony's café. I remained very close friends with Sheila Haines, but she lived further away in Earlsfield and was a little more reserved than Wendy and I tended to be. Wendy, as said, lived the other side of Balham in Bedford Hill. Her father was a silversmith and worked in the City of London; her mother also went out to work as did her older brother. Similar to some of the homes already mentioned the Goodship home was yet another one where I could go to relax. The Goodship family even managed to cope with my eccentricities, like the time Wendy and her brother held a party at their flat. I went along to it with a full set of Pakistani clothes – shalwar, kameez, shawl and oriental jewellery – in a bag. I had borrowed these from Naheed, a friend I met at Camberwell Art School where I went to study following grammar school. I must have been about seventeen or eighteen years old and intended wearing these clothes at the party. Mr and Mrs Goodship were preparing to leave the flat in order for Wendy, her brother and the expected guests to have the freedom of the place but they were still around when I arrived. I went into their bathroom and changed into the Pakistani costume. When I came out my appearance must have been completely out of character with the spirit of the intended party but the family never battered an eye-lid. I suppose I was attempting to be adventurous and "with-it", not realising I was attention seeking and too up-front. Thankfully I got cold feet just before the other guests arrived and rushed back into the bathroom to change back into my ordinary clothes which I knew were a bit shabby for a party, and probably another reason I had considered wearing "fancy dress".

Wendy and I went to many social events together and sometimes went on double dates with boys we knew. I think our special friendship was cemented after we had endured each other's vomiting fits. On a trip to Southend one day it was Wendy who over indulged with food and drink from the beachside stalls and was sick on the return train-journey home. I helped her sort herself out. Similarly Wendy helped me when I over-indulged at a party or dance one occasion. These experiences gave us the feeling of being blood-sisters. We were both determined to enjoy ourselves as much as possible, kitting ourselves out as best we could in the latest fashionable gear and going along to dances and socials hoping to meet boys in the process.

We had several romances in our teenage years but nothing heavy or serious. At one time we dated Peter Killick and Brian Reynolds, two local young men. At the beginning, I paired off with Peter, while Wendy went with his best friend Brian. Peter's father was a docker working in Bermondsey Docks. He believed children should strive to achieve more than their parents had done before them. As a consequence, Peter was proud of the fact that he was training to be an accountant in a white-collar career with better prospects than his father had had before him. Brian was training in banking, so he too had good job prospects. After a couple of dates we swapped partners and carried on longer under the new arrangement. I have a feeling Wendy with her attractive looks and personality was probably the favourite of both boys, so with Peter, being the better looking of the two boys I suppose it was inevitable that they should end up together.

Wendy Goodship took this photograph (circa 1963) at a dance

I am sitting between Peter Killick, on my left – who I think heard of the dance through his work connections – and Brian Reynolds on my right. I am wearing a striped shirt-blouse with a shoestring tie and my hair is cut in the Cleopatra-style, all fashionable at the time.

It was with Wendy, Peter and Brian that I attempted a long walk from London Bridge to Brighton one day. Being an enthusiastic organiser I think it was once more me who suggested the activity. In the early 1960s walking was not particularly in vogue but meeting challenges was becoming fashionable and a 47-mile trek between London and Brighton seemed a decent enough challenge to me. We set off as a foursome from London Bridge in the early hours of one morning, each carrying a backpack containing food, drink and other necessities. We wore what we considered sensible clothing. At first it was a laugh and good fun, and we saw parts of London in a whole new way passing through on foot as we did instead of in a bus or train as was our custom, but as we trudged through Surrey we started to find it more and more difficult to drag our feet along behind us. As evening drew near, we found ourselves approaching Redhill, Surrey, and realised we had to take a long break – previously we had only stopped for short breaks. It was becoming quite cold but we managed to find a bus-shelter to rest in and must have fallen off to sleep because suddenly we were woken up by the sound of hushed voices and scary lights flashing all around us. It was unsettling until we realised the Territorial Army were on manoeuvres in the area. This, together with the blisters on our feet and general weariness, made us realise we could not continue. As soon as daylight approached, we set about finding the necessary public transport to take us back to London and our homes.

I can clearly remember one boy I met as an adolescent even though I only went out with him on a couple of occasions. His name was Wayne Gardiner. Wayne as a name was unusual for an English boy in the late fifties early sixties and leads me to suspect his father may have been an American GI. Wendy and I met Wayne and his friend at a dance one evening, and the four of us immediately hit-it-off and got on well together. The two boys invited us back to a dance they had heard about being held in a church hall near their home in Wallington, (or possibly Beddington) Surrey. They picked us up on the appointed day and escorted us to the church hall. When we stepped inside, I was impressed by the really good atmosphere that had been created by some church youth leaders in a very ordinary community building – lights were dimmed, modern music was being played on the stage and there was a certain amount of alcohol with plenty of other refreshments. The room was attractively decorated and it must have been Halloween because I remember pumpkins, artificial cobwebs, witches' hats and other paraphernalia around the room. Everyone had a great time. Afterwards Wayne and his friend brought Wendy and me back to Balham. Wendy's parents were out and so we all went back to her place to drink coffee and snog on the sofa. I was chuffed that Wayne was the one who fancied me, because for once he was the more handsome of the two boys. Wendy was usually the one who had the "best of the bunch". In addition to his good looks, Wayne came across as a thoughtful and intelligent person, so it surprised Wendy and me when we learnt he was on temporary release from a Borstal (or perhaps approved school or detention centre). He explained that he hated it there and would never get himself in that situation again, although he was reluctant to say how he had managed to find himself there in the first place. As the evening progressed Wayne's friend began to get agitated. He knew Wayne had to report back to his centre by a certain time or he would forfeit future privileges and off-site passes. Wayne was reluctant to make the move, even though his chance of catching late-night public transport was fast disappearing; he was happy where he was. When the boys did eventually go it was too late to retrieve the situation. Even with a lot of luck Wayne would not have met his deadline. Wendy and I never heard from the boys again and I have often wondered what happened to them when we separated. It might have been my imagination but I was sure Wayne felt a bond with me in the short time we were together.

For some reason, I was able to go to two holiday-camps in 1962. I don't know whether my parents were particularly affluent that year, but not only did they take me on holiday with them to Pontin's Holiday Camp, at Bracklesham Bay, West Sussex, together with Lillian and John and the Walworth crowd who had arranged the holiday, but I also managed to go to Maddieson's Littlestone Holiday Camp, in Kent, with Wendy. Perhaps I paid for part of the latter myself, with the money I had saved from my Saturday and school-holiday jobs – I am not sure now – but I do remember having a great time at both camps. I was seventeen years old and feeling very independent, although obviously I was not, having no steady income or home to call my own, but at least on holiday I could forget the problems of living in my parent's flat and imagine I was managing my own life and making my own decisions.

Although, I went to Bracklesham Bay with my immediate family and their friends – with whom I had little in common – I soon joined up with a group of young people from the Anerley and Penge area of London, my father's childhood home although he did not know them. They had come to the camp as a party and had no trouble enjoying themselves, making new friends and assimilating me into their group. In fact as there were more boys than girls in their group, I think they were glad of another female member. When I was at Littlestone Holiday Camp with Wendy the two of us were swiftly incorporated into yet another group of young people, who, like the Penge-Anerley crowd, had come along together as a party. In the following photograph Wendy and I can be seen with this group drinking in one of the holiday camp lounge bars. Behind us are two guitars belonging to members of the group. When there was no other distraction we would sing along to the playing of these guitars with the folk ballads and popular songs of the day.

The group at Littlestone Holiday Camp Wendy and I joined. From the left of the photograph, going around the back row are – first a girl whose name I cannot remember, Jeff, Tony, Brian, me, Wendy and Peter – and I have now forgotten the names of the other three in front.
I think the cameraman must have caught us unawares by the startled look on some faces.

Before going to the camps, I was able to make some up-to-date clothes, including the bright orange dress with two black frills running down the front on the right side, seen in one of the following black and white photos. Being part of a group was, and still is I imagine, a big part of being a teenager – sharing jokes, playing pranks on each other, having sing-alongs, dancing, playing tennis and joining in other sporting activities are so much more fun with a group you know.

When I left Clapham County School to go to art school in 1962 my social life began to shift to friends I was meeting there, and unfortunately I saw less and less of Wendy. A few years later in 1966 following a whirlwind romance Wendy married a Greek or Greek-Cypriot young man who had been living in London. I did not know about it until it was all signed and sealed, and when I saw her afterwards, she felt I should have been more enthusiastic about her news. I was obviously not as overjoyed as she would have liked me to have been. Within a year of the wedding the couple had a lovely baby boy who they named Marcus, but before he was very old, he had to experience the break-up of his parents' marriage. At this point Wendy confided in me that her honeymoon in Cyprus (or maybe it was mainland Greece) had been wonderful, she had been treated like a princess, but on returning to England her husband turned into what some imagine to be the old-fashioned stereo-type of a Mediterranean man – a womaniser who looks on his wife as his possession, believing she was lucky that he had married her. Separation was inevitable. Wendy and I had been conditioned both at home and in school to be self-assertive, independent women. Neither of us would accept total submission to a partner. After a time of celibacy, then a few affairs, Wendy met Tom. The couple set up home together in Mitcham, and eventually married. I found Tom a likeable young man if somewhat volatile, coming as he did from Romany stock. Despite their somewhat erratic relationship Wendy and Tom seemed to love each other and were still together last time I saw them. By then they had brought two or three daughters into the world.

FOOTNOTE – On meeting Wendy more recently I learnt that after several years of marriage she and Tom did eventually separate, but they have remained in positive and amicable contact with each other.

PONTIN'S BRACKLESHAM BAY HOLIDAY CAMP, 1962

Sitting in a camp lounge. **LEFT** to **RIGHT**
Dad – Mum – Lillian –? – ? – John

My sister Jill (centre) winning the children's fancy-dress competition dressed as a witch.

Two group photos of our party at the Bracklesham Bay Holiday Camp. The first one shows the women of our party with my mother third from the left in the back row, Lillian is fifth from the left, and I am frontrow far left. The second photo shows the men of our party with my father in the front row, second from left, helping to hold up another member of the group.

Two more photos taken at Bracklesham Bay Holiday Camp showing members of the group that "adopted" me. The first shows (not in order) Tony, Colin, Sally (just seen), Allan, Clive, Wally, John, Nick and me. (Gill is missing and so is probably taking the photo.) The second photo was taken at a camp theme event "The Dessert Island Evening". Wally the pirate has rushed into the ballroom capturing me and the girl behind. Tony is in front of him wearing a hula-hula outfit.

Christian Faith 1961

My teens were full of contrasts, misery at home and great fun with friends outside. I went out with Wendy and other friends as much as I possibly could but also continued going to Immanuel Church and its youth club where I felt an affinity with the atmosphere and its members. I have admitted before that I was finding it difficult to understand and accept the beliefs and practices associated with my faith. How could we be sure Jesus really lived on earth, anyway? How did we know the stories of the virgin birth, resurrection and other hard-to-believe miracles were true? What was wrong with me hating my mother and father for their attitude to me? Why shouldn't I live in an uninhibited way, go by my natural instincts and throw self-discipline and temperance to the wall?

It must have been shortly before or shortly after my Christian confirmation at the Holy Redeemer Church, Streatham Vale, that these doubts really set in and seriously buffeted my mind. Despite the negative thoughts I was having I continued to pray and read the Bible on a regular basis. There came a period when I was so desperate that I knew no human being on earth would understand what I was going through, but I still held the hope that there might possibly be a "Listening God". I remember feeling suicidal on occasions and can recall praying that either my mother or I would die to end the dilemma. I cannot pin-point an exact time but I know there was a moment when God did in fact become very real to me. It was the same time that I prayed, "If you are there God, please come into my life." I actually began to experience God taking control, and my general outlook changed in a dramatic way; the mysteries of the Christian faith started to become clearer and more comprehensible and Bible texts began to hold personal messages for me and clarify situations. I know I continued to make mistakes, take wrong decisions and probably misunderstood some of the spiritual prompts I was being given, but basically I knew I was being guided and supported by God's power, not my own anymore. I have never doubted God's existence since that time. There have been moments when I have been spiritually confused, I have experienced weakness, been greatly unhappy and knowingly side-stepped divine guidance, but my faith has never been destroyed – even when being accused of hypocrisy, which I am ashamed to admit has actually been the case on many occasions, or of clinging to a primitive out-dated philosophy. Many good things have only come about as a direct result of my trust in Christ, the Son of God, my Saviour. I am a born coward, and should anyone at any time physically torture me I might conceivably deny my faith verbally, but no one can take away my inner knowledge and conviction.

Outwardly my life did not change much after my spiritual rebirth. I still appreciated and saw the same friends as before, both those outside and those inside the church, I continued trying to be modern and a free-thinker and continued to experience stalemate in my family situation, but now I was allowing my newfound faith to influence my general planning and decision making. This more personal faith helped me interpret things going on around me, and to choose what action to take. One part of the Bible in particular seemed to speak out to me after my conversion; it was the story of Abraham's spiritual calling and his first journey of faith when he left behind his known home and extended family to follow and trust in God's provision alone. God was to be Abraham's only source of comfort and security; I knew this principle was meant for me. You might think it was not difficult for me to emotionally walk away from my home and family, (though not literally at this point in time,) having little if any relationship with my parents, but in my heart I suppose I continued to hope my mother would eventually show some sign of wanting and loving me. I would have done almost anything to find this spark of love in her, but I was now gaining strength to put this thought aside for the time-being and set out to explore new spiritual territory and to meet challenges with God's help.

I believe my Christian awakening must have happened about the age of sixteen, before I took my O-Level public examinations at school. I found any form of examination nerve-racking, but I remember quite specifically praying for strength to take the exams and trusting in God to guide me through the whole assessment period. A few months before the O-Level examinations I did as much revision as I could, and spent hours going over lesson notes and the set texts, realising my lesson-work had deteriorated in quality and quantity throughout the preceding couple of years. I was determined to get as good a result as possible and rushed to members of staff trying to retrieve notes to help me fill in the gaps that I found I now had in my subject note books. Lining up outside the exam room on the first day of the exam period was extremely stressful. I waited with other pupils outside the classroom for the member of staff who would be invigilating our exam to let us in. My hands and knees were trembling as I clutched my writing utensils close to my body. Once inside the room I managed to keep my wits about me, and tackled the written questions in a reasonably organised manner. As the examination period progressed it became more and more difficult to study at home for the next day's exam, and so on several occasions I revised into the early hours of the morning when it was quiet. After this traumatic period I waited with other schoolmates for our results to be published, and I have already described how I received mine through the post while at a Baptist summer school in Cilgwyn, Newcastle Emlyn.

My O-Level results were quite pleasing considering my steady fall in achievement since the third year, or year nine as it now is. I had passed five subjects, English language, French, mathematics, Latin and geography – but failed English literature, German and science. I had already chosen to stay on at Clapham County School following the O-Level examinations, although I do not think this pleased my mother much. She let it be known she would rather I went out to find a good, steady, secure job, such as bank-clerk as my friend Wendy was about to do. I suppose the money I would then have given her out of my wages for my keep would have been useful. To her credit she did not pressurise me and I remained at school into the lower sixth form to study four main subjects, namely A-Level geography, A-Level art, A-Level religious education and O-Level economic history. How these subjects would fit in with a future career I had no idea. Originally I had wanted to be a nurse, and had gone to Clapham County with this intention – it was the reason I had joined the Junior Red Cross cadets – but now I was not so sure. I was finding it difficult to face blood and gore, in fact I had become quite squeamish and I suppose I was also developing new ideas and ambitions. I know it was my Christian faith that helped me choose my final A-Level selection because I took account of Christ's teachings about using one's talents. This inspired me to choose geography as one of my subjects because I had scored better than I thought I deserved in my O-Level geography exam showing I might have a natural bent for this subject. In relation to art I had only given it up at O-Level because it was considered by some to be a less worthy subject, but I had enjoyed my art lessons in the past and taking the subject at A-Level would develop this interest further and seemed to make sense. The choice of religious education as my third A-Level subject more or less confirms the notion that I had become a fully committed Christian by this time. I think O-Level economic history may just have been a timetable fill-in, but the lessons would be with Miss Rayner who I admired.

I lasted one year in the Lower Sixth form at Clapham County Grammar School. The rows at home were intensifying and I could not concentrate or study. In addition, many of my close school friends had left at the end of the fifth form. I came to realise I had to get out of the academic environment for my own sanity. My general health was reasonably good but I was beginning to get anaemic and I had had a few mild migraine attacks, possible symptoms of anxiety. I was really enjoying my artwork at school and wondered if transferring to an art school might be the answer. I could be creative and explore ideas without spending hours on prescribed factual research. Students could apply for a place at art school from the age of sixteen, so I began to make moves to see if one would accept me. Mrs Pell the art teacher helped me gather a portfolio of work, and even my mother helped by contacting a local art school, namely Camberwell Art School. Here I was hurriedly called up for interview. This institution was nearing the end of its student-selection process for the coming academic year but still had a few places to offer. Joe Dixon, Head of Intermediate Studies, was the person who interviewed me. I remember him looking through my sketches and paintings and picking out a picture of a cabbage I had drawn. I had tried to copy it as faithfully as possible, every vein and blemish on every leaf. "Someone who has the patience to copy this sort of detail deserves a chance," he said, and so I gained a place in Camberwell Art School for the academic year beginning September 1962.

Chapter 6

Camberwell School of Art and Crafts, Peckham Road, S.E.5. 1962-1964

My first taste of student life at Camberwell Art School was not as carefree as I would have wished. It was tinged with anxiety because I would have to miss the first week of the academic term due to my previously arranged holiday with Wendy to Littlestone Holiday Camp. Surprisingly the authorities did not seem to think one week would make much difference to my studies and I was able to negotiate my late entry, but I was conditioned to feel guilty if I missed any deadline or target; added to this guilt was the fact that I would have to miss important induction sessions such as the one where we would be introduced to the life-study class. Other than strippers in nightclubs public nakedness was still a cause of some embarrassment to most in the 1960s. I learnt later from my peers at the art school that they had gradually been initiated into the life-class during their first week; first the female model had posed for them fully clothed, then she posed topless and lastly she posed completely naked for the first year students who were present. Would I blush and go red when I joined the life class? Would I be able to draw the figure without inhibition?

As it happened, I settled in to the life-class and other aspects of Camberwell Art School without any problems. There was certainly no sexual innuendo to the life-class sessions where everyone's effort was put into producing a meaningful artistic composition. The fact is I don't think anyone could have had erotic feelings in the life class at Camberwell Art School even if they had wanted them. The art school had trouble hiring models and some of the individuals hired were most off-putting. One was an over-weight, mature woman who was oblivious to the world around her. She had what we would call these days learning difficulties and special needs and she broke the code of nudity as a model by wearing a baby's bonnet on her head, and she sometimes carried a doll around with her. Another male model was an aging tramp who brought his dog along to the art sessions with him. The poor canine creature would lick the sores on his master's body as we drew and sketched him. There was one particular model I did admire though. She was an elderly lady who had been a dancer in her earlier years. Her body was wrinkled but she had kept herself in really good shape and she was extremely knowledgeable with a keen intellect. She was friendly, dignified and non-opinionated.

The other students in my year group at Camberwell Art School were a real "mixed bag" coming as they did from different backgrounds and different parts of England, although quite a few were Londoners like myself. On the whole everyone was friendly and it was easy to integrate into student life. Art students in the early 1960s were expected to undertake a two-year Intermediate course before going on to specialise in the two-year National Diploma of Design course (the NDD). The Intermediate course proved to be a very good grounding, and many aspects of art and craft were tackled. I had lessons in ceramics, art history, art philosophy, basic design, calligraphy, sketching, painting, lithography, sculpture, architecture and anatomy, both the theory and the practice. It gave me and other students a chance to assess where our strengths lay before choosing our specialisation for the NDD. Most of us took the Intermediate course very seriously and in our group we had at least one mature student who had given up a good professional career to join the programme. In addition to most Camberwell students being dedicated and conscientious we also knew how to relax and socialise, and at the beginning I found little prejudice and few social cliques within the institution.

It was not long before Jillian became one of my close friends at Camberwell Art School. Jill was married to a paratrooper called Dennis Maude, and the couple had a little daughter called Brigid. Dennis was away from home much of the time on tours of duty, and Jill and Brigid were temporarily living back at Jill's parents' home, in Abbey Wood, South East London. Jill had been encouraged by Mr and Mrs Pemberton, her parents, to return to full-time education in England in order to gain a qualification. It emerged that Jill had for a time lived abroad in Cyprus with Dennis in army quarters. Here apparently she learnt, (and consequently passed on to me,) how to fry Christmas sprouts with almonds for extra taste, and how not to be too generous to beggars. She told me a vagrant had come to her door in Cyprus one day and "Jill being Jill" she offered him what food she had and a little money. The next day there were many, many more such individuals finding their way up the path of her Cypriot home. I do not know why Jill did not continue to live in military accommodation with Dennis. It may have been her choice or maybe the option was taken away from her. As an individual I found Jill a little reserved and unpretentiously sophisticated, and so it was a surprise to me when one Christmas holiday, in Dennis's absence from the UK, I accompanied her and Brigid to Dennis's family, who lived in Bromley, Kent. The Maude family were so different to the other acquaintances in Jill's life, her family and friends. They were overtly working class or as my mother would say "rather coarse." I suppose with different priorities and approaches to life, added to the frustration of Dennis's absence, it was inevitable that a loud, blazing row began to break out between Jill and the other members of the Maude family. It was over something and nothing and thankfully soon passed with everyone calming down and making a real effort to get back to normality for the sake of little Brigid.

I speculated that Dennis, with his strong character and charm, must have swept Jill off her feet when she was still quite young, before she had time to realise what was happening to her. I met him a couple of times when he was on home-leave. He was a likeable enough rogue and certainly handsome and charismatic, and must have done well for himself career-wise being among the few to be accepted into the ranks of the paratroopers. After her short reunions with Dennis Jill was always emotional, and although she was not prone to sharing personal details, she once told me she knew Dennis was unfaithful to her when he was away but she felt he loved her and would always come back. I did not share her confidence but said nothing. Several years later, Dennis retired from the paratroopers and bought a yacht in which he sailed off into the Mediterranean sunset with a new female partner in tow. The last time I saw Jill, she was renting a smart flat in an exclusive part of Bath, Somerset. It was lavishly furnished and there were original, framed cartoon-sketches on the wall leading up the stairs, designed by an artist of the Punch Magazine. The last I heard of Jill she had found a new partner, and little Brigid had reached and passed her Age of Majority.

A few students in my year had come down to Camberwell from Manchester, and had known each other previously. Their financial situation and general attitude to life was similar to many others on the course, that is to say they were materially poor but gregarious, generous and carefree. Where they did slightly differ to most of us at the beginning, apart perhaps from the older students, was that they tended to be very self-assured and had few social boundaries. Their moral code was as open and free as was soon to follow with the Flower Power movement of the late 1960s. They enjoyed life without commitment or responsibility. Despite this apparent rejection of convention and traditional boundaries the Manchester students did not set themselves up as superior, and they did not try to influence anyone else into their culture. They were thoughtful, caring and mixed with others easily. One occasion that comes to mind, and emphasises the generosity of the Manchester students happened when I was walking along the road with some of them one day. The group included a young couple who I particularly admired for their optimism and pragmatic approach to life. When they realised an unplanned baby was on the way they looked on it as an opportunity rather than a problem despite it occurring right in the middle of their studies. Together the pair worked out how they could both complete their studies and raise the baby at the same time. None of us on this day in question had much money; it was lunchtime and we were feeling quite hungry. The prospective father began fumbling in his pocket and managed to find a few coins with which he bought a large fruit malt-loaf from the bakers. He broke it into pieces and began to share it around. At first, I refused to take a piece, feeling his heavily pregnant partner needed a bigger share, but he wouldn't hear of it. It was almost Biblical, like the feeding of the 5,000. This act was typical of the generosity that I found at Camberwell Art School. Money was short for most of us, but goodwill was abundant. Another occasion I remember that emphasises lack of finance was the bottle-party held at the digs of Derek Vernon. There were no glasses to drink from, they were a luxury in most student pads, but neither was there panic. Old, clean, dry jam jars were quickly found and used. The wine and beer we had brought along to the party tasted just as good – if not better.

Once while travelling on a bus during my Camberwell art student days, I met Penny, my friend from Mitcham. She noticed I was not wearing any stockings or socks in the middle of winter. It must have been in my second year when I had left the family home and was living in digs and trying to manage on a small student grant. She was appalled, and immediately took out a ten-shilling note from her handbag and handed it to me to buy a pair of stockings for myself. She was out at work by that time, and receiving a reasonable wage, but I still did not want to accept the money. She insisted however, and eventually I took it.

There were a few students on the Intermediate course who could boast good financial backing. They either came from a wealthy family who supported them, or had a sponsor of one kind or another. I believe Barry Guppy may have been one such student. He certainly looked as if he had come from a privileged background and never appeared to be short of resources or equipment. A few decades later, I came across a smart ceramics studio-shop in fashionable Lyme Regis, Dorset, with the name Barry Guppy over the door. It displayed polished, high-status pottery making it easy for me to speculate that his business too may have benefited from some kind of family financial backing. Another male student on the course who I recall as being fairly affluent was light-heartedly teased by some for having previously attended a prestigious finishing school or private college. It had helped him attain the appropriate academic level he needed to be able to enrol in a recognised higher education programme. He was a likeable young man and so his peers were pleased the extra tuition had paid off. Most of us however came from much poorer backgrounds. I was by no means an exception in having to drastically economise during my student days.

Poor or not we had a good social life. Once in my first year at art school I took my old school friend Wendy with me to an art-student party. I am not sure who told me about it or who had invited me, but it was held in a multi-story house at the bottom of Clapham Common, Southside. At the time I understood the property was owned by the Fantoni family. When I arrived at Camberwell Art School Barry Fantoni had been a student there for some time. I was told the reason for this was that he had changed the direction of his studies once or twice. He was a well-known figure and very popular. I was fortunate to encounter him on a personal level on at least one occasion. I had been having problems with one of my prints in the lithography room and without hesitation or request Barry Fantoni who was the only other person in the room came over to help me. Years later I heard him speaking on the radio. He was talking from America about literature; in addition to his many other interests he had become an author and book critic. Several years ago I saw a magazine article on Barry that led me to believe the house at Clapham Common where Wendy and I had gone to this party was the same as the one visited by Paul McCartney of Beatles fame, and where he had practised one of his new musical numbers; however on reading further articles (some of which are appended below), it seems I was wrong. It was another later property owned by the Fantoni family where Paul McCartney had been entertained.

PROFILE OF BARRY FANTONI

Some facts about Barry Fantoni gleaned from the internet.......................

Barry Ernest Fantoni was born on 28th February 1940 of Italian descent. He became a recognised British writer, comic strip cartoonist and jazz musician, and was known for his work on "Private Eye", where he created Neasden F.C. that appeared in the mid-1960s. He also became a shareholder in the company that owns Private Eye, Pressdram Limited.

Barry's other accomplishments include publishing books on Chinese astrology, being a satirist, play writer, music composer and a jazz musician. His involvement with the media began in the 1960s, following his studies at Camberwell School of Art. He first joined the staff of Private Eye Magazine as a cartoonist and columnist, and then wrote scripts for the BBC's ground-breaking satirical show "That Was the Week That Was". He became a television star in 1966, hosting the fashion and music programme, "A Whole Scene Going", where Twiggy made her television debut, and where Barry himself was voted Television Personality of the Year. He debuted on BBC Radio Five Live's "Fighting Talk" on Saturday 27th January 2007, scoring 28 points and finishing last, (the programme's tradition for a debutant). He was also a guest on Private Passions in September 2007, the weekly music discussion programme hosted by Michael Berkeley.

Barry Fantoni's self-confessed obsession is music. It led him to adapting some of his home for his musical instruments that were beginning to take over his four-bedroom Victorian terrace house in Clapham where he moved to in 1976. He had all Ronnie Scott's saxophones, Ronnie's horns, four (other?) saxophones, four clarinets, dozens of recorders, guitars, and banjos. His instruments far outnumbered his furniture and he knocked down the internal walls on the ground floor to create an open-plan studio for duos, trios and quartets. There was little soundproofing in the house and Barry had to think carefully about his neighbours when friends gathered to play. His neighbour on the left was a woman who made wedding dresses in her attic; neighbours on his right were five City men who were off the premises at dawn and back at midnight, which helped his situation a little. (n.b. I now believe this house is probably the one where Barry entertained Paul McCartney, Pete Townsend and Ray Davies, who dropped by to join in some of the jazz sessions over the years, and not the Clapham house where Wendy and I attended a party. Our venue probably belonged to another member of the Fantoni family.)

At the age of 67, Barry was still playing jazz three nights a week at the Chelsea Arts Club, the Duke of Cumberland at Parsons Green and the Archduke, next to the Royal Festival Hall. In addition he was still contributing to Private Eye. At this time he was also seeking to downsize his home and wanted to move to a smaller studio space. He put his Clapham house on to the market through estate agents Douglas & Gordon for £600,000.

The Clapham party I took Wendy to was a little out of our depth. As claimed, we went to many parties and social events and had many friends, but were still not nearly as worldly-wise as the people we rubbed shoulders with at this party. The rooms of the house were dim and I noticed a small side room (or large cupboard) where a mattress lay on the floor. Wendy and I saw at least one amorous couple dart into it at some point during the evening. Although not one of the in-crowd Wendy and I were not ignored by the other guests, especially the people I knew from art school. We were made to feel welcome and no one tried to persuade us to copy them or their habits. At some point, someone came over to ask if we wanted "a smoke". Being rather partial to OPFFs (other people's free fags) at the time, I said I wouldn't mind one, and was told someone in the next room had some for sale at ten bob (i.e. ten shillings) each. I realised then he was not talking about ordinary cigarettes. Wendy and I had already seen some of these alternative cigarettes glowing unusual colours in the dark, and realised they were marihuana. The person who kindly informed us of the bargain did not hang around to persuade us further. That was the whole atmosphere of Camberwell Art School everyone was respected for their own convictions and no one was expected to conform to another's life-style. You were an art student and so you and your friends were one of the crowd, whatever your choices and preferences. This was a different situation to the one I experienced towards the end of my National Diploma of Design studies, when I felt the culture at Walthamstow College of Art was becoming a little too exclusive.

One girl I got to know fairly well at Camberwell Art School was Anna. She invited me to go back to her home one weekend to stay with her and her family in Rochdale, Lancashire. As an art student Anna was more reserved than most, and you wouldn't have guessed she was an art student merely by her appearance. She did not experiment with her clothes and left her fair hair straight and un-styled. She did not seem to worry much about her rather blotchy complexion either. This lack of attention to visual matters was more than compensated by Anna's lovely personality and she got on well with everyone. When I saw her in her home environment, I realised what she had to contend with on a personal level and why she probably had little concern for her image. Her mother had terminal cancer and had little hair on her head as a result of treatment. Anna, her mother, father and brother all tried to keep cheerful, but it was obvious there was a lot of sorrow behind their smiling faces. They lived in a small terraced house, and money must have been in short supply because although they made me very welcome and had gone to a lot of trouble to ensure I was looked after, dinner was only a very economic stew with lots of potatoes and other vegetables, and very little meat. I do not know whether I enjoyed the weekend or not. I certainly enjoyed the walk I went on with Anna, across the Pennines following a Roman road, and I enjoyed seeing Rochdale town with its historic Co-operative buildings, but I did not like seeing the anxiety of the family. I think Anna's mother was very proud of the fact that her daughter had gained a place at a London art school; it is possible she did not live to see her daughter graduate.

In my first year at art school, while still living with my parents, I travelled to Camberwell by bus each day. From home, I would walk up Yukon Road to Balham Hill, and from there catch a bus to the Oval, Kennington. I then transferred to another bus that took me down Camberwell New Road to the art school. On these bus journeys, I was joined by other Camberwell students who lived in and around South West London. Three of my regular fellow-passengers were John Quickenden, Michael Bishenden and John Draper who lived in or near Tooting. They were great fun and I enjoyed their London sense of humour and down-to-earth approach to life. At the beginning art school was a big adventure for most of us and we were fired up with enthusiasm and new ideas. John Quickenden was very tall and good looking. He always dressed smartly and fashionably and I had a feeling he took a fancy to me at the beginning, but if he did nothing came of it. Michael Bishenden was also quite tall, and although not as handsome as John, was nearly always smiling and cheerful despite having a more passive nature. Michael must have eventually made up for his apparent lack of personal drive however because a few years later I saw his picture in an art magazine assisting in the studio of an established artist. Positions like this were only given to graduate students who showed potential, and were ostentatiously creative. The third member of the trio, John Draper, was shorter in height than the other two but like Michael was always smiling and cheerful. He had what I considered a brotherly nature and seemed to be more into joking than into flirting and romancing with girls. Michael and the two Johns were best of friends, and always interacted positively with each other. They also had the knack of cheering everyone up around them. Our bus journeys were always enjoyable affairs, full of laughter, as were the times we met each other in and around the art school.

Another art student who lived on the Tooting-Balham border, and who sometimes travelled on the bus to the Oval with us, was a young man (name since forgotten) who lived in Du Cane Court, situated the Tooting Bec side of Balham Station.

Du Cane Court © Jim Linwood – Wikimedia

Du Cane Court was, and still is I believe, "a prestigious sought-after set of residential apartments in landscaped surroundings". Following its completion in the 1930s it was regarded so highly that even Adolf Hitler, when he saw the design decided it would be an ideal place for his administrative headquarters in England after his imagined invasion of the U.K. and the winning of WW2 – a fact which I am sure our travelling companion was well aware. This young man kept himself a little aloof from the rest of us art students on the bus. I think our high spirits, joking and banter did not equate with the more refined image he would like to portray for himself.

At the beginning, I counted two of my best friends at Camberwell Art School as being Ann Oliver, a Welsh girl from Treorchy in the Rhondda Valley, and Naheed Jaffrey (or Jaffery) a Pakistani girl who was temporarily living in Knightsbridge with her family. These two were very close to each other and nearly always seen together. They looked an unlikely pair of confidantes and I was never quite sure of their relationship, but neither did I care. Ann looked as though she might have been a mature student. She certainly looked older than most of us although this may possibly have been because of the way she dressed. She was small of stature, rather plain looking and unfeminine, while Naheed was tall, attractive, fun-loving and dressed as fashionably as she could within the restrictions of traditional Pakistani costume (a set of which I borrowed for the party at Wendy's house as previously described). Ann was the much-loved only child of elderly parents. She once took me to stay with them in her Welsh home for a weekend. Although elderly her parents were young-at-heart, lively and hospitable, which surprised me because Ann herself seemed rather serious and dour. On this visit, I was taken out and about in the region; I heard the famous Treorchy male voice choir sing and did some sketching on the local slag-heaps which by then were being reclaimed by nature. I was also taken to see some of Ann's relatives, including a woman about thirty to forty years old who was dying of tuberculosis. She was bed-ridden and constantly had to turn her head from visitors to relieve her lung-congestion into a bowl. I remember this meeting vividly because of the way the woman managed to keep a strong Christian faith despite her terrible suffering. In the 1960s many Welsh people were still benefitting from the after-effects of the Christian revival that had spread through the Welsh Valleys in the 1930s; many still kept a deep faith and conviction. Ann's parents were lovely people but not particularly religious, and Ann herself was definitely not that way inclined. She was quite intellectual and I think she saw the Christian faith as outdated and unwanted.

Naheed came from a Muslim Family. On the one and only occasion I broached the subject of religious faith with her she uncharacteristically appeared to have a closed mind and wasn't open to discussion so I went no further. Naheed's father worked for the Pakistani government, and was staying in London with his family to complete an embassy assignment. I believe Naheed, like Ann, was also an only child. The family's temporary home was a luxury apartment behind the Harrods Store in Knightsbridge. It was not only used by the immediate family but by extended family members, friends and helpers. I think Ann stayed there quite a lot, but I only remember visiting once along with another close friend at Camberwell, Julia Wheeler. Naheed's uncle was a famous actor (possibly the well-known Indian actor Saeed Jaffery – though I am not sure). He was staying at the apartment when we visited and I recall overhearing other guests talking about his performing accomplishments.

On the day of my visit to Naheed's Knightsbridge apartment, Julia and I went first into Naheed's room to share gossip with her and Ann and to look at Naheed's jewellery and other items. We then joined other guests in the main reception room for a large buffet meal that helpers were laying out in serving dishes on a central table. Guests were beginning to walk around the table and fill their plates, and we four girls followed suit. Before we sat down on one of the chairs around the edge of the room with our plates, Julia had an accident. Like me she was probably feeling a little self-conscious but unlike me who managed to sit down without a hitch, she had the misfortunate of tripping and dropping her plate of food all over the floor. Luckily it was soon mopped up by one of the helpers, but the incident must have embarrassed her. My embarrassment came later towards the end of the meal when most guests had finished eating. A couple of male helpers entered the room with a cut-glass bowl containing a delicacy covered with foil. I was the first one they approached. One of the men lifted the foil and waited for me to take a portion of the substance from the bowl. I was not sure what to do but I took the little silver serving spoon provided and lifted out a few tea-spoonsful of the thin thread-like substance from the bowl and placed it on my plate. When the servants went on to serve the other guests, I noticed they took very little of the substance, only about a level teaspoonful each. I soon realised the reason why when I tasted it. It was extremely strong and pungent; I had obviously been over-indulgent with what was considered an expensive luxury commodity.

A small insignificant incident concerning needles and thread seems to have been the cause of my friendship with Naheed and Ann being terminated. One day, I needed to do some emergency mending but did not have a sewing kit with me at the art school. Knowing that Naheed and Ann were about to go out for lunch I asked them if they would mind buying me some needles and thread from a shop along their way. They readily agreed and on returning handed the items over to me. I tried to pay for them, but they refused my money. I continued to press for them to take the money and they continued to refuse. Then – in what I thought was a jokey, jovial light-hearted manner – I insisted they took for the cost of the items from the money I had ready for them in my hand. Ann in particular seemed to take offence at this and afterwards she and Naheed never responded to me in the same friendly manner again. It had always been my mother's habit not to be beholden to anybody. Whenever she visited a relation or friend, she would always take something with her to contribute towards her refreshments; she did not like owing anybody anything. I remember her taking butter, bags of sugar and other groceries to Aunt Lizzie when she visited her in Tooting, or when she left me there to stay for a few days. This was probably a hangover from the austere days of the war and post-war years when everyone was required to pay their way and share what rationed food they had. The needles and cotton incident was insignificant but proved a landmark in my relationship with these two girls and also in my understanding of different people and different attitudes. In hindsight I think Ann may have been looking for an excuse to distance herself and Naheed from me. She seemed to be getting more and more possessive about their relationship, and in addition I was probably not Anne's preferred choice of companion anyway – naïve, childish and comparatively ignorant as I was.

Apart from Naheed, there were only a few other non-British students at Camberwell Art School when I was there. Although few in number they added interest and colour to our cultural life and increased our awareness of international affairs. Two of the foreign students had been sent to our art school by their home country, Malaya. They were to follow the same two-year Intermediate art course as the rest of us, but unlike most of us were using it as a stepping-stone to a career in architecture. Character-wise, the two men could not have been more different from each other. Ram (short for Rahman) was from Kuala Lumpur City. He was sophisticated, worldly-wise, and got on well with everyone. I believe he had a wife back home. He possessed a terrific sense of humour and was always open to new ideas. He even ventured into the Christian Union meetings at the art school once or twice despite his Muslim background. He was also quite happy for us to call him by the shortened version of his name, knowing it was easy for us to remember and say. His fellow countryman however was not so accommodating. He came from a rural area of Malaya, was polite, reasonably friendly and approachable like Ram, but unlike Ram very restricted in outlook, and not very flexible in his thinking. He seemed happiest keeping to what he knew. At his request, we called him by his full Malaysian name, (since forgotten) and fellow students had to be careful not to offend him in any way. If we were not sure he would understand what we were doing or talking about in his presence we would discontinue for fear he would misinterpret our intentions. He was not an aggressive person, just extremely defensive.

Perhaps, of all my Camberwell friends Julia Wheeler was the one with whom I shared the most. Her family lived in Tonbridge, Kent, and Julia was another who took me on a couple of weekends to stay with her family at her home. The Wheelers were established business people, and seemed fairly affluent. I believe Mr Wheeler was a fruit importer. Once again, this family were far from snobbish and I did not feel out of place when I was with them. Something insignificant struck me as odd though. It was the way Julia ate her apples. She would eat everything except the stem – flesh, skin, pips and hard pip-case. It surprised me because my mother had strong dogma about such things as eating – and eating an apple in this way was definitely reserved in her mind for poor and starving people. As Julia and I could be open with each other I asked her one day about her unusual habit, and she gave me some reasonable answer that I have since forgotten

When Julia arrived at Camberwell she was already engaged to be married. Her fiancé was a young man from her hometown. In general you would have thought Julia's life was well mapped out and orderly. She planned to gain the necessary qualifications she needed for a professional career, save for a home with her fiancé, and then marry the man she thought she loved. Her family must have been very pleased with this because the fiancé's family like their own was Roman Catholic and from an established background. After a couple of years at art school all this changed when Julia met and fell in love with a student enrolled on a post-graduate art course at the Royal Academy of Art. He was an American, from Texas. After a whirlwind romance Julia married him and soon after became pregnant. I had moved to another art school by this time but visited the couple after the baby was born. They were living in a rented flat in Whitechapel and appeared to have adopted a Bohemian style of existence despite both having had a privileged upbringing with all mod cons. When I saw them, they were leading a minimalistic life-style, and Julia's husband had made a crib for the baby out of spare palettes and wood he had found in Whitechapel Market. I believe Julia's parents accepted their daughter's new direction in life but it must have been strange for them adjusting to a whole new set of circumstances. It was Julia who I was sitting with, before her marriage, on top of a double-decker bus on Friday 22 November 1963. I especially remember this occasion because she turned to me and said, "Have you heard that John Kennedy has been shot dead?" confirming the notion that we all know where we were when we first heard of the American president's assassination in Dallas, Texas. Julia, as a Roman Catholic, was probably particularly affected by this historic event; it being the assassination of the first Roman Catholic president of the USA.

FOOTNOTE – My attempts to reconnect with Julia have proved unsuccessful. It is just possible she might be the one I discovered on the internet living in the USA with a female partner in a civil partnership, having had a career in psychiatry and having worked for a period in a New York Clinic. I think I found this reference on the now defunct Friends Reunited Message Board and so I have no way of double-checking.

Julia occasionally came along to the Christian Union meetings at Camberwell Art School where I as a believer had become a regular member. About six to eight of us used to attend the weekly CU sessions. I am not sure who started the group. A slightly older person seemed to be in charge when I first arrived, but he soon disappeared and an art student from our year, Beryl Aitken, took over. Beryl was staunchly religious, but also realistic in outlook and had a good sense of humour. She lived in or near Kidbrook, South East London, with her mother and older sister. She had been a pupil at Kidbrook School, the first comprehensive school to be established in England.

I imagine the Aitkens may have worshipped at a rather fundamental evangelical church because Mrs Aitken in particular seemed extremely overpowering when it came to expressing her beliefs and views. Thankfully Beryl was more open and sensitive to other people's situations and feelings. It came to light that Beryl's father had not long into his marriage proved a liability, and Mrs Aitken was eventually left to bring up the two girls on her own. I do not know the full story; Beryl was wise enough not to divulge the details, but I speculated that bad marital experiences must have embittered Mrs Aitken who unreservedly threw herself into preaching her interpretation of the Christian message, encouraging her daughters to do the same. I am not saying Mrs Aitken was insincere but I think she should have been more aware of the needs of others. Fortunately Beryl was not judgemental or narrow-minded; she let things take their natural course and did not try to force issues. Beryl was a good friend in general, and her sense of humour was the characteristic I looked for in my friends. Together with her mother and sister Beryl became a member of an organisation called Operation Mobilisation (OM). She eventually married one of OM's English coordinators, a young man called Derek Virgin, who was a member of a well-known 1950s Somerset cricketing family.

LEFT Julia Wheeler in a man's shirt used as her artist's smock, and Beryl Aitken in clay smeared jeans, outside the scaffolded entrance to Camberwell School of Art and Crafts. **BELOW** Me, Julia and Beryl sitting on the steps of the art school the same day, taking a break from our ceramics class.

Another member of Camberwell's Christian Union was Derek Vernon. He came along to the meetings out of curiosity to begin with, but after attending a few sessions had a personal experience similar but not identical to mine. One night he woke up and found himself praying. God to him then became real and meaningful, and he realised he had entered a new spiritual dimension. Derek's family home was in Derbyshire, where he had been brought up by his mother and an aunt after (I assume from odd comments I overheard – and there is a possibility I may have misunderstood them) his black GI father left England to return to the USA. I think I am right too in believing Derek had attended the famous Manchester Grammar School before arriving in Camberwell. He knew and was friendly with the other Manchester students, but probably because his home was in the next county, he did not seem part of their inner circle.

Following four years at Camberwell Art School, and passing his Intermediate Examination and the National Diploma of Design, Derek went on to be one of the first students to take a Master of Fine Arts degree in England. To do this he transferred to Reading University, where he invited me to visit and stay with him at his digs one weekend. He took me around the town and its environs and I experienced some of the student life Reading had to offer. My eyes were again opened to new places and new prospects.

Derek made good progress at Reading, and gained his MFA. Following this he found temporary work as a studio-technician for an established artist to acquire the connections and practical experience he would need to further his career. I lost touch with him soon after, but met up with him once more when he was living in Brighton, Sussex. He was married by then and had a baby daughter called Hebe. To support his family and his artwork he had taken on a job as chef in the town. He had also attached his father's surname to his own, calling himself Derek Vernon-Morris. Recent research on the internet shows Derek is now well established in the Art World.

PROFILE OF DEREK VERNON-MORRIS:

I have taken this updated information from the internet and hope the details are correct........... Following his N.D.D. qualification at Camberwell, and his MFA degree at Reading University, Derek studied in Paris and went on to gain a PhD. He has been a tutor in University College, London, and Sussex University, and displayed his work in venues such as Sao Paulo, Brazil. He has two children, a daughter who is a "Sign Language" communicator and co-writer of a book on traditional and contemporary print-making, and a son who has helped him build the family tree where links to Scandinavia, Yorkshire, Derbyshire, Lancashire, Scotland, Kenya, the Caribbean and France have been found. He was also involved in a few other occupations while in Brighton. He enjoyed being head chef in a restaurant, in the construction business, in Landscape Gardening and in a mid-distance driving along the South Coast. His leisure pursuits are travelling abroad and around the UK, jazz, opera, Latin, and Caribbean genres.

Many friendships were forged at Camberwell, but Christian Union members seem to have had a special bond. After going our separate ways we tended to keep in touch with each other far longer than most other students did. Friends at Camberwell had different philosophies and beliefs and my social circle was not exclusive but it was my friends in the CU who gave me the greatest comradeship.

Camberwell Art School CU linked with other London art school CUs. This not only helped to reassure us as minority groups within our institutions, but also widened our social circle. There was a Christian revival among artists and art students in the 1960s. Some of the individuals concerned became quite high profile, and used every opportunity and artistic talent to share their faith openly and publicly. A few even featured in the media. In particular I remember a newspaper article about a group of Christian art students evangelising down the fashionable Carnaby Street in the West End. It was in "The Daily Mirror", 5 July 1966. The picture accompanying the article showed students striding down the street dressed in their usual, casual art-student gear, with guitars and Bibles in hand ready to sing and talk to the tourists, shoppers and storekeepers. Other Christians, like Anne Roberts, were inspirational in other ways. Anne was a highly skilled student at the Royal Academy of Art but was quieter in her demonstration of faith. She proved a great support to fellow Christians and others she happened to come across her, me included.

I got to know four boys who were members of the Hornsey Art School CU well, and they became firm friends. One of them was Stephen Pegg who specialised in furniture design. He was tall, fair and handsome, and lived with his family in Southgate, London. It was not long before he attached himself to me making every effort to stay close by my side wherever and whenever the opportunity arose. He never got as far as asking me out on a date, but as Christmas approached, he sent me a beautiful, expensive card with a personal message inside and his address, 79, Selborne Road, Southgate, N.14. All clues pointed to the fact that Stephen was about to take our friendship further, when fate intervened. Richard Naylor, a surveying student and friend of mine at Walthamstow where I had moved to study following my Intermediate course at Camberwell, decided to pick me up in his car and take me along to an inter-college CU meeting, one that was for students of various disciplines, not just art. Richard not only arrived with me at the venue but remained attentively by my side talking to me non-stop. When Stephen arrived, he stared at me across the room and must have got the wrong idea, because after that he avoided me like the plague. I reasoned that if he could so easily misinterpret situations, he was not worth getting involved with anyway. Sometime later when I met one of the other four young men from Hornsey Art School, I learnt that Stephen had had some sort of emotional trauma or crisis – which I took to be a mental breakdown. If true this would explain his over-sensitivity.

Unfortunately, as a young woman romancing with the opposite sex, I experienced several similar episodes to this one. I seem to have been attracted to, or was found attractive by, successful, handsome young men with happy, loving and outward-going personalities who later proved to have some sort of mental or emotional disorder. Maybe my own stressful childhood made me a magnet for this type, with me having similar emotional wounds to them. In my early twenties I attracted the attention of an extremely handsome young man in Walthamstow. He was tall, blond and handsome with classic features and a strong masculine physique. His manners and personality were impeccable and he had a good steady job with prospects. He lived with his mother, stepfather and several brothers and sisters in a large rented council house, (formerly two separate houses) in The Drive, Walthamstow, E.17. I was flattered that he appeared to be so in awe of me, but fortunately I discovered in time, before it was too late, that he was schizophrenic. It was a very sorry sight when a friend and I visited him in the local mental hospital (probably Claybury Hospital or Goodmayes Hospital – the two closest institutions to our home in Walthamstow at the time). I was so glad I had not become involved with him because I do not think I would have been able to cope with his problems, or supported his very special needs.

Yet another example happened when I was in my first teaching post. My path crossed that of another young professional. Our interests and involvements were similar and it was obvious we had mutual attraction. Without any canvassing on my part friends noted and reported back to me what I already knew, that he could not keep his eyes off me. Staring, however, and participating in a few shared projects, was as far as our relationship went despite friends trying to encourage the romance. I became frustrated and began to look for attractions elsewhere because although I was assertive in many ways, I still believed it was the man who should make the first move in romance. It is possible a young teenage girl we both knew interfered, and caused trouble between us. I know of at least one occasion where she reported something back to him that I was supposed to have said, but quoted it out of context in a way that would cause doubt and mistrust. Anyway for whatever reason nothing materialised and our paths eventually separated. He went on to have an interesting and challenging career but never married. I do not think he was homosexual; my guess is that he was just extremely shy despite outwardly appearing to be gregarious. I have since wondered whether he might have been sexually groomed and abused as a child or young person. The last I heard of him he was in his late middle age, and had not long before suffered a severe nervous breakdown, but thankfully had come through it.

Eventually I outgrew my attraction to unsuitable admirers and suitors; my later admirers and boy friends were less vulnerable…

ANYWAY – leaving behind my accounts of specific art school friends – which led me to reminiscing about relationships in general – I will return my thoughts and experiences at Camberwell Art School.

Rubbing shoulders with celebrities at Camberwell Art School reignited my overdeveloped ego. One of my art tutors was Euan Uglow, who had at least one of his paintings exhibited in the Tate Gallery. On a few occasions, I was tutored by the famous

Kitaj. In fact, many mentors and tutors at Camberwell were established, well-known artists. They taught as a means of keeping in touch with fellow artists in education, and having a steady income to supplement their sales of studio-work. In my opinion some were also interested in the perks of the job, hero-worship and free sex with ambitious students. You could identify these tutors because they did not appear overtly interested in students from non-descript backgrounds who still had much to learn about art and life in general. (I am not sure if this was true of Uglow and Kitaj. I seem to recall Uglow being quite understanding and supportive of my artwork on a couple of occasions, so I think he at least was one of the conscientious tutors.)

For my lectures in History of Art, I was fortunate to have Dr Michael Podro as my tutor. He was far more formal than the other staff at Camberwell Art School, probably because he was more of a theorist than a practising artist. Most of us referred to him by his full academic title. We knew he was someone important by the respect that was paid to him by other members of staff. At the beginning of Dr Podro's course of lectures with a new student group, he would issue each student with a copy of EH Gombrich's book "The Story of Art". I kept mine for years, finally losing it in the 1980s. Since those Camberwell days Dr Podro has been involved in many national projects, including at least one of the government's Hansard Committee debates.

PROFILE OF PROFESSOR MICHAEL PODRO

This is an updated profile of Dr Podro gleaned from the internet, including his involvements following the time he spent at Camberwell Art School, ...

Dr Michael Podro CBE, FBA, is a renowned British art historian, and considered to be a leading philosopher of art. He is widely acclaimed for his writings on art and psycho-analysis. Michael Podro was the son of Jewish refugees from central Europe; the family surname was shortened from Podroznik to Podro. He was born on 13th March 1931 in Hendon, Middlesex (now in the borough of Barnet), and attended Berkhamsted School, Hertfordshire. He served in the R.A.F., read English at Jesus College, Cambridge, spent a year at the Slade School of Art and read philosophy at University College, London. He gained a PhD in philosophy and history. He has been a lecturer at Camberwell School of Art and Crafts, the Warburg Institute and Essex University. Among his best-known works are: "The Manifold of Perception", "Theories of Art from Kant to Hildebrand" (1972) and "Critical Historians of Art" (1982). Dr Podro became a trustee at the Victoria and Albert Museum and was a fellow of the British Academy. He has two daughters from his marriage to Charlotte Booth, and died 28th March 2008.

Another famous person I saw during my Camberwell time was Lord Snowdon, the former Anthony Armstrong-Jones who had married Princess Margaret in 1960. He looked quite casual when I saw him arrive at the main entrance of our art school one day. He did not come with an entourage of assistants so I assume he had not come on official business. As well as famous visitors and tutors, the regular art-criticism event we had was often led by famous artists such as Peter Blake. It was he who on one such occasion highlighted my contribution, appearing to compliment it. He began this formal art-criticism by talking negatively about some of the other paintings on display suggesting they appeared a little too preconceived, inhibited and conditioned. He then turned to my primitive depiction of a child looking lost in a wild and rocky landscape and said something to the effect of "although this painting is unpolished it shows an immediate response to a situation". I had little confidence in my work. The small oil painting I had produced was the best I could do in my situation. I had hardly any former experience of oil painting before arriving at Camberwell, no support from my family, few painting tools to hand, and no real place to work. I thought my painting was a poor effort against the others on display.

Now that I was mixing with some renowned individuals, I began to get arrogant. This was exhibited at my church youth club in Streatham one day. A well-known art critic had been invited to talk to our YP group one Thursday evening. I sat listening to the woman with an air of superiority. Eventually she asked if we the audience had any questions we would like to put to her. I responded by calling out and asking her opinion of Annigoni's 1957 portrait of Princess Margaret. It had recently been in the news for some reason, and was being heavily reviewed in the newspapers. I hoped she would be positive, praise it and go into raptures about its execution. This would make my fore-knowledge a sign of someone who was "in the know". Instead, I was carefully put in my place as the woman quietly said, "Did you mean – Annigoni?" pronouncing the artist's name with its correct syllabic emphasis. I wanted the floor to swallow me up. I was an art student and should have been aware of the correct pronunciation. This incident was only one of several where my growing ego, coupled with poor general knowledge, caused me embarrassment.

LEFT
Annigoni's 1957 portrait of
Princess Margaret

Streatham Hill, S.W. 2. 1963

At the age of eighteen, I was able to benefit financially from a Major County Award. This was an annual grant of money issued by the then London County Council to students who had achieved a certain degree of academic success and wanted to continue into higher education. It was intended to help these individuals buy some of life's necessities and live semi-independently. As my relationships at home were either non-existent or counter-productive, I realised I had to make a clean break, leave home and live as independently as possible. I was fearful and lacked confidence but realised I had no other choice; with this MCA grant I might conceivably be able to rent a room somewhere. I knew I would be forfeiting contact with my brother and sister and some of the home comforts I had been used to. Philip was twelve years old by his time, and developing into a real character. By nature he was perhaps quiet but certainly not timid. I felt close to him but met with frustration whenever I tried to interact with him; my mother always seemed to be there interfering in the background. Jill was not yet six and I knew if I left, I would miss out on much of her childhood. She was beginning to gain the puppy fat I had suffered as a child. Mum was frequently taking her to the doctor's for health problems. As an adult, I have since pondered on the possibility that our mother may have suffered from Munchausen's Disease, making her dwell on the physical deficiencies in her children to gain the attention she craved for herself. Despite Jill's real or imaginary health problems Mum developed a very close and lasting emotional tie with my sister.

My decision to go-it-alone was guided by the Bible. I recorded previously that I became very familiar with Abraham and his journey of faith leaving home, family and comforts to fulfil God's plan for his life. I had already partially done this in the emotional sense now I had to do it in a practical way by leaving the Balham flat I had known as my home for the past eight years. I may have been rather naïve in my interpretation and use of the scriptures but it worked for me, and that is what matters.

Also previously mentioned was the fact that it was Brian Snellgrove, my friend at Immanuel YP, who helped me find digs at this point in time. He had seen an advertisement for a lodger who was required at a flat in Streatham Place, and told me about it. I had tried to find lodgings myself but had only been able to locate a rather grotty bed-sit in a building managed by a rather unsavoury character somewhere in Streatham Hill. The tenants who had posted the advertisement Brian had seen were offering a room with bed breakfast and evening meal for just £3.10s per week – very cheap – even for those days. The flat turned out to be part of a large Edwardian building set back from the road east side of Streatham Hill Road, not far from Streatham Hill Bus Garage. It was at this garage that three years earlier I had encountered another of London's warped, opportunist men. It is surprising that I was not put off sex and men altogether! Incidents like the one about to be described were not uncommon, many London girls suffered them, but they still tended to shock me probably because of the bad experiences I had had with my father, and knowledge that I could not productively share these things with my mother.

The incident in question occurred on one of my journeys to an 8 o'clock Sunday morning Holy Communion Service, at Immanuel Church, Streatham Common. I must have been about fifteen years old. The 118-bus service was restricted at weekends, and so on these occasions I would have to leave home at around 6:45 am, take a walk along Cavendish Road, then Poynders Road and Atkins Road to Streatham Place. I would then wait at the Streatham Hill bus garage for an early bus travelling towards Streatham Common to come out. This particular morning, there was a professional looking gentleman already at the bus stop. He was dressed formerly in city suit and loose raincoat, and held a newspaper in front of him. When he saw me approaching, he lowered the paper and exposed a full view of his genitals through his opened trouser flies. There was nobody else around. I tried not to panic and stood some distance from him. Thankfully a bus was not long in coming out of the garage and I was able to escape. I was too shocked to tell the bus-driver or anyone else. They might not have believed me anyway.

After this diversion.......................

The flat I went to view near the bus garage was on the ground floor. There was another flat in the basement, a second one on the ground floor, and one or two flats on the first floor. The tenants who were willing to take me into their home were a married couple who had a young daughter about six years old. If I remember correctly this little girl had to move into her parents' bedroom to leave me the only other one in the flat. Although the rooms were few in number, they were quite spacious and clean. The young wife was friendly and welcoming, while her husband was older, certainly fatter, and seemed to be very much in control of situations and his family. I planned to move in as soon as I returned home from Lee Abbey Youth Camp in the summer of 1963. I had organised it so that when I arrived back to Cavendish Road, Balham, I would go straight indoors, pick up a bag which I had already packed and hidden, and leave for good – having given no prior warning of my move to my parents. It would have been a kind of revenge-act I suppose, and not very Christian. I reassured myself on this point by believing it would not greatly worry my mother; she often said how glad she would be to get rid of me – but I also knew my action would dent the precious image she had of herself as a caring, self-sacrificial, perfect mother. How would she explain my sudden disappearance to friends and relatives? While at youth camp I had a twinge of conscience and felt guilty about this course of action. I decided to write my mother a letter explaining what I was about to do. The letter must have sounded very self-righteous, saying such things as "I will try to forgive you for all the pain and hurt you have caused me", etc. I duly posted the letter and assume she received it.

On the Saturday of my home-coming, I went into the flat, picked up the bag I had hidden and grabbed a few other necessities in the process, including a couple of old towels from the bathroom. My mother, father, Philip and Jill were around somewhere, probably in the front room, but no one approached me or said anything. No one tried to discuss what I was about to do. Sometime later when I met up with my mother again, she mentioned the taking of the towels, and talked about this as though I had committed some terrible crime, but this did not make me feel guilty or an ungrateful daughter as she would have liked. I considered that taking of a couple of towels, from a place that was meant to have been my home, insignificant in the general scheme of things.

Soon after my move I emptied my Post Office savings account, the money that had been given to me over the years by relatives for such events as birthdays, together with some of the wages I had accrued from my casual work. As I saw it if I was to trust God to look after me, as He had done for Abraham, I should not be dependent on, or tempted by safety nets – financial or otherwise – especially if things were to get tough. With the money from my savings I bought a black leather coat, very fashionable and hopefully very practical for keeping me warm through the cold winter, and a Lambretta motor scooter for a cheap means of transport. The scooter was bought on the advice of my new landlord who told me he knew of a real bargain going cheap. It turned out to be the complete opposite, a "rust-bucket" and complete waste of money. I had made the mistake of trusting an untrustworthy person. This landlord knew exactly how to spot a naïve, gullible young person. He must have realised I was especially vulnerable, with my family situation as it was. This same person made a sexual pass at me not long after I had moved in. He came into my room one day, which did not have a lock on the door, and tried to kiss me when his wife and child were not around. I do not know how, but thankfully I was able to ward him off on my own, and from then on when in my room alone I propped a chair under the door-handle and hoped this would keep him out. I was never quite sure how much the young wife knew about her husband's amorous leanings, probably little if, as I suspected, she was totally intimidated by him. I saw no benefit in telling her what had happened, it would only have added to her worries; instead I immediately began to look for alternative accommodation.

While still at these digs, I encountered another uncomfortable incident. This occurred as I was sitting in the living room with my landlord and his young daughter one day. He managed to catch a dragonfly and proceeded to pull its wings off. After seeing the creature wriggle around on the floor for a while, he killed it painfully and slowly with a flame from his cigarette lighter. He did all this in front of me and his young daughter with a smile on his face leaving me absolutely sickened. My mother could be cruel, but only when she couldn't cope with life or needed to get her own way over something, my father lost his temper on occasions, and some other people I knew had hard, uncaring, and hurtful ways – but no one who I knew loved pain for its own sake as this man did. With hindsight and more knowledge I now realise he may have endured a traumatic childhood himself for his thinking to be so twisted, but it still does not excuse him for his actions, or take away his personal responsibility.

A black leather coat like the one I bought with my savings

A Lambretta scooter – the icon of the 1960s, but mine was old and rusty and lasted only a few months.
© Clem Rutter-Wikimedia

It was blatantly obvious I could not stay much longer in this flat. In one way it was a pity because my financial contribution seemed to be desperately needed by the family, and the woman tried so hard to feed me as best she could with what she had. Nevertheless it was my good fortune that not long after these described incidents Brian told me of a room that had become vacant in the house where he was a lodger. I am not sure how long I had been at my digs in Streatham Hill before moving into the new digs in Barrow Road, Streatham, it seemed like ages but it could only have been a matter of weeks, probably from the beginning of September to the end of October. I doubt whether I could have survived emotionally much longer with my predator landlord. Jean Hinton the newly appointed youth leader at Immanuel Church YP came along in her car to help me transport my few belongings from Streatham Place to Barrow Road, (possibly number 24, Barrow Road – if my friend Karen's memory is correct). I am not sure how I had managed to acquire it but somehow I had in my possession a bottle of Channel No 5 perfume, a real luxury item for one who was surviving on a small student financial grant. I remember the item because I could not have secured the stopper on the bottle properly and by the end of the journey to Barrow Road Jean's glove department, where it had been stored, smelt like an evening at Covent Garden Opera and I had lost my prize possession.

Barrow Road, S.W.16. 1963-1964

My new landlady in Barrow Road had links with Immanuel Church, although I cannot recall her attending services there on a regular basis. She rented out four rooms to single young people on a half-board basis in the lodging house she owned. I suppose it was her way of helping others while at the same time receiving a small steady income for herself. Brian was obviously one of the lodgers, Philip, a Chinese student another and a semi-professional young woman – whose name I have since forgotten, possibly Margaret – was the third. I was now the fourth.

I found the other female lodger a very proud person. She was especially proud of the fact that she had been educated at a private residential school run by the Freemasons. From this I imagine she may have been the daughter of a Freemason who had been killed in the war. She was also proud of her olive skinned South African boyfriend who she said was an Afrikaner. Little attention was paid to this fact at the lodging-house despite mixed race relationships still being a rare thing in the 1960s – even elsewhere at this time I do not recall anyone ridiculing or discriminating against couples with different ethnic backgrounds. My fellow female lodger and her boyfriend were ardent supporters of the anti-apartheid movement which I had not heard of before meeting them. It was still a relatively new organisation in the 1960s.

BRIEF HISTORY OF ANTI-APARTHEID from details found on the internet:

On 29th June 1959, in response to an appeal by Albert Luthuli, the Boycott Movement was formed in London. It was a forerunner of the Anti-apartheid Movement and was attended by South African exiles and their supporters. It attracted support from students, trade unions, the Labour, Liberal and Communist parties. The person who summarised the purpose of this movement was Julius Nyerere, who said the movement was not asking the British public for anything special, merely to withdraw support from apartheid by refusing to buy South African goods. When the Congressional Black Caucus was established in 1971, anti-apartheid formed a major part of its policy. Its first bill concerning apartheid practices was introduced in 1972, by Ronald V Dellums, but it was to be another decade before the Comprehensive Anti-Apartheid Act was passed in Congress; at least fifteen bills had been passed by CBC in its attempt to ban apartheid practices.

My new rent would be £4.10s a week, one pound more than I had previously paid. I think that at the beginning my Major County Award grant amounted to about £4. 17s 6p per week. This was meant to go towards accommodation, fares, study materials, toiletries, medication, clothes and all other necessities. Most students were financially supplemented by their parents, but in the first few months of my leaving home I had no additional money whatsoever. Each week before I did anything else with my allotted quota of money in my Barrow Road digs I would put £4.10s aside for my new higher rent, and then I would put a further half a crown (i.e. 2s.6d – two shillings and six pence) away in a drawer, incredulously this was to go towards a summer holiday, a luxury I felt I could not forego. I was anticipating a further visit to Lee Abbey Youth Camp in the August of 1964 and realised I would have to find all the money for this myself. I began saving half a crown a week to this end. (Nearer the time I planned to boost my savings with money earned from holiday casual-work.) On paper, it was impossible for me to budget within the five shillings I had left each week; my requirements far outstretched this amount. The only answer I had was to put the remaining coins back in my purse and only dip into it when absolutely essential. Just like the cruse of oil in the Bible story there was always just enough money to see me through to the end of the week – but only just! In an earlier chapter I recalled how Penny gave me ten shillings when she saw me without stockings one winter, and how I shared a malt loaf with a group of students one lunchtime, and there were also many occasions when I walked the four or five miles between Barrow Road to Camberwell Art School to save the fare. They were frugal days but very happy ones and they proved to be a good teacher of values and priorities.

During the first few weeks I lived at Barrow Road I still had the dilapidated Lambretta scooter that I had bought with the encouragement of my previous unscrupulous landlord. Philip my fellow lodger took me out on it once or twice, trying to teach me how to ride it. On the first occasion he ensured I was positioned properly on the seat and explained the controls, after which I started up the scooter-engine and gradually rode off down Barrow Road towards Estreham Road. What I did not know was that Philip was only partially sighted. He did not see when I began to wobble on the scooter, or when I fell off. Eventually however after much perseverance and the gaining of some skill and confidence I began to ride the scooter to and from art school each day. It was certainly cheaper than using public transport, but on the first day it began to splutter and decelerate as I rode it up a hill near Crystal Palace. I had been changing up the gears instead of down as I should have been doing. Thankfully a businessman in his city suit walking on the pavement was kind enough to stop and give advice, showing me what to do. The bike did not last long; it kept breaking down and was too old to be repaired.

My new landlady's breakfasts and evening meals meant I did not go hungry. She served good wholesome home-cooked food, and usually offered seconds. She even provided cakes and cocoa in the evening. It was like a dream. I had never been looked after so well before with regular meals and routines. During this period, I began to put back the excess body-weight I had suffered as a child but lost in puberty. In addition to my frequent uptake of second helpings at meals in my digs, the canteen at Camberwell Art School sold large mugs of milky coffee and large jam doughnuts which, unwisely and for cheapness sake, I substituted for a balanced light-snack some lunch-times when I could afford it. I put on pounds in weight during this period and didn't think it mattered. I had all the friends I wanted and life appeared to have turned for the better; I did not realise the problems I was storing up for myself physically and mentally While staying in Barrow Road three particular incidents come to mind. One was my father coming around unexpectedly just before the 1963 Christmas. He came on his pop-bike, (a motorised bicycle), with my brother Philip sitting behind him on the luggage-bar holding a box of Christmas goodies for me. Apparently my mother had discovered my address, and I imagine it was she who arranged this delivery, although it may have been my father. Despite my father's past disturbed behaviour and the fact that I hadn't exchanged greetings cards or spoken to him properly for several years, I was pleased it was he who had come around to my digs and not my mother; he tackled matters far more diplomatically. My mother's unrealistic outlook, untrustworthy statements and neurotic ways ensured dialogue between us nearly always ended in verbal warfare. My father and Philip did not stay long, but I was pleased they had made the effort.

Many years later I learnt my mother had gone into a deep depression following my departure from Cavendish Road, and had barely left her bed for several weeks. Wisely or unwisely she did not let me know about this. I suppose it may have been a sign of a deep love she had for me that she could not express. She had had so many opportunities to talk to me and meet me half way, but never did. Maybe her personal problems were too complex for her to make the move – perhaps guilt was causing her to be so unapproachable. I now realise broken relationships, grief, bereavement, her own confusing childhood and other circumstances may have all played a part in causing the problems she experienced in her later life. She always claimed to have had an ideal childhood, and certainly seemed to have been spoilt, being a much-wanted daughter after three sons and her mother's separation from her husband in WW1. I have seen many early photographs of my mother as a child and teenager in Hollywood type poses sitting on a stool in dancing outfits – ballet shoes, tutus and so on – obviously the darling of the family, and as a child, she enjoyed the benefit of a family car, and had the magical Christmases she continually referred to. The problem was that while she reminisced over past times, she often overlooked current blessings, and the good things that were happening around her at the time. I have since wondered whether these attempts to convince us of an ideal childhood were a ploy to cover up something less admirable she wished to forget. I do not think I will ever understand her even now she is dead. Something went wrong somewhere, and I realise my actions must have exasperated rather than helped the situation.

The second incident I can recall from my Barrow Road days was contacting my mother about money. I didn't want anything from her, or to be in touch with her again, but I remembered her once saying that the endowment payments she collected for me from the Canadian Bank each month were meant to cover my studies and would last as long as I was in full-time education. Suddenly it dawned on me that this money might still be available, (and perhaps wickedly I also wondered if my mother might be pocketing the money for herself). My enquiry must have come at a time when she was beginning to overcome her depression because my letter met with swift action and it was not long before everything was sorted out, and I began to receive payments of a few extra pounds each month, which helped my situation enormously. The money came to me by post and so I did not regain personal contact with my family which suited me fine as I was still inwardly smarting. Much later I learnt my mother had had to swallow her pride and go back to my old grammar school to see Miss Viner, my old headmistress, to ask her to sign papers confirming I remained in full-time education. Unlike me Miss Viner was already aware of my paternity. At a later Quandam meeting, in the 1980s Miss Viner revealed that the school had unsuccessfully tried to persuade my mother to tell me the facts of my birth while I was still a pupil at the school, and going through my disaffected phase. As was her norm, Miss Viner was only too willing to help my mother with the documents, but looking back it must have taken my mother some considerable effort to re-establish this Canadian serviceman dependent's pension.

I am sure my general immaturity must have shown itself in many ways during my stay at Barrow Road, including the third incident that comes to mind. Apart from childishly making a pig of myself with seconds at meal-times and the suppertime refreshments, I also impulsively decided to tart up my room one day. I applied gold spray-paint to the disused fireplace and the ceiling rose. I had not consulted my landlady beforehand because it had not occurred to me that I was in someone else's home and the facilities there were only on loan to me. Soon after this attempt to rejuvenate my room, the landlady's daughter came around to see me at the house. She gave me a thorough dressing-down for my ill-considered action and told me what she thought of me in no uncertain terms. I think her mother was either too shocked or too timid to talk to me herself, but the daughter's input more than compensated for her mother's passivity.

It was probably convenient for me that soon after this incident I had to move on from Barrow Road. My two-year Intermediate art course at Camberwell Art School was coming to an end. Somehow I had managed to pass the end-of-course examination taken in the June or July of 1964; now I was ready to specialise within a National Diploma of Design course. Originally I had been thinking of pursuing Graphic Art as a specialisation. It was the in-thing in the 1960s, and proved a gateway to success for many that used it to get into the illustration and commercial art business where a lot of money could to be earned, but I began to question my motives. Did I want a comfortable job or to follow my Christian conviction that I should be developing and using my talents? At this point in my education I thought Fine Art was more my forte. Future financial prospects in this field however were poor unless (to my way of thinking at least) you were someone who was prepared to submerge your body and soul 100% into the artists' culture, absorbing all the habits and practices that went with it. I felt I could not do this. Nevertheless, I decided to follow my spiritual prompt not knowing where it would lead. Had I chosen Graphic Art I might possibly have been able to remain at Camberwell Art School where a few places for that department were still available, but Fine Art was a different matter. Camberwell had an excellent reputation for painting, ceramics and sculpture, and shared many of its lecturers with the Royal Academy of Art. Students from all over the country were vying for an NDD place in the Fine Art department at Camberwell Art School. I stood little chance of being a successful applicant and was forced to look for placement elsewhere...... To be honest it is questionable how much real talent I had in this field anyway, but at that point in time I thought I had, and by following my spiritual guidelines I was led into some wonderful places and experiences that I am sure would not have happened had I been guided by more materialistic inclinations.

Chapter 7

Flat 4, 77 Church Hill, Walthamstow, E.17. 1964-1966

In September 1964, I found myself heading towards the South West Essex Technical College and School of Art in Walthamstow, London, E.17. ready to study for the National Diploma of Design in Fine Art with Lithography as a subsidiary subject. It seemed to be my fate. This college was the only one that had been recommended to me by a tutor and it had immediately accepted my application. The South West Essex Technical College and School of Art (S.W. Essex Tech) was in the north east part of London, the opposite side of the capital city to the part I knew and was familiar with. In fact I had not even heard the name Walthamstow before 1964; it might just as well have been a foreign country. The underground Victoria Line that would eventually stretch from Walthamstow to Brixton was under construction however, and was beginning to put Walthamstow Central, one of its termini, on the map for many of us who lived south of the river. When it was completed a few years later, it proved an invaluable asset for me, greatly facilitating my movements between Walthamstow and my friends in South London. However, I had to wait for this until the completion of my NDD course at the local art school, a year in Bournemouth undertaking a post-graduate ATD course, and my return to Walthamstow to take up a teaching post in 1967.

Three decades later I was surprised to learn that I did in fact have some strong ancestral links with Walthamstow, and the borough of Waltham Forest. The following appendage is an article I wrote in 2008 for Walthamstow parish church. The church was celebrating the 900-year anniversary of its earliest known foundation, and had asked for articles on any known historical link with the old parish church. I was able to use my newfound family-tree knowledge to submit the following article.

Appendices 4. 900 Years of Family Celebrations
ST MARY'S CHURCH WALTHAMSTOW.

On 3 September 1787, my great-great-great-great-great aunt, Hannah Rounding, married John Pluckrose in the church of St Mary the Virgin, Walthamstow. Hannah had been christened in the church of St Mary the Virgin, Woodford, Essex, on 26 June 1768, where her father and mother had previously married on the 23 January 1761. Robert Rounding, Hannah's father, had been born in Gainford, County Durham, in the year 1738. He later moved to Woodford, where he met and married Hannah's mother, Ann Gray. Hannah's uncle, Timothy, her father's brother, moved to Woodford around the same time.

Robert became landlord at the Horse and Well Inn, Woodford Wells, and was there from 1769 to 1791. He was also elected as constable in the local court from 1769 to 1771, and in 1784 became over-seer of the poor. Robert and Ann had at least five children born to them in Woodford; Thomas in 1762, twins Richard and Robert junior 1763, Hannah herself 1768 and Anne 1769. Hannah's brothers

Thomas and Richard went on to establish the Epping or Essex Hunt. And as such were mentioned by the famous Wanstead poet Thomas Hood, in his long comedy poem "The Epping Hunt".

EIGHTEENTH
CENTURY
COSTUME

©Wikimedia
commons

SOME HUNTING FACTS GATHERED FROM EQUINE PUBLICATIONS In

1785, the Essex Hunt was founded by J (J=a miscopied T for Tom) and D (D= for Dick, short for Richard) Rounding. They were Masters and Chief Huntsmen in Essex, although hunting had been carried out in the district almost a century before, when a pack of hounds were brought down from North Essex and Norfolk to the Epping Forest area. When the Roundings retired in 1805, new regulations were drawn up for the Essex Hunt. It had previously been a non-subscription pack, and members had used their own hounds for the hunt that consisted of friends and neighbours who joined the Roundings in pre-arranged hunts. The MFA (Masters of Fox Hounds Association) did not exist then, and there were no formal boundaries for the hunt, although it is noted hunt members could only travel a few miles from where their hounds were kennelled in any case.

POSSIBLE ORIGIN OF THE ROUNDING SURNAME

It is curious to note that to date, unlike most other English surnames, no reference can be found to the name Rounding before 1648, when Mary Rounding, daughter of William and Abigail, was christened on 24 May 1648 in Stepney. This was the time of strong Parliamentary allegiances and the beginning of the Civil War. Christopher Rounding is documented as having been christened in St Giles, Cripplegate, 1667, and there was a Rounding wedding in London in 1692. After this the Rounding clan seem to have moved and settled in Yorkshire and the north, where they thrived and multiplied.

Speculation is that they may have been puritans or parliamentarians who adopted the name Rounding mid-17th century. Following the Restoration and the growing influence of the Monarchy towards the end of the 17th century, many puritans decided to move north for safety. Here the Roundings mixed with the Fox family of Quaker fame, and the Rich family who were aristocratic Puritans. The Roundings were not without wealth themselves, as wills and land ownership in Yorkshire and County Durham will testify. In 1817, Hannah's nephew – another Robert – sold land back in Ingleton, County Durham, for £1,440 – a fair sum of money for those days!

Hannah and John went on to have their own family – Anne Pluckrose, born 1788, Robert 1790, John (junior) 1792, Hannah (junior), 1795, Thomas 1798, Richard 1800 and William in 1807.

All the children were born and christened in Woodford, Essex.

In 1841, according to the census, Hannah and her husband John were living in Forest Side, Chingford, and John was a shoemaker. Hannah died in 1845 at Woodford Bridge.

Looking back I realise how fortunate I was to have put my roots down so easily and successfully in my new environment. One of the ladies at Immanuel Church, Streatham, (possibly Miss Downing my old Bible Class teacher,) had without my knowledge contacted the vicar of the Walthamstow parish church and asked if anyone in the congregation could put me up during the early days of my relocation to his parish. Canon Kenneth Druitt the vicar, (and later rector,) of St Mary's Church, Walthamstow, replied saying there was a young teacher Miss Susan Rowe who sub-let a couple of rooms in her Church Hill flat, and by chance one had recently become vacant. After some discussion I accepted the offer of accommodation in this flat imagining I would move on as soon as I could find more suitable digs – somewhere I could do my own thing and paint my pictures to my heart's content. My temporary accommodation lasted for the whole two years of my NDD course at the art school in the S.W. Essex Tech. I was extremely happy in Susan's flat and it became a real and much-loved home.

My room in the flat had previously been used by a tenant called Lynette who had recently moved away from the area. Lynette was not English, possibly Malaysian, and held a semi-professional job in central London. I imagine she must have been older than Susan and my other flatmate because Lynette had to touch-up the grey bits in her long black hair. I knew about her long black hair from a photograph she left at the flat, and I knew about the hair dye because of the stains that were left on surfaces in my inherited room. Lynette had obviously been a stable member of the flat's trio; now Susan and my other flatmate had to adjust to a younger, scattier art student as the third member of their team. They coped well and I found myself with a wonderful new family. They did much to increase my self-esteem. During my time in Flat 4, 77, Church Hill, Walthamstow, there were one or two changes with the person who was my second flat-mate but Susan remained in situ the whole time, providing continuity and a happy environment for all who entered our home.

Susan taught in the local church primary school. She was a conscientious professional and loved her work, but she made sure she had a full social life outside her job too. She especially loved meeting people and pursuing new interests. She had a great sense of fun, was realistic, had a modern outlook to life and dressed reasonably fashionably. I learnt that her childhood home had been in Plympton, Devon, where she had been part of a loving family. Her father was a Cornishman whose family had been involved in the foundation of the famous Farley's Rusk Company. She must have inherited her tall build, black hair and blue eyes from her paternal Cornish ancestry. Her mother was originally from Liverpool, and was a very shrewd, practical and intelligent woman. I am not sure whether Susan got her thrift from her mother or her father but I remember her once buying a coat at a jumble sale, removing its lining and inserting it into her favourite coat back home, because the lining of that had become tatty. She was teased about this economy for some time. Not only did Susan have many friends in Walthamstow but she also had family living nearby. Her older sister Deirdre lived in Leyton with her husband, the Rev Geoffrey Thomas, who was vicar of All Saints'

Church, Melbourne Road, Leyton. E.10. The couple lived in All Saints vicarage with their two daughters, Susan's nieces.

My 1971 drawing of St Mary's Primary School. E.17.

This is where Susan taught when I lived at her flat in Church Hill.
The building has since been redeveloped. It is no longer a church school
but a church community centre called the Welcome Centre.

In the two years that I lived in Church Hill, I learnt how to share, collaborate and be independent where necessary. I experienced living without a sense of guilt hanging over me, and increasingly was finding the world to be an exciting place. One small benefit of this newfound independence was my appreciation of food in a whole new way. In the flat the three of us usually had our Sunday dinner together, but the rest of the time we prepared our own meals, and for this I had to learn economy and thrift. I am not sure whether one particular recipe I concocted was good or not, but it served a purpose. I would boil Brussels sprouts, puree them and add a teaspoon of marmite to give added flavour. It provided a thick cheap broth. I also found a recipe in a magazine for making a tasty curry out of a tin of pilchards and some other easy-to-find ingredients. The result was quite delicious and I managed to fool several friends who ate it with me. They enjoyed it so much they were amazed when I told them the very basic ingredients that were required to make it.

I believe Delza Boyle may have been the other person in the flat when I first arrived. She was definitely there at some point, and I think it was at the beginning. She was a lively character, full of ideas and enthusiasm despite having a questionable background. I gained the impression that Delza's family and past situation may not have been straight forward. In addition, although she was a fully trained midwife and health visitor, she was employed in a less high-profile NHS job while living at the flat. From the odd comments I accidentally overheard, I speculated that Delza may have been in trouble with hospital authorities at some point in her career, and this might conceivably have been connected to the mismanagement of drugs – but I cannot be absolutely sure. There was an unspoken code at the flat not to pass knowledge on just for the sake of gossip. I only wish I had continued to live by this code. My natural instinct was, and still is, to tittle-tattle; Susan however supported friends and associates to-the-hilt and kept confidences. She had a personal strength that helped her remain positive in most situations. It was this

163

characteristic that gave Delza, me and others the chance to come to terms with any of our previous problems, and move on with our lives.

Another person who came to be a second tenant, (possibly the one who followed Delza,) was Christine Callaghan. I found Christine's personality overpowering, and felt she was probably even more difficult to live with than I might be. She was tall and blond and wore a fixed smile. Her father was headmaster of a private school in Solihull, but you would never have thought this from Christine's unsophisticated ways and poor organisation. She spoke well and had good general knowledge, but her standards were slovenly and she could not think beyond the immediate situation. I considered her a very introvert person. In the flat we all put a small amount of money into a communal kitty for general groceries such as milk, bread and for cleaning materials. Christine was known at times to take over-and-above her portion from the shared items in the fridge, not worrying whether the next person had sufficient milk to make a cup of tea with, and so on. It seemed as though Chris wanted to grab as much as she could, while she could. I wondered whether she might have suffered some emotional abuse as a child. I had suffered from bad parenting myself but at least I think I managed to retain a sense of fairness. In my opinion Christine was also close to becoming a hypochondriac. She couldn't cope with even a common cold without believing she was at death's door. She appeared unable to face life on her own, and seemed desperate for attention.

I cannot be certain about Chris's occupation. I think she was a primary school teacher like Susan. I do however remember her ritualistic religious practices. Apart from occasionally attending St Mary's Church she also attended the strict Baptist church in Church Hill that at that time had its own church building and a definite strict-Baptist culture. Chris was very careful about covering her head in prayer and worship, avoiding certain substances and following some other recognised religious observances. This was no real problem to me, but somehow Chris's holier-than-thou image amused a few people who thought she was being superficially pious. Eventually Chris became engaged to be married to a trainee priest in the Church of England. This became the centre of her world; she could not think or talk about anything else. She was totally obsessed with her new situation. I suppose it is not surprising that I, with my own personal insecurities, found Chris's mannerisms difficult to deal with. I needed temperate individuals around me with balanced emotions, but it surprised me to discover that even Susan was beginning to find the situation a bit of a strain. Susan could get along with almost anyone – even me! Christine must have been one of Susan's few disappointments in maintaining social harmony within the flat. There was no big row or heated discussion but Susan encouraged Chris to find somewhere else to live. Susan and I did not dislike Chris, or she us; she was not deliberately trying to be awkward but her presence was just too overpowering. When she left, we kept in touch with her and she reappeared to visit us once or twice.

FOOTNOTE – I have recently found some negative comments on the internet about a Mr H. B. Callaghan, a former headmaster of Cedarhurst School, Solihull. I imagine this may have been Christine's father, and if so his behaviour as described in the posted memoirs could explain Christine's resulting personality.

The tenant who arrived after Christine was Pat LeMay. She was "a dear"; much loved by everyone, inoffensive and non-assertive. She probably found me hard going as a flat-mate at times, opinionated, assertive and strong-willed as I was, but Pat never showed any sign of exasperation or annoyance. She was easy to talk to, well organised, tidy and thoughtful – quite the opposite of Christine.

Pat did not have a very good personal history. Her mother had died when she was a teenager, and being the eldest child of the family she helped her father look after her younger sister and brother. At some point Pat's father remarried, and from local gossip, (Pat would never be judgemental herself,) it appears the stepmother was the stereotype of the fictional wicked stepmother of fairy stories – power grabbing, unsympathetic and a control-freak. A short while after her father's remarriage Pat's younger sister married her childhood sweetheart. The young couple had a baby boy but tragically, while he was still a toddler, his mother, who Susan and I had grown to know quite well, died suddenly from health complications; although grieving Pat managed to support her distraught brother-in-law and young nephew in practical and emotional ways. To add grief to grief not long after this Pat's young brother began to get himself into bad company and then into trouble with the police. Those who knew the family guessed he was probably rebelling against his stepmother and the difficult situation at home, but this was no comfort to Pat who was trying to get him back into good habits.

Friends could not believe how much tragedy one person could have in their life, especially to a person who was so kind and caring. Throughout these problems Pat's one constant friend was Simone Coombs. The two young women were almost inseparable, and they were both very active members of the church despite their other commitments and responsibilities. Simone eventually took up full-time paid church work, married and moved away, but she continued to keep in touch with Pat whose faith never floundered despite the bad things that had happened to her. Many years later I heard that Pat herself had married, and that her husband was a diagnosed schizophrenic. Only Pat could be self-contained and strong enough to meet such a challenge. I saw the couple together once and they looked very happy but they must have had to deal with some really tough incidents as a result of the mental illness.

Being three flat-mates living under the same roof in Flat 4, 77 Church Hill, and having such different backgrounds, interests and characteristics, it is surprising what a good atmosphere there was in our flat, even most of the time Christine Callaghan was there. Susan sometimes mentioned if I forgot some responsibility or chore, but she did it in a non-confrontational way and talked to me as an equal making me feel valued. We shared the household chores and did them in a rota; one week one of us was responsible for cleaning the kitchen, another for cleaning the dining room, and the third for cleaning the bathroom, the following week we moved on to a different room – and obviously we were all responsible for cleaning our own bedroom. I had the little box room with a Dormer window at the front of the building. It was big enough for a bed, a small cupboard, a mirror, my junk and a few of my on-going oil paintings.

As time went by Susan decided it might be best if we hired a home-help to do the basic cleaning in the communal rooms. All of us were beginning to lead busier and more hectic lives with increasing professional and personal involvements. Housework was taking a back-seat and routine becoming a bit of a problem. After discussion and agreement, Susan hired a cleaning lady who came in once or twice a week to do one- or two-hours' housework. We shared her fee between us and this proved another boost to my snobby streak. In my estimation having a char was a prestigious asset. The woman seemed to serve us well at the beginning, but then on a couple of occasions when I unexpectedly came back to the flat on breaks from my art school lectures and sessions at the S.W. Essex Tech, which was within walking distance, I found the lady just relaxing or eating a picnic lunch. To add to my suspicions her initial excellent cleaning results started to diminish. I did not interfere or say anything; I knew Susan would become aware of the situation and deal with it far more adequately and diplomatically than I ever could, and she did.

We had a phone in our flat, one of those traditional black, Bakelite ones. In 1964 it was still not common to have your own personal telephone. In my estimation under a quarter of the British population had one in their home at this time, and mobile phones were certainly not heard of. Our telephone number was COP 1963. COP stood for Coppermill, with our flat being in the area surrounding Coppermill Lane. The Post Office who owned the telephone network had not reached the point where it could implement full number coding. Our four-digit telephone number, 1-9-6-3, was also easy to remember because 1963 was the year prior to my arrival at the flat. Once again, the telephone meant I could boast that I had access to an item of social significance. The only time the telephone proved a problem was when Susan noticed our quarterly bill rising steeply and not matching the money we put into the box on the table. (We used to time our calls and put the appropriate amount of money into the box at the end.) A couple of times we had to share the excess payment between us. I began to take extra care monitoring my calls, realising I might inadvertently have underestimated one or two of them, but it soon became apparent that most of the excess charges were down to Chris Callaghan who was the third tenant at the time. During term-time her boyfriend was away at theological college and she would phone him regularly and get carried away in long conversations. At the end of these calls she would forget to check the time, or work out exactly how much she owed.

It goes without saying that Susan had a good relationship with all our neighbours in the other flats at 77, Church Hill, and community life was very pleasant. The letting agent for the property was a man who had an unwritten policy of only renting to professional or working people that he felt would appreciate the accommodation and prove reliable and responsible tenants. He would not be allowed to be that selective today! He acted on behalf of the Leggett family, the owners of the building, who also owned a well-known local furniture business.

Flat 1, on the ground floor, was the largest of the five flats in 77 Church Hill. A working couple with two young children lived there. They were very friendly and we sometimes popped in to see them. Once they passed on an unwanted sideboard to us. It was in good condition but the couple would not take any money for it. Flat 2 was also on the ground floor. This was rented to a single woman. Her flat had its own entrance straight into the back garden, whereas the other flats, although having a personal inner door, had to share the house's main front door and the communal back door that lead out into the garden. The woman in this flat eventually married a divorced man with a disabled toddler son. I believe the wedding was not that grand, with few guests and relations attending, but Susan went out of her way to find an expensive perfume and presented it to the bride as a wedding gift from the three of us in Flat 4. She wanted the woman to feel her wedding was an occasion to celebrate. Flat 3 was a one or two bed-roomed flat on the first floor, and rented to a young couple. The other bigger flat on this floor, with three bedrooms and three communal rooms, was ours. The attic flat above us, Flat 5, was rented to an older middle-aged man. All tenants shared the small back garden and residents would sometimes meet there to gossip while hanging washing out on the line.

Church Hill was at the hub of old Walthamstow. The girls' grammar school was just over the road from our house, and the ancient parish church was a short walk away up the hill. Apart from the parish church it was quite a religious road, because in 1964 there were at least four churches on our doorstep – the old parish church where Canon Druitt presided, a Strict Baptist church that Christine Callaghan attended, a Church of the Nazarene and a London City Mission Hall that was up Prospect Hill, a road that adjoins Church Hill at the Y junction. Not much further away were Methodist, Baptist, Open Brethren, United Reformed and Roman Catholic churches. Our flat was also only a short walking distance away from the well-known Walthamstow Market. All I had to do to get there was walk down to the bottom of Church Hill, cross over Hoe Street and straight into the High Street opposite where stalls were laid out for trading on Thursdays and Saturdays.

LEFT. Me with Penny Smith outside 77, Church Hill, on one of the days she came over in her car to visit me with Karen Fagan.
RIGHT. Karen posing with me outside 77, Church Hill, the same day.

LEFT and **ABOVE.**
Susan Rowe and Pat LeMay hanging washing out to dry in the garden of 77, Church Hill.

Being a mile long and well patronised in the 1960s, Walthamstow Market had become internationally famous. It was known as the longest market in Europe and sold excellent greengrocery straight from Covent Garden, good hardware, haberdashery, material and well-made clothes straight from the East End factories and sweatshops that had over-produced for the major London stores they supplied. Most essential commodities could be bought in the market in the 1960s. When I re-visited it a few years ago I found it in a poor state. Few familiar sights remained, and few worthwhile items were being sold. Tubby Isaac's traditional seafood stall was still there as was Manze's Pie and Mash shop, but little else. In the 1970s the local council started playing politics with the market and as a consequence in 2004 you could find stalls down the High Street most days of the week. Previously Londoners had prepared themselves for a good shop on one or both of the two traditional days. Shoppers would arrive with their bags early in the day ready to spend their money and meet friends. It was quite an event and a good social occasion. In 2004 many of the stalls sold only cheap, gimmicky, trendy or profitable gear such as mobile phones, CDs, DVDs, poor-quality gifts and badly made teenage fashions. Stallholders were arriving late, some setting up their stalls as late as ten or eleven o'clock in the morning. I had to manoeuvre my way between their vans and barrows as I tried to make my way safely down the road. These newer stallholders did not have the right skills, background or culture to run a successful London market stall. They did not seem to understand the graft and organisation that is necessary. In the past all stalls would have been set up and running by 7 a.m. to catch potential customers on their way to work or wanting a quick purchase before the start of the day. Other Londoners would arrive soon after, and the market would remain open and busy till about 3.30p.m. when stalls would begin to clear up and close.

Waltham Forest Council in the 1970s believed the traditional Walthamstow stallholders were keeping a closed shop and not giving opportunities for newcomers to join them. It speculated there was a particular prejudice against foreigners in the market. I believe this was a misconception brought about by a few ambitious councillors who wanted to make a name for themselves as being promoters of inclusiveness. My experience was the opposite of their understanding. Many of the old traditional East London stall-holders had come from refugee or under-privileged backgrounds themselves and in my view were more considerate than most in understanding the needs of newcomers. Obviously there are always exceptions. A small minority of stallholders may have been racially offensive at one time or another. These individuals were usually sorted out by legal means or through natural de-selection by the other stallholders. I feel strongly about the unjust image the politically correct councillors propagated during this time. I experienced some of the biased propaganda myself when teaching in Leyton in the 1970s. I worked with Margaret Wheeler, wife of a Waltham Forest councillor. More than once I heard her condemn the market stallholders suggesting they were bigoted and biased and once heard her imply something to the effect that they needed to be taught a lesson. I came to suspect this must be the party line of the recently emerged New Labour movement. I am glad I was able to enjoy the best of the market as a young student in the 1960s. I bought some beautiful materials at cost price to make clothes and furnishings, and found most of the gear I needed for my artwork in the wonderful market that I knew.

FOOTNOTE – The political gaff of Prime Minister Gordon Brown in May 2010, during the lead up to his party's defeat at the General Election where he ignorantly and erroneously called a concerned woman "a bigot" is in my opinion further proof of the tunnel-vision and prejudice of many New Labour individuals.

Walthamstow is on the edge of Essex and Epping Forest, and this proved a bonus for me while studying there. I was taken by friends such as Joyce Weston, who I met at the art school, and her parents around some nearby picturesque rural locations. I was taken to High Beach, Queen Elizabeth I's Hunting Lodge, Connaught Waters and nearby towns and villages such as Waltham Abbey, Nazeing, Loughton, Theydon Bois, Abridge, Ongar, Greensted and Bumbles Green. Some of these places could even be reached by bus or by the Central Line underground trains, and proved invaluable places for my sketching and painting expeditions. Another friend at art school took me one day on the back of her motor scooter down the High Street, past the old Coppermill, to the river and the canals of the lower Lea Valley. It was really countrified then and had a community of people living gypsy-style on river barges – so unlike South London where I had grown up. After my initial dubious feelings about Walthamstow I was growing to love the place, see its advantages and feel it was truly my home.

South West Essex Technical College and School of Art, E.17. 1964-1966

South West Essex Technical College and School of Art was housed in a large impressive building in Forest Road, Walthamstow. It had been erected 1938. On entering the grounds of the college from Forest Road you first crossed over an extensive green area before being confronted by a grand flight of steps leading up to the main entrance of the building. In hot weather, students would sit out on these steps socialising and sunbathing in their study-breaks. The college was close to Walthamstow Town Hall, the Assembly Hall and other administrative buildings which were just as architecturally impressive. This part of Walthamstow was the borough's attempt at regeneration in the 1930s, but WW2 and other setbacks halted the progress for at least the next couple of decades. Most of the educational courses held at the college when I was an art student there were technically or commercially based – surveying, foundation architecture, catering, secretarial, engineering and so on. Our art school was only one part of the institution and based on the ground and basement floors to the right of the main entrance as you went into the lobby.

South West Essex Technical College and School of Art, now renamed Waltham Forest College

Walthamstow Town Hall, now Waltham Forest Town Hall.

Walthamstow Assembly Hall.

I liked the additional space I now had at the new art school for my lectures and studies, but I couldn't help noticing that the teaching staff there, although qualified, were less professional than those I had been used to at Camberwell Art School. Some of the tutors and lecturers at Camberwell may have operated with less than moral integrity, especially in their relationships with students, but the institution boasted the patronage of some highly accomplished artists, and most of the teaching staff were au-fait with the latest developments in the world of art having direct or at least indirect links with the Royal Academy of Art. I came to realise that there were in fact some competent artists and tutors at Walthamstow too; a few even had links with the Royal College of Art, but they were in the minority. Apart from this loss of prestige I found it difficult to adapt to the different approach to visual representation in my new art school. Inspiration at Walthamstow was based on hot, warm and cold interpretations of colour and movement, a Royal College of Art tradition, whereas Camberwell was fired up and inspired by the Royal Academy of Art, and artists such as Victor Passmore and Sir William Coldstream. Camberwell was more concerned with control of visual space and portrayal of depth through dimensional plotting. This sudden change confused me. Had I had a more intellectual or artistic background I think I may have been able to cope with it a little better. During the whole five-year period of my art education I think I only managed to pick up a few very basic brush-techniques and vaguely learnt how to assimilate a few optical effects. With hindsight I wish I had been taught in a far more practical way at my art schools. Their attempts at a philosophical-psychological approach to art, and their leaning towards abstraction and making a statement, were too airy-fairy for me.

In relation to lithography, my subsidiary subject, I hated the mess of the different preparations required for processing in this medium. Being a messy, disorganised person already, I got into such a state ploughing through the various stages and procedures of lithography. Often the original inspiration of my print was lost completely by the end. If I managed to create any sort of order with shape, texture and colour in my final print I felt I had been successful.

Not all my experience at the S.W. Essex Tech was depressing. The institution had one or two caring tutors. One was Maggie Green who lived with her partner, the painter Michael Green. Both had graduated from the Royal College of Art and both exhibited occasionally in the Royal Academy's Summer Exhibition. Maggie seemed to take a personal interest in her students. It was she who, after I joked with her and a group of friends about my blossoming weight, commented "How disgusting!" She was not being rude or cruel; she was just trying to make me see sense, realising I was becoming self-destructive and needed to take serious account of my situation before it got out of hand. It was no good my joking about the problem. Maggie then shared with us how she managed to keep her weight down by sucking a polo-mint when she felt the hunger pangs. I took her comment to heart and it was the beginning of my journey into personal awareness and self-discipline.

Fellow art students at Walthamstow were friendly but not nearly as individual as those I had known at Camberwell; far more of them still lived with their families and were inclined to be more conventional. In the end my closest friends at S.W. Essex Tech tended to come from the college's inter-departmental Christian Union, and were studying within a variety of subject disciplines. Joyce Weston however was one friend in the CU who happened to be an art student like myself and also in my year group. At the beginning of my first term, following enrolment, I saw a wall-poster in the college advertising the college's CU. It gave times and the place of meetings. I went along to what I thought would be the first CU meeting of the term, but only one other student bothered to turn up. He was a newly enrolled foundation-architecture student called Raphael Djkota, a Ghanaian. My imagination began to run riot. Were Raphael and I the only two committed Christians in the whole college? Would we be able to revitalise the CU? How much Christian outreach would we be able to attempt on our own with our heavy study schedules etc., etc.?

Thankfully it was not long before Raphael and I discovered the Walthamstow CU did not actually commence its meetings until students had had the opportunity to settle into the new term and into their new subject courses. We also learnt we would not be the only CU members in the college; there were several others. We found this out from the CU leader who we eventually managed to track down. He apologised for the misleading poster and said he would keep us informed of the situation from then on. He explained that there were good procedures in place to support a CU on campus, although when we did eventually congregate for the first official CU meeting of the academic year we were met with confusion. The room that had been allotted to us was completely inappropriate and had to be changed. Our CU leader was an older student from the surveying department. If I remember correctly, he was married, lived nearby and worshipped at Wadham Gospel Hall which at that time was an Open Brethren church; however he was in his final study year which meant that after he had given CU members a kick-start he began to disappear from the scene to prepare for his final exams. Thankfully the remainder of us, many new to the college, had no trouble gelling together and organising ourselves into what we considered a reasonably lively body of students. We certainly had good rapport with each other considering the many different situations and educational disciplines we came from.

Some members of the South West Essex Technical College and School of Art, Christian Union, 1965.

LEFT to **RIGHT** Richard Naylor (just in view), Me, Joyce Western, Judie Foskett Dave Pritchard, someone only identified by a few wisps of hair, Raphael Djkota, David Hope.

It was inevitable Joyce Weston and I would soon become good friends through our artwork and our CU membership. Joyce lived in Chingford, a short bus-ride away from the college, initially with her parents and then with a couple of lodgers. The house she lived in belonged to Mr and Mrs Weston, but when they decided to move on, they allowed their daughter to remain there while she completed her studies at the local college. They also arranged for two other students to rent the two spare bedrooms and Joyce used this rent money to cover her living expenses. Before Mr and Mrs Weston moved away, I was able to spend Christmas Day with them, Joyce and Joyce's boyfriend in Chingford. I still have a vision of setting out early on the morning of the 25 December 1964, and walking from my flat in Church Hill down Howard Road towards Forest Road, and then on to Chingford. That year there was actually a layer of snow on the ground Christmas morning. As I walked down Howard Road towards the Bell Pub, I could see the whitened roofs and snow-coated trees of Epping Forest in the distance. It was sad that I could not enjoy Christmas with my own family, but at least I had a good substitute and I could not complain.

Joyce's boyfriend, Tony Playle, was a year or two older than she was and already out at work. His good looks were complemented by a great personality ensuring I did not feel intrusive or a wallflower when around him and Joyce. Tony had become a Christian through going to a meeting with Joyce at her Open Brethren church, Ridgeway Hall, in Chingford. The couple were overtly compatible and definitely in love, but still managed to include me and others in their social plans. During my period of study at Walthamstow I seemed to have had mostly platonic boyfriends rather than romantic ones. I had a crush on one or two young men and one or two had a crush on me, but it was rarely mutual except for the brush with Stephen Pegg already recorded, and a boy I met at a party in

171

Susan Barnes flat (to be outlined later). I do not think I had a memorable romance during my whole two years in Walthamstow and was limited to a few low-key dates.

Two of the members of the S.W. Essex Tech CU I grew to know quite well. They were the two Rogers, namely Roger Monk and Roger Kennell. This was partly due to the fact that in addition to attending the CU the young men also joined in many of the activities at St Mary's Church where I worshipped. They were surveying students and I found them good company and fun to be with. This platonic friendship lasted several years, and when I returned to Walthamstow to teach I and my friend Jenny Beard went camping with the two Rogers in the Brecon Beacons. We had an enjoyable holiday with shared highlights, activities and many laughs but definitely no romance. Roger Kennell eventually married Doris Hallett from St Mary's Church, and the couple went to live in Braintree, Essex. Roger Monk married a young woman he met in the place where he went to work following graduation.

In addition to the new friends I was making at the S.W. Essex Tech, I kept in touch with old friends from Camberwell Art School, especially Julia Wheeler, Derek Vernon and Beryl Aitken. It was Beryl who introduced me to Operation Mobilisation.

Operation Mobilisation 1965-1967

I believe it was 1965, a year after moving in Walthamstow, that I went on my first summer crusade to Austria with Operation Mobilisation in the summer break, (although it may have been 1966). OM was a movement trying to motivate young Christians to evangelise and share their faith with others. Its concept and origin was American, and consequently it tended to be a bit loud and assertive in approach and a little prescriptive. Many OM members were caring and inspirational but a few I met were dogmatic and narrow-minded. I did not feel completely at home with all of OM's paraphernalia, but OM was an ecumenical movement and provided me the opportunity to meet and work with other Christians. Another reason, (if I am to be entirely honest with myself,) was that it offered opportunities to travel.

The practice of OM in England was to organise several weekend conferences and evangelistic events throughout the year, in various parts of the UK, and then to concentrate its members on a major evangelistic thrust into mainland Europe during the month of August. The UK conferences usually involved lectures, times of prayer, Bible Study and sessions where members were sent door-to-door to engage local people in conversation about the Christian message. One of the ploys to gain the interest and attention of householders was to show them the Christian books we had on us for sale, and which we carried around in shoulder bags. We hoped the titles of the books might catch their imagination and lead them into meaningful discussion. Sometimes we gave the books away for free if the person we were speaking to seemed to have a genuine interest, but could not afford to buy a book. It was impressed on us that OM was not a moneymaking organisation.

The first weekend I went away to one these OM conferences, it was held in Urmston, Manchester. On arrival I and other members were divided into groups and billeted out to local churches whose congregations gave us accommodation and generally looked after us. My group was billeted with members of a Strict Brethren congregation, while others were billeted at Baptist, Anglican, Methodist, Pentecostal, Open Brethren and other evangelical churches. I had been made aware of some of the ways of Strict Brethren through Chris Callaghan and her association with a Strict Baptist church who supported a similar culture, but now I was about to experience it first-hand. When my group and I prayed with our hosts, and went to their Sunday service, we had to cover our heads and our knees with scarves. It was the day of the mini-skirt and knees were seen by Strict Brethren as provocative. The homes where we stayed had no televisions or other such distractions and family members kept to strict prescribed roles within their home. Apart from having a different outlook on life to the majority of Christians our hosts were kind and friendly and my group did not mind joining in and respecting their ways while we were with them.

After a period of involvement with OM I did some independent door-to-door evangelising around my own neighbourhood. This was the result of OM encouraging its members to be full-time active evangelists. I remember doing it in Streatham and so this was probably early1964, before my move to Walthamstow. I clearly remember going and knocking on local doors, sometimes with a friend but sometimes unwisely on my own. It was rewarding work if potentially dangerous. For some reason, I remember one person in particular who opened the door to me. His name was Mr Lord. He was a young family man with black hair and olive coloured skin. I guessed his ancestry may have been Mauritian or Ceylonese. He seemed to be an open-thinker and I thought he might probably have come from a nominally Christian background but had let his faith lapse. I did not ask him too many questions or do any stereotype Bible-bashing, but I did leave him with a few books to read and hoped they might interest him enough to lead him on to a more committed faith.

It was envisaged by leaders that the British OM conferences and mini-crusades would encourage members, especially students in further or higher education and others able to make themselves available for the whole month of August, to participate in the great European mainland summer crusade. Those who put their names forward for this were not asked to pay anything towards their keep during the four weeks, but it was heavily recommended they prayed and trusted God to send them – one way or another – a personally predetermined sum of money which could be donated to OM's general funds. OM was sponsored and backed by a group of rich American Christians who I believe provided the core-finance for this project, however most OMers prayed for and received enough money to cover a fair proportion of the costs they would be incurring while away. The leader of OM was a fiery young American called George Verwer. He had a second-in-command, who I can picture well but whose name I have forgotten. These two were supported by a close-knit team of middle managers, one of whom was an Englishman called Ron Penny. I liked Ron because he was a Cockney, with a Cockney sense of humour and outlook on life. He was easy-going but still able to meet any challenge or crisis in a positive manner. George Verwer and the other American leaders were more serious. They seemed to have set responses to most situations. I'm sure the Americans were well meaning, and they certainly kept the show-on-the-road, but I kept my reservations about using them as my spiritual mentors.

I chose Austria as the destination for my summer crusade because I knew a little of the German language from my schooldays and hoped this would help me while in the country. Perhaps a more selfish incentive was that Austria seemed a romantic country for me to visit. Other OM members chose or were selected to go to France, Italy, Spain, Yugoslavia and a few other mainland countries, the majority of which were nominally Roman Catholic while OM leaders and members were, almost without exception, protestant-evangelical Christians. Rightly or wrongly OM leaders believed that the European countries to be visited were not encouraging their population to make a personal search for faith and commitment to Christ.

At the beginning of each summer crusade leaders and participants would congregate in one place to take part in a grand pre-crusade conference that lasted a few days. George Verwer's main European headquarters and recruitment area was England, but many participating in the summer crusade had been drafted in from other continental protestant countries such as Finland, Germany, Sweden and Holland. In addition to these participants a band of young American and Canadian Christians came from "across the pond" to join in, and so England proved not to be such a convenient place for this initial gathering. Resources in England were expensive and commuting was particularly costly, especially when it came to taking vehicles and personnel across the English Channel for the start of the crusade on the mainland. It was soon realised that the European Lowland countries would provide better and cheaper accommodation, were more central and a better choice for holding the summer conference. Warehouses in the Netherlands were consequently rented for meetings, accommodation, administration and anything else connected with the conference. After the conference most of the warehouses were returned to their owners, with one or two being retained until the end of the month to act as headquarters and points of reference for the OM teams spreading out across the continent. Most members had to sleep in barrack-like conditions during the conference, but the first year I attended I was fortunate; instead of sharing warehouse accommodation with hundreds of others, I was billeted out to the home of some local Christians.

The conference for the 1965 (or 1966) crusade was held in Rotterdam, Holland. I was billeted near the conference centre at the home of a lovely Dutch couple and their elderly mother. Christine Freake, another OMer, was billeted with me and the two of us became good friends and remained in touch for many years following the crusade. Our hosts in Rotterdam gave us an attic room for a bedroom. Although not rich, they did everything they could to make us feel welcome. Our room was light and bright, and every care was taken to ensure all our personal toiletries and other needs were supplied. For breakfast, we had a beautiful table laid out before us with many different breads, cheeses and cold meats on it. Each morning, something new seemed to be added – bananas, eggs, sausages and so on; we had more than enough but did not know how to tell our hosts. We wanted them to know how much we appreciated their hospitality and so tried to eat as much as we could but had to leave each morning feeling well and truly over-indulged. I believe the family belonged to and worshipped with the Salvation Army, I say believe because they spoke little English and we no Dutch. Following the crusade Christine and I corresponded with the family through translated letters. A few years later we were surprised to learn the couple had had a baby son. They looked more or less middle-aged when we were with them and imagined the wife was well passed childbearing age, so we were particularly delighted to receive this piece of news. During our short period in Holland I came to realise how much that country had suffered in the war. Several young people of my age and older had missing limbs, brought about I imagine by their mother's wartime traumas and food deprivation in pregnancy. Anneka was one such person. She was a participant on the crusade and had only one hand and lower arm. Despite this, she did not seek sympathy and managed to join in most of the normal activities.

Lunch and evening meals were provided at the OM conference centre. We never quite knew what to expect. It was emphasised we had to live by faith. In other words, there were no planned dining arrangements and we had to depend on what became available on a day-to-day basis. Once a local benefactor gave huge churns of natural live yoghurt to the conference leaders. I had never seen it in this condition before. In fact at that time yoghurt was not very much in evidence in English shops at all. The yoghurt was distributed around to us in large pudding bowls and we were allowed some sugar to sprinkle on top. Another day a farmer gave us some chickens for food, and there were regular deliveries of black bread from anonymous well-wishers. Whatever was donated the Americans always made sure they had their peanut butter at hand; large catering-size tins of it were to be found in the kitchen areas. They loved to spread it thickly on their bread – with jam on top of that! The rest of us soon picked up the habit. It's a good thing the travelling and work of the summer crusade was arduous, or we would have put on a lot of extra pounds in body-weight. Fortunately I lost some of the weight I had been putting on previously by joining in shared activities such as scrubbing and cleaning the conference facilities, lifting heavy equipment and pushing broken-down vehicles en route to our European destination.

The first summer crusade conference I attended was perhaps a little overpowering. As I have reflected, some individuals enjoyed organising and controlling others a little too much, Beryl Aitken's mother being one. Mrs Aitken had come along on the crusade as a mature-helper and chaperone, part of the traditional American Christian culture. She had very definite ideas about what members should and should not do. Being a rebel, I would not conform just for the sake of it and was glad that I only had to see Mrs Aitken in Rotterdam; after the conference she was put on another team to mine to be their chaperone. In prayer meetings a few OMers had a definite prayer-style, and tried to persuade others to copy their body language and mannerisms. Some OMers even set themselves up as unofficial leaders and tried to take centre stage. I think they thought they were God's gift to the World Church. On the other hand there were also many humble and sincere Christians on the crusade, and on the whole OM was a really good experience. Crusaders learnt a lot from each other and there was no compulsion to be stereotyped. During my time on the crusades I learnt how to put faith into a practical perspective; I saw many answers to confirm prayer works and learnt the Christian life can be really invigorating if placed above mere personal satisfaction.

A few years after meeting Christine Freake at the OM conference she married Patrick (Pat) Castens who she had met through other OM involvements. The last time I saw this couple they had three sons and were living in Milton Keynes, Buckinghamshire. I went to stay with them a couple of times during my student days and early teaching years and enjoyed their friendship. Chris and Pat's wedding is another of those occasions I will not forget. Christine's family home had been in Tollington Park Road, London, N.2. where she had lived with her parents and brothers before marriage. The Freakes were not a wealthy family but Mr and Mrs Freake made every effort to ensure their daughter had a wedding to remember. Her six younger brothers, (she was the eldest sibling and had no sisters) were all kitted out in smart, plain suits with ties and white shirts. The wedding service was a moving straightforward affair in a small local Pentecostal church where the family worshipped. It seemed to be a liberal church, not over-emotional and over-loud as some Pentecostal gatherings tend to be. Many of the church's congregation were at the service and later at the wedding reception.

The large room that was used for the reception had been thoughtfully prepared by the family with the help of friends, and the wedding breakfast set out attractively on a large table in the centre of the room. Everything you might want was there. Presentation was not over-fastidious with masses of frills and fancy trimmings but the overall appearance was very elegant. It couldn't have been a happier occasion. Unfortunately some years later I heard Mr and Mrs Freak's own marriage had broken down. I believe, (though cannot be 100% sure) that Christine's father left his family to be with a younger woman he had met at work. The news shocked me because he and his wife appeared to be so happy and compatible. Mrs Freake was a really nice person who dressed well and was good looking in a modest sort of way. She had a very neat figure considering the number of children she had had. I thought their faith, family life and situation were unshakable – but apparently not.

After the conference in Rotterdam I was assigned to a team travelling to Lintz, in Austria. I watched as the trucks were loaded up for the journey with general provisions and our personal luggage. Back in England we had been told to take only the bare minimum of essential items and only practical, sensible and useful clothing. Suddenly one of my bags split open and a pair of my shoes fell out. They were not sensible walking brogues but fashionable stiletto heeled shoes. Ron Penny was there and laughed as he picked them up and put them back into the bag. Chuckling to himself he made some dry comment about "the feet of discipleship". Only he could put a rather irresponsible OMer at ease in this way, and see the funny side of the incident.

Our team travelled through Germany with members of another team in one of OM's rickety old trucks that kept breaking down. Each time this or other vehicles went wrong we would have to pray hard because English speaking mechanics and money for repairs were sparse, and some divine intervention was usually required. Frequently on such occasions an unexpected coincidence or mini-miracle would occur to put us back on the road again, and sometimes we would find some sort of benefit had been gained from our inconvenience. We might have heard a useful piece of information while waiting, or met someone needing our help, or someone prepared to listen to the Christian message. These O.M. journeys to and from our mainland destinations usually took more than one day and conditions were primitive. When we needed toilet facilities, and there was no obvious sign of a village, the trucks would stop at a remote spot on the road. Girls would jump out of the lorry one side and boys the other, walk to opposite sides of the road and find woods to relieve ourselves in. We would sleep when and where we could on these journeys – on one occasion in a sympathetic farmer's hayloft. Sometimes we scrumped apples and other fruit from orchards where and when we thought the owner would not mind. Unfortunately one year I picked up intestinal worms from this practice, probably from a fallen apple I had picked up rather than one taken from the tree. The problem was dealt with on my return to England…….

My team finally arrived in Lintz. It was led by an American girl called Greti Graber, and an English boy called Malcolm. I think Greti's parents had been born in Austria, and had immigrated to the USA before the war. Both of our leaders were competent and helpful. Greti in particular had a sunny disposition that kept everyone happy. Our team was certainly international, consisting as it did of American, Dutch, German, English and Welsh members. Willi and Dietmar were the two Germans boys on our team, and were as different to each other as chalk is from cheese. I could often be found laughing and joking with Dietmar, although he was the one who spoke hardly any English and could not understand my poor attempts at German, but this did not stop us communicating in other ways. We had a similar sense of humour and irony and would frequently burst out in giggles together at some comical incident. Willi on the other hand was far more serious. He spoke good English and we communicated on that level, but on little else. Rosie was the live-wire of our team. She was English and yet another person I had no trouble relating to. In fact the only person I found difficult to be with was Ann, another English girl. Looking back, I realise I should have dealt with the situation better and probably would have done had I had better social skills. Ann appeared to me to be one of those people who always wants to be superior and in charge. She was older than me and more experienced in Christian outreach but I certainly did not want to follow her lead all the time. Once when she was trying to get me to do something that didn't suit, I refused, and we ended up in an argument. After this I tried to ignore her but she insisted we had a talk. We sat down on a bench outside the house where we were staying and she asked me to pray with her. She said we should both pray for forgiveness and confess our shortcomings. I was suspicious, feeling this was a contrived situation and not a natural or genuine spiritual prompt. I did not want to end up a puppet, given to following prescribed rituals; rightly or wrongly I walked away.

The OM Linz Team

TOP ROW Left to right = Kristina, Roswitha, Heidi, Johan, Willi, Greti, Malcolm, Ann.
KNEELING Left to right = Me, Rosie, Dietmar. (Photo possibly taken by our Welsh member.)

In Lintz, our hosts and chaperones were Heidi and Johan Van Dam, a young married Dutch couple who led a small protestant mission-church in the town. I think the church had a Baptist foundation, although it might have been Lutheran. The Van Dams and their small congregation were well integrated into the Lintz community despite being a minority group, belonging as they did to a protestant church in a Roman Catholic country. Members of their church made every effort to mix with and be part of the community. They had good local contacts and the Van Dam's had made many friends in the area. Excluding my personality clash with Ann, Lintz was a good experience and adventure. Daily routine was hard work but we felt we were doing something worthwhile, and when relaxed our team was usually found in high spirits.

For Christian worship we attended services in the Van Dam's little church. I cannot now recall if the church had its own building or if services were held in a house or other building. In addition to church services we also had our own OM prayer and Bible study meetings organised by Greti and Malcolm. Among our leaders' other responsibilities was the drawing up of our schedules for the door-to-door outreach programme. Most weekdays after the morning meeting we would go out in twos calling on houses and meeting local people. We would introduce ourselves and show them the German language Christian literature we had in our bags. We would explain the purpose of the books saying that some were for sale, but that we also had others that we could give away if they were interested. I was surprised at how many of the Austrians responded positively to our effort; mostly we experienced smiles, friendliness and a genuine interest in our work. Occasionally we felt we had actually managed to help some people who wanted to talk about matters that concerned them.

I have forgotten what living-accommodation we had in Lintz. It was probably very basic, just two dormitories, one for girls and one for boys, either in the Van Dam's home or in a local community building. I am confident the Van Dams would not have been far away from these dormitories because as I have said OM implemented a strict chaperoning policy, but during the day we were not heavily supervised and often left on our own. I remember sharing in the cooking and other chores in Lintz. Once I had a disaster when put in charge of the laundry. I was washing the team's clothes by hand in a large tub, and not being very experienced at that sort of thing I put several items of clothing together that should have been kept separate, including a bright red garment that coloured the hot water red and some of the other garments too. When I took the items out to hang them up to dry the Welsh girl in our team (not in the photograph, and whose name I cannot remember), almost broke down in tears. Apparently she had spent months before the crusade saving up enough money to buy some decent clothes, including a complete set of new white underwear with a pretty lace-edged petticoat. All this underwear was now pink. I did not know what to say. Roswitha saw the incident and said to the victim in broken English, "Never mind, you now have pretty rose-coloured underwear!" This did not help. I admit the underwear had dyed a perfectly even colour, and was indeed a pretty shade of rose pink, but it was not the colour-preference of its owner.

In Lintz, our team got to know some of the local families. Most of them were farming families, and their life-style was basic but well organised. They had few mod cons but their existence was full and interesting. It was nothing for parents to have twelve children in their family, and eight was quite normal. I remember one mother regularly taking her large brood of offspring up the mountain path to the lake for relaxation and swimming. She was still young looking with a good figure that I envied; she even wore a bikini at the lake. I couldn't help but wonder if I would look anything near as good as she did when I reached her age. In spare time local families could often be found sitting with friends in their orchard-like gardens talking and sipping fruit juice under the shade of the trees. I was with a few other members of our team at one such gathering when a neighbour came along with a large plate of cinnamon apple blintzes to celebrate our visit. They were heavily spiced and had been taken straight from the oven. I had never tasted such heavenly fruit-filled pancakes before; they were delicious.

The next OM summer crusade I went on the following year was also to Austria, but this time the introductory conference was held in Belgium, not far from Ostend. The warehouses here were bigger than the ones we had used in Rotterdam and so more of us, including me this time, slept in them overnight on the floor in sleeping bags. After the conference I was put on a team travelling to Freistadt, a small mediaeval Austrian town on the Czechoslovakian border. There must have been some administrative blunder however because our team was left solely in the care of two young single people. Once again, the pair consisted of an American young woman and an English young man. Teams normally were sent out with a couple of older OM members, or were met at their destination by an older, married couple who would supervise throughout. Despite this blunder our team had excellent leaders who were well able to ensure a good team atmosphere without social complications. The male leader was an undergraduate at Cambridge University. I cannot recall his of the female leader's name, but I do remember the nickname of the male leader's friend on our team. He was also a student from Cambridge and called Sandy – unsurprisingly because he had sandy or ginger coloured hair! These two Cambridge students were quite charismatic and were part of a large company of Cambridge University students who had come down to participate in the OM summer crusade that year. They added intellectual credibility to what some outsiders might have considered a group of fanatical religious-maniacs on a crazy venture. I assume Cambridge University must have had a very good and lively Christian Union in the1960s.

The picturesque town of Freistadt did not have an established protestant church to support our work and so we set up camp in tents on a mountainside just outside the town. The very first night there we endured a storm. Thunder and lightning crashed and flashed over us and torrential rain poured down. Nearly everyone and everything became soaked – our bedding, our clothes and most of our belongings. Next morning, the leaders took us down into the town to try and cheer us up. They found a local gasthaus, or inn to buy refreshments for everybody. Officially OMers were meant to forego luxuries such as visits to restaurants and cafés, but the leaders felt our situation demanded the guidelines be ignored on this occasion, and at the gasthaus they ordered hot tea for everyone. The landlady of the establishment was dressed in Tyrolean style clothes and she brought in a tray of mugs containing what looked like steaming hot black tea for us to drink in her lounge. She was smiling, and obviously enjoyed the company of young people. Wrapped in blankets and shawls retrieved from our less-soaked luggage we warmed our hands on the mugs and began to sip the tea. It was heavenly, but we soon realised it was heavily laced with rum. There were two Dutch girls on our team who belonged to the Salvation Army and had taken the Tea-Total pledge. They had gratefully drunk some of their beverage before realising its contents. The landlady and her husband had taken pity on us, and laced our drinks at no extra cost to warm us up without realising the implications. This couple proved more than friendly, and to cut a long story short, following a conversation with our leaders they offered our team two large rooms in their gasthaus absolutely rent-free for the duration of our stay in Freistadt.

I learnt that the landlady was German-born, and this may have helped with her international, interdenominational empathy. I do not know if she was originally a Protestant or a Roman Catholic, but she certainly supported the OM effort as did her husband. Staying at the gasthaus meant that we were in the heart of the Freistadt community that we wanted to serve. Alcohol was definitely off limits for the team from then on, but on the very first day, returning to our tents slightly drunk, disorientated, fumbling and shuffling to collect the remainder of our belongings and take them down to our new accommodation, we were more than appreciative of that initial alcoholic gesture. Cynics might say the storm was just a coincidence, but our team would point out it happened at the right time and in the right place to achieve maximum benefit for our team.

Unlike the other OM teams on the 1966 (or 1967) summer crusade, our group became quite liberal in attitude and practice. I suppose it may have been a reflection of the Cambridge University student culture that emanated from our male leader and Sandy, or due to the fact that we were operating without the oversight of less-flexible older individuals – but somehow we managed to avoid the dictate of American, fundamental, orthodox, puritan Christianity practised in most other OM teams. To give two examples of this our team often paired off in mixed couples for door-to-door work, and at our prayer meetings we were not inhibited by ultra-modest rules and regulations – girls did not hide away all their feminine charms and boys treated girls as equals. Nevertheless we were highly directed and motivated and did not allow ourselves to be distracted by any in-house or out-house flirtations. We developed into a very strong, modern, caring fraternity. On a couple of occasions I was paired with the male leader for door-to-door evangelism; like me he seemed interested in art and architecture and one day the two of us managed to take a few minutes break to explore a local highly decorated Roman Catholic church. While we were inside admiring the setting and artefacts my need to impress came into play. Trying hard to remember my art history lectures I boasted to my companion that the structure of the church "looks seventeenth century to me!" When we left the building, there was a plaque outside giving the date of construction as early twentieth century – so much for my general knowledge!

Our team's Christian outreach sometimes extended beyond the ancient walls of Freistadt, and we travelled to neighbouring villages and towns to call on the residents there. Wherever we went, we followed the same procedure; first telling the householders who we were and what our intention was, then showing them our literature to see if they were interested in buying any of the books or in discussing the Christian message. OM work may appear similar to that of Jehovah Witness practices, but at the pre-crusade OM conference the difference was explained. The Jehovah Witness movement apparently has a strong commercial foundation, and encourages members to be involved in prescribed patterns of outreach, deflecting from the belief that inspiration comes from the Holy Spirit on a personal and minute-by-minute basis. We were told we should be motivated by love and not finance or perceived acts of redemption. Doctrinal differences between some of the other cults and sects that have sprung up in the wake of orthodox Christianity were also explained. Most OMers that I knew loved meeting people and engaging in doorstep dialogue. In order for me to do this in Austria, I had to try hard to remember the schoolgirl German I had learnt, and supplement it with extra vocabulary picked up along the way. It proved quite a challenge. When we met residents, we tried to avoid contentious subjects such as – the Protestant refusal to accept the Pope's ultimate authority on earth – the importance of Jesus' mother in the Gospels – the practice of praying to or for the dead – calling priests father – and so on. Our team felt a deep affinity with many of the believing Christians we came across in Austria, many of whom had a real, strong, meaningful faith and taught us much about sincerity and honesty.

THE KEFERMARKT ALTARPIECE / KEFERMARKT FLUGELALTAR:

The ornate triptych at the altar in St Wolfgang Church, Kefermarkt, Austria was carved between 1490 and 1497. The artist has not been identified, and he is merely known as, "the Master of the Kefermarkt Altarpiece". This triptych is considered to be one of the main works of Gothic art in German speaking Europe. Together with the Pacher Altarpiece in Wolfgang Church, Salzkammergut, Austria and the Veit Stoss altarpiece, Krakow, Poland, it is acknowledged to be one of the three most important surviving altarpieces of the late fifteenth century.

LEFT some sketches I made in the church. ABOVE the triptych. © commons – Wikimedia

Voluntary work with OM was not total graft. Maybe it was due to our particular leaders in Freistadt, but our team was able to enjoy one or two mini-outings, one being to Kefermarkt, to see the beautiful carved rood screen in the church there. Our leaders were wise to recognise that intermittent periods of R and R (rest and relaxation) are good for morale and team-building.

In both Lintz and Freistadt our work seemed to be appreciated by several individuals. One of the families we met and made friends with in Lintz was going through a difficult time. A young member of their family was extremely ill, and died while we were there. It was a sad time for everyone but we felt privileged when, as a team, we were invited to contribute to the funeral service. We accepted without hesitation being only too pleased to join in the family's final act of farewell. Following discussion with the family we chose to sing the Christian hymn "When Peace like a River" at the graveside. We sang it in German and spent time beforehand practising the correct pronunciation of the words. The funeral service was a very moving affair, but among the tears and sadness was a real sense of hope and faith. I believe our team's small effort brought some comfort to the mourners. This hymn frequently returns to my mind today, and when I hear it sung by a choir or hear it in the media my spirit immediately returns to that family in Lintz.

DESL FAMILY
Photo possibly taken in the year 1959.
When we met the family the children's ages were Alfred 19 ½ Veronika 18 Ernst 16 ½ Rudolf 15 Gertrude 14 Ernestine 11 Karl 9 and Waltrand 8.

Freistadt was the town where we came into contact with the Desl family There were ten in the family including the parents. They were loving and caring individuals not only caring for each other but also for those they came into contact with. We did not realise it at the time but the mother was terminally ill. She died not long after our return to England. Despite his grief the father sent every member of our team mementos of his wife – a copy of her funeral card and a picture of the family in earlier days. The children had lost a cherished mother, but at least they knew she loved them and that they were born to parents who wanted them. I have often wondered how the Desl children coped without their mother but am confident the older children would have helped their father with the younger ones, doing their best to fill the gap their mother's death had made. Occasionally I try to visualise what the children are doing now, hoping their adult lives reflect and copy their parents' good example.

Freistadt was also the town where I met the Steininger family. I became especially friendly with the eldest daughter Huberta. She was only a young teenager at the time but seemed interested in the work of our OM team and me in particular. I believe she saw me as some sort of older sister figure. She was very pretty and much more sophisticated than the average girl of her age in Austria, and so I am sure her interest in OM was not the result of loneliness or boredom. Her characteristics ensured she was popular with peers and she was not looking for social distraction, something to belong to, or in gaining some sort of credibility. I found it flattering that she wanted to be associated me and the team. She joined in one or two of OMs activities, and her parents and young twin sisters also took trouble to make us feel welcome in their town. The Steiningers were a comparatively small family for that part of Austria. I wondered whether the problem might have been to do with Mrs Steininger's health, although if it was, she did not show any signs of it and I learnt later that she lived to a good old age. When the summer crusade was over, and our team was ready to leave Freistadt, Huberta presented me with a linen handkerchief. In the corner was an embroidered illustration of Zwettle, another picturesque historic town in the region. Being sentimental I still have the handkerchief in my possession today, though like me it is showing its age.

LEFT. The Steininger family in Freistadt at the twins' first communion.
ABOVE The Zwettle handkerchief that was gifted to me

Apart from Operation Mobilisation, there were a few other voluntary youth groups working in mainland Europe in the 1960s, and our team came across one such group. Like us its members consisted of young people in their late teens and early twenties, but unlike us they had been given a manual work-assignment, not a Christian evangelistic one. Most of this team were British and they believed they had been sent to Austria to help in the reconstruction and repairing of facilities belonging to poor rural communities in the aftermath of WW2, and the upheaval that had been caused across Europe. Unfortunately they found themselves re-surfacing the driveway of a large house belonging to an affluent town mayor. They did not consider this part of their contract, and were most aggrieved and very angry.

All in all being a member of OM was something not to be missed. One weekend when I was with an OM mini-crusade in England I did some off-the-cuff soapbox preaching in a public place and thought I was rather good at it. I even over-heard a couple of older men from OM talking to each other on the pavement a few yards away confirming my thoughts, but I did not feel I was being natural. I did not want to become centre-stage or look for human admiration. I realised I could easily be drawn into a role of self-importance and self-promotion by being so ostentatious. Looking around at some of the newer worship-groups in churches these days I wonder if some of the young people and leaders there have been tempted into the image-culture. When I see exaggerated body language and looks of ecstasy on faces, I wonder if it might be for the benefit of those around rather than a spontaneous reaction to a spiritual prompt.

Friends and Family

During my two years living at Flat 4, 77, Church Hill, friends from South West London made several visits to see me, and Susan made every effort to ensure they felt at home in our flat. She was a natural hostess, never putting on airs and graces and treating everyone with respect. She would often share laughs with visitors and took an interest in their lives. As a consequence of her open light-hearted manner she occasionally left people bemused. Derek Vernon, from Camberwell Art School, was one such person. He came over one day and while sitting in the front room drinking coffee and chatting with me and friends, Susan said something to him that sounded as though she was talking to a child. It was only the usual unmonitored, off-the-cuff banter that we often exchanged in the flat, but it took Derek by surprise. When Susan left the room, he appeared indignant and laughingly referred to her as a "silly-old-cow", obviously feeling she had been patronising. Like many art students of the sixties Derek sometimes took himself a little too seriously. I am glad to say he soon realised Susan was a genuine character, not the Joyce Grenville figure he was beginning to imagine.

Bunny (Susan Barnes) was another friend from South West London who I kept in contact with for a long time as the earlier account of my visit to her and her husband in Zambia confirms. Before her marriage however, following her formal education and the beginning of her career, she moved with some friends into a flat near the Fairfield Halls in Croydon, Surrey, and I have mentioned that I attended a party there. On the day in question it turned out to be a very enjoyable get-together of gregarious young people. Guests had the opportunity to meet old friends and make new ones; good food, drink, modern music and dancing were in good supply and I wore my latest, very trendy outfit – a black velvety all-in-one cat suit with long sleeves, high neckline, bell-bottom trouser-legs and a zip all the way up the front. I had managed to make it from a modern design-pattern on an old sewing machine.

The party went well, and I spent nearly all my time dancing, eating, drinking and socialising with a young man who turned out to be one of Susan's flat-mates. He was handsome, had a nice personality, and we got on really well together. The party continued into the early hours of the next day. When we as guests felt we could not keep up the social pace any longer we flopped down on the floor, chairs or sofas, with whatever cushions we could muster, and slept as best we could. Next morning we began to make our way home. My party-partner tried to make arrangements for us to meet again but I would not commit myself. I liked him very much, and found him extremely attractive, but I wasn't sure it would be practical to further our friendship. A few days later a large bouquet of beautiful flowers arrived for me at 77, Church Hill, with a message from the young man asking me to contact him. Bunny had given him my address. Wisely or unwisely I decided not to respond because I knew that with someone like him it would not be long before I allowed my heart to rule my head, and if this happened, I would have no chance of finishing my studies and gaining future independence. Any distraction would have been too much for me at that point in time; I was only just keeping focussed on my work as it was. I wanted a proper boyfriend, but this was not the time. When Susan Rowe saw the flowers at the flat, she said it was a shame my admirer was going to be disappointed. She was a romantic at heart, and felt it was a pity that someone making such an effort would not be rewarded.

By 1965 and 1966, mainly through my Christian Union connections, I knew art students I considered to be good personal friends in most of the main London art schools – Camberwell, Goldsmith's, the Royal Academy, St Martin's, Hornsey, the Royal College, Wimbledon, the Slade and so on. We often joined together and supported each other in Christian outreach events. I have already described my friendship with Stephen

Pegg and his three friends at Hornsey Art School, and it was one of the other three, a ceramics student, (name since forgotten) who invited me and a few others to go to Essex and help support a Christian youth outreach event there one holiday time. His family lived in Black Notley, near Braintree, Essex, and most weekends during term-time he would return there where he belonged to a lively youth group at the local church. This group, together with others in the area, were organising the event and I agreed to be one of the volunteer-helpers. As a consequence I was offered accommodation for the duration of the weeklong event and found myself billeted with Ann and John Smith at their farmhouse, Greylag, on Hubbard's Farm, situated between the villages of Shalford and Panfield in Essex. Meeting the Smiths was the beginning of another long-term friendship. I came to know Ann and John and their extended family well. Ann was a year or two younger than me but we had a similar outlook on life and as with my other friends she had a good sense of humour. Ann had married John when she was still young, 17 years old if I remember it correctly; John was her senior by almost eleven years. Their home was a newly built modern detached farmhouse on land belonging to John's father, the owner of Hubbard's Farm. John and his brother would inherit the farm one day.

I think Ann and I complemented each other's aspirations. I was flattered by the fact that I had a friend who was well established in the farming community, knew about agriculture and country life and had an interesting family background. Ann on the other hand might possibly have been flattered by the fact that she had a friend from the city who was reasonably well educated, fairly trendy and knowledgeable about one or two contemporary issues. I stayed with Ann and John as a guest in their farmhouse several times after this outreach week. On one of these occasions, just before Christmas, I went out to sketch in one of the farm's barns while the recently killed turkeys were being plucked ready for the Christmas market. I remember this occasion well because it was extremely cold. The cold went up from the concrete floor, through my Wellington boots and into my legs. I was determined to finish my drawings but was almost paralysed by the time I had finished and tried walking back to Greylag.

During my stays at the farmhouse, I would sometimes accompany Ann when she visited her parents in Bocking, a suburb of Braintree. Ann had grown up there in a large Georgian house which she, her parents and sister shared with her uncle, aunt and cousins. The two families ran a bakery business from the property. The main house incorporated a baker's shop at the front, while the bakery building was sited just behind the house. The whole set-up fascinated me. Often Ann and I would arrive there when morning refreshments were being served in the kitchen, a large room behind the shop. Bakers, deliverymen, shop assistants and other workers would wonder in for their break, and enjoy the tea, coffee, bread, buns and other things that had been laid out on the large central table by Ann's mother and aunt. The smell of food on the table was complemented by further heavenly smells coming from the bakery outside. These smells, together with the soft lilt of the East Anglian accent that I heard all around me as people chatted made for an enchanting atmosphere. Before returning to Greylag, Ann would take some cakes and loaves from the shelves in the shop to store in her freezer back home. I was told by Ann that the chapel next to the bakery and main house was a Brethren chapel with a Kelly-Lowe foundation. I think I am right in saying her family, the Boileys, owned the chapel, and were responsible for leading its small congregation – though I never attended a service there myself.

My visits to Ann and John enabled me to discover yet more quaint Essex villages, this time to the north of the county – Thaxted, Finchingfield, the Barfields, the Easters, the Rodings, Castle Headingham and Weatherfield among them. Ann loved to get out and about and so we often went on trips to these places. I had already grown to love the rural villages in south Essex, around Walthamstow, and now I was appreciating the more northern ones, some of which were reminiscent of the scenes in Constable's paintings. It was while staying on the farm, around about the year 1967, that I began to learn how to drive a car. One day Ann was driving across the farm fields with me beside her. We were going to meet John who was working on his tractor in a field, and taking him his packed lunch. When we arrived, he was not ready to stop and so with spare time on our hands Ann turned to me and asked if I wanted to take over the wheel of her car. We were on private land and I did not need a license so I spent the next half hour learning how to manoeuvre pedals, gears and steering wheel. I had to drive across open, bumpy, fields to do this, but Ann was a good tutor and very encouraging. Learning the techniques of driving became very much part of my agenda from that day on. I was in my first teaching post at the time, and being able to drive my own transport proved more than useful.

John's parents, Mr and Mrs Smith senior, lived under the same roof as each other, but led more or less separate lives. Sometime later I discovered the reason for this. When John and his brother were small, their toddler sister died, falling into a tub of scolding water being prepared by their mother for their baths. I do not know all the details but gather Mr Smith senior blamed his wife for the death of his only daughter, and from then on, the couple were man and wife in name only. Ann and John worshipped in a non-conformist chapel, but I do not think it was the same one that John's father attended, and Mrs Smith attended Braintree parish church. They were a Christian family but had not found a way to forgive and live harmoniously together.

The Bakery Business, Bocking, Braintree.

The home of the Boiley family in the 1960s.
The baker's shop at the premises can clearly be seen at the front of the house, while the bakery itself behind the house is obscured. The corner of a building that is just seen to the far right of this photograph, (behind the small brick wall) is the beginning of the Kelly Lowe Chapel.

Ann and John Smith looking towards their newly built house, Greylag.
They are standing in front of one of the old farm vans and holding their Bibles...probably because they are about to go to, or have just come from, a Sunday church service.

Like some of my early would-be boyfriends it gradually emerged Ann herself had some emotional problems that needed addressing. As time went by, I inevitably got caught up in some of the fall-out from these. I had to learn where and when to get involved – if at all. Sometimes I could help, but other times I knew only Ann herself would be able to resolve the situation. Rightly or wrongly I felt Ann should have been more single-minded and focussed; it would have saved her and others a lot of trouble. Despite the problems, Ann remained a good friend and a caring person. She loved her children and John unconditionally. Taking on a lot of responsibility at a very young age might possibly have been part of her problem. Last time I was in touch with her she and John had five children, four sons and a daughter, and were still living in the Braintree area. Whenever I have made contact with Ann and John, they have continued to be warm and welcoming, and they have managed to keep together despite some traumatic moments.

Relations with my own family had remained more or less non-existent, until at some point during my stay in Church Hill, Walthamstow I heard from Aunty Kit that my mother had cancer. Immediately I made an effort to get in touch with my family again. It is possible Aunty Kit exaggerated the situation making it sound more serious than it was in order to seek reconciliation between me and my mother – although realistically any form of cancer in the 1960s was potentially dangerous. It emerged that my mother had cancerous womb fibroids and needed to have a hysterectomy. I saw her a few times over this period, and we made partial peace, but even after her treatment and recovery our relationship remained extremely stressful. It was like facing a war zone every time I set foot in 192, Cavendish Road, Balham, S.W.12. I tried going back just before Christmas after her recovery. It was only for a day or two, but the looks my mother threw me and the remarks she made helped me feel like an intruder the whole time. Others who called in to see her were made to feel welcome and told to help themselves to the festive food and drink that lay around the flat in fancy bowls and decanters. The one occasion I fancied and asked for a glass of sherry I was made to feel greedy and an opportunist. A real fuss was also made if I had any sort of accident; a real likelihood with my inborn clumsiness. While there I brushed up against a plastic tea-dispenser attached to the kitchen wall and partially broke it. You would have thought I had done it on purpose by the way my mother reacted. All these incidents made me grow a thick emotional skin. Even today I find it difficult to take responsibility or to feel guilty for my less praiseworthy actions. If someone brings a failing or mistake to my notice, I shrug it off and do not even bother to try and excuse myself – making up I suppose for the time when I could do nothing right.

With my self-imposed exile partially broken I tried to make myself useful, and took my young sister Jill out for a day trip on a couple of occasions. She was not six years old when I left home and I had missed seeing her early development; taking her out to places like Central London partly helped to compensate for this. Jill was a tubby little girl, and by 1965 was the centre of our mother's world. Philip was then a teenager, semi-independent and not needing our mother's attention so much. Without another son to indulge in (Mum's self-confessed gender preference), Jill was the next best thing. It is not surprising Jill and I were tubby children. We were over protected and molly-coddled as toddlers. The situation changed for me when I began to rebel, but Jill's placid nature and sympathetic understanding of our mother's needs helped her keep our mother's affection. Jill has always deeply loved our mother, but like me sometimes wondered if mum over-dramatized some of our childhood health problems. In Jill's case this meant frequent referral for medical check-ups and tests.

FOOTNOTE – Jill has since made up for her tubby childhood by keeping her figure in excellent trim as an older woman. When she was 40, she could easily be mistaken for a trim 25-year-old.

Trafalgar Square, London. 1965

This photograph was taken during the period when I was living in Walthamstow. It was one of the occasions I took my young sister out for a day-trip into Central London.

The Christmas tree behind us suggests the photograph was taken early December, and we are pictured feeding the pigeons with tubs of seed bought from the stall behind us. This activity was permitted then, but now banned for Londoners, visitors and tourists alike.

I have come to realise Jill needed all the additional parental attention she could get after my dramatic departure from the family home, because as noted my mother went into a deep depression that kept her bed-bound for several weeks following this event. It must have been very confusing for a little girl like Jill, and it was not long after this that Jill was diagnosed with the condition petit-mal, following which my mother decided to go into Jill's bedroom and share it with her. This sleeping arrangement continued for many years and may have been the excuse Mum needed to distant herself further from the husband she did not respect, the man I wrongly believed at the time to be my natural father.

LEFT Philip and Jill circa 1963, sitting on the doorstep (sited in Yukon Road.) of the family's flat 192, Cavendish Road, Balham,
ABOVE Philip and Jill playing on a homemade trolley-cart. The double gate behind is the entrance to the shop's yard, and the single gate beyond this is the one belonging to the family flat.

Like his sisters Philip too was a regular visitor to the doctor's surgery and hospitals as a child. He did in fact suffer a few very real semi-serious illnesses such as pleurisy, and some complications resulting from an accident he had as a toddler when he rode his little three-wheeler bike along the passageway of the Balham flat and forgot to stop at the top of the stairs. This accident left him with a permanent loss of smell and taste.

As years went by my mother began to leave my father in Balham and take holidays alone, with friends or with Jill – and later with Jill's young daughter Carley who was born in 1975 – but definitely not with Dad! In 1980 she was on holiday with Carley in Weston Super Mare, when my father died. He had become ill before she left Balham for the holiday, and it was serious enough for him to be admitted into Tooting Bec Hospital as an in-patient. She received the news of his death at the holiday-camp where she and Carley were staying, but remained at the camp until the end of the holiday. She excused this action with comments such as "What good would my early return have done?", "I needed time to pull myself together and compose myself for the rest of the family!", "An early return would have spoilt Carley's holiday!", "I was not that close to Len the last few years of his life anyway," etc., etc. I found these excuses really difficult to accept. Perhaps I should not think the worst of her. It is just possible she was confused, guilt-ridden and depressed and that was the only way she could cope with the situation, but my gut feeling was that she was being purely selfish, and finding dramatic reasons to explain her actions and gain sympathy.

The relationship between my father and me is another thing that has already been carefully outlined. We hardly exchanged a word from the moment I discovered his Peeping-Tom activities in Balham until he appeared at my digs in Barrow Road, Streatham, when he came with my young brother to deliver the Christmas package. We exchanged a few words then and had limited dialogue from that time on. The next memorable occasion, also previously recorded, was when my father tried to make amends for his unacceptable actions and purchased gifts of matching pendants for me and my mother. This happened when I was living in Walthamstow, and it was while I was in Walthamstow that he made a big effort for my 21st birthday party, something I describe in detail further on. I was also pleased when my father was willing and available to "give-me-away" at my wedding in 1976.

During the breakdown of our relationship however I felt an enormous sense of rejection, in particular with the cessation of his birthday cards to me – even though I no longer sent him one and was probably the main instigator of the alienation. As a child I had always received a card from both parents, and my mother had begun the practice of storing and keeping all her children's birthday cards from one year old onwards. When older I continued this practice myself, and so the loss of my father's card seemed particularly poignant and hurtful. Dad's first priority at all times was to please my mother and keep the peace. I am not exactly sure when he said it – probably towards the end of his life (and he certainly was not trying to backstab my mother who he nearly always praised) but he once muttered, "I think if it was not for your mother we might have got along better together."

During his last years my father left the Co-operative Society grocery trade and become a night watchman. My mother thought this was a far better occupation, especially where pay was concerned. She was continually pointing out to my father that other men, already in that line of business, were enjoying a far better standard of living than they were doing. In reality my father was just not suited to his new occupation. He was a "people's man", and gained satisfaction from performing recognised face-to-face services; he liked helping customers and solving their problems. The nocturnal duties of his new job meant he had no customers and he had to work alongside several shirkers who chose night work to avoid being supervised. Despite these problems my father persevered and my mother was able to buy the small car that she had craved over the years. Unfortunately it was never put to use. Dad began to experience mental breakdowns making him unable to drive, and Mum did not have the opportunity to learn to drive herself. Leonard Harold Lewis died July 1980, just before his 64th birthday.

St Mary's Church, Church Hill, Walthamstow, E. 17. 1964

Friends in Walthamstow were my stability and substitute family. I still saw old friends back in south London – old school friends, Camberwell art student friends, Immanuel youth club friends and others – but now I had several new friends, some of whom belonged to the young people's group I joined at St Mary's Church. Similar to Immanuel YP members, members of St Mary's youth group covered a wide range of ages, interests and backgrounds too, and still managed to have a lot of fun. I was especially pleased that St Mary's youth group organised round-the-houses carol singing in the lead up to Christmas, as Immanuel YP had done. About twenty of us would meet in the evenings before Christmas and walk around local streets and housing estates singing Christmas carols as we went. We would dress up in bright coloured scarves and gloves and wear comical hats; some would bring along torches and lanterns. We would sing enthusiastically from the carol sheets provided by the church. Most residents seemed to appreciate our efforts in the 1960s, even if they were not churchgoers or Christians. Many would smile and put money into our charity boxes. After a few hours singing we would reward ourselves by going back to the church hall or someone's house for mince pies, coffee and even the occasional glass of sherry or wine for those of the right age. Canon Druitt at St Mary's Church was Tea-Total. He had seen suffering caused by indulgent drinking in the period between the world wars, especially in the poorer parts of London, but he was realistic knowing most of the young people in his church enjoyed a tipple or two and wouldn't be persuaded otherwise. We enjoyed many outings and social events at St Mary's youth group, both formal and informal, but we also appreciated the more serious Bible studies and religious meetings of the church that gave opportunity to air views, exchange ideas and pose questions.

Susan Rowe held one such Bible study group in our flat. I remember clearly one member who belonged to it. He was Frank, a young man in his mid or late twenties. He had recently become a Christian through the work of a national Christian crusade, possibly a Billy Graham Crusade. Frank was a breath of fresh air within the group. He was honest, down to earth and once again had a great sense of humour. He was also a heavy smoker. When he realised most of the Bible study group did not smoke, without any prompting from us he refrained from lighting up in the meetings but instead went out of the room into the garden for a fag-break every so often. We never talked to him about his habit. At that time the dangers of smoking were not widely understood and it was a common pass-time for many individuals, especially young people. As Christians we could not see how initially smoking would interfere with his newfound faith and believed that as time went by Frank's own conscience would guide him as to what was right and wrong for him personally. Another Christian group in the area however, who were also in touch with Frank, did see a problem. They were a high-powered Bible-bashing group from another local church who considered themselves charismatic and appointed by God to show others the errors of their ways. They began to pester Frank about his smoking and his interference with God's Temple (i.e. his body). They probably told him that he should get Christ's victory over his habit. As a consequence Frank became very guilt-ridden and eventually to every-one's surprise and grief committed suicide. It seemed a terrible waste of an individual who otherwise appeared emotionally well balanced, and who was an asset to any group he might be part of.

Not in our house group, but in another part of the St Mary's network were the Gordon sisters, Elaine and Carol Gordon (or Ellie and Vicky as they preferred to be known) and their friend Jo. It was through their acquaintance and going to one of their parties that I met my husband-to-be several years later. Ellie, Vicki (and I think Jo too) were involved in Sunday School teaching, and as I had for some time wanted to do something practical with my faith in Walthamstow I thought it would be a good idea if I continued with the Sunday school teaching I had begun to do in Streatham. With this in mind I offered my services to the vicar, Canon Druitt. At first, he was a little wary, probably wondering what my motives and abilities were, but eventually he must have been positively persuaded because not long after he invited me to fill a gap in one of the Sunday school teaching teams. Ellie was the enthusiastic leader of this team. She would get down to the children's level bouncing up and down with them as they sang choruses, and entering into the mood of the Bible stories that were being told. Vicky, her younger sister, was also competent and easily gained the children's interest and attention. I enjoyed my time teaching in St Mary's Sunday school and made yet more friends among families of the Sunday school children, two of whom had Caribbean backgrounds.

The first of these Caribbean families was the Joseph family. Hyacinth and George Joseph were originally from Antigua. They had two boys, Terry and Vere, and a daughter, Kimberley. Later they adopted Hyacinth's niece, Anna, giving Kimberley a much-loved stepsister. All of the children were regular Sunday school attendees and when I visited their home, I was made welcome and treated like one of the family. I admired the way they were so well organised, despite Hyacinth and George both having to go out to full-time jobs to earn a decent living and pay their mortgage. As a family, they nearly always sat down together for meals, and their house was kept spotlessly clean and beautifully decorated. Some years later, Kimberley was chief bridesmaid at my wedding, and later still my husband and I attended her wedding when she married Mark Bowers, an Antiguan businessman and member of the Antigua cricket team. The wedding was a very grand international affair with friends and family of the Josephs and Bowers travelling from such places as Liberia, the Caribbean, USA and mainland Europe to be there.

The other Caribbean family I grew close to in Walthamstow was the Robinson family. They were temporarily residing in the borough while Rupert furthered his studies in surveying at the S.W. Essex Tech, to gain a higher qualification. Joyce his wife supplemented her husband's Jamaican Government financial grant by working as a nurse in London. They had four children who they brought to England with them, together with an elderly relative Aunty Pearl, who helped with child minding and housework. Like the Josephs, the Robinson children too were regular attendees at St Mary's Sunday school, and Joyce and Rupert joined in as many church activities as their other commitments would allow. A few years later, after the family had returned home, I visited them there in Kingston, Jamaica, and had a wonderful month-long holiday. In 1991 I returned for a second time, this time with husband and sons in tow.

I could spend hours talking about the various people I met in Walthamstow, but will concentrate for the time being on the vicar, later assigned as rector, and his four rather unique curates of the mid-1960s.

Kimberley Joseph as my chief bridesmaid in 1976, and behind her, to the right, Rachel Banks, Deirdre Gaynor and Susan Banks.

Photograph taken in the Robinson's garden in Havendale, Kingston, Jamaica.

Canon Druitt was a parish priest in the old Victorian mould. He was outwardly stern and authoritative but, as I came to realise, had a real soft centre. It gradually became apparent to me and a few others that Canon Druitt understood more than most the needs of ordinary people – the problems of disaffected youth, the despair of down-and-outs, the depression of people who had fallen on hard times or met tragedy of one kind or another and the helplessness of individuals who had a strong personal weakness they felt they could not control. This part of his character was not generally known. It was only discovered by accident by the few who found out about his unpublicised acts of kindness and compassion – instances where he had anonymously put envelopes of his own money through the letterboxes of needy people, helped single teenage mums who were suicidal or reassured individuals who felt they had committed the worse possible sin under the sun and were beyond any kind of redemption. Unfortunately his usual reputation was that of a tactless old man who said and sometimes did inappropriate things. On occasions he appeared to verbally bully people, especially his young curates.

With hindsight I believe the cause of Canon Druitt's tactlessness may have been his own background. He had never married and it was rumoured that as a child, he had had an over-bearing father. When his mother was windowed, she went to live with her son until her own death. It was Mrs Druitt who took on an unmarried mother as their housekeeper following her son's appointment as vicar of Walthamstow, and move to the Walthamstow vicarage. Violet Scott was this housekeeper, and Daphne Scott her young daughter. Both went to live at the vicarage and later in the new rectory when it was built. In old age Canon Druitt was pressurised by the church authorities into retirement, his mother had been dead for many years by then but he had continued to provide food, accommodation and a small wage for Violet never querying the sometimes rather large housekeeping bills she presented to him. He was always considerate of her needs and welcomed all her friends into his home. Following retirement Canon Druitt paid Violet a good rent to lodge in her recently acquired house.

Portrait of Canon Kenneth Harold Druitt.

Not long before Canon Druitt's enforced retirement, Violet in her middle-age had married a terminally ill widower who died within months of their wedding. He left Violet the Walthamstow house he and his former wife had lovingly maintained and furnished over the years. In my opinion Violet had a big chip-on-her-shoulder. She was the daughter of Salvation Army parents and had been born with a harelip and other complications. Her illegitimate baby came as a further disappointment to her very religious family who I was told had all but abandoned her. It must have been good fortune that led Violet to the notice of Canon Druitt's mother, culminating in employment and a secure home for her and her child. Despite this she continually complained that she stayed at the vicarage under sufferance. She felt hard done-by and moaned about the injustices she believed she suffered at the hands of everyone around her. Initially I had seen Violet as a very friendly, understanding and caring person, but later found her to be a persistent liar and manipulator of people. I have seen Canon Druitt spoil Violet like a daughter, and Daphne like a grandchild. He frequently gave way to their demands and willingly bought them expensive presents for Christmas and birthdays. He also spared no expense at Daphne's wedding celebrations when she married – but the older Canon Druitt became, the more offensive and intimidating Violet got towards him, as my husband and I witnessed when we visited him at Violet's inherited house one day.

It is no wonder Canon Druitt had little chance of relating to people as equals with his limited background. He was all right if he was totally in charge, or if he could be of service, or if he was being told what to do – but in my opinion he was lost in team and collaborative situations. Once he was approached by the church authorities to see if he was interested in becoming a bishop. He refused believing he could give better service as parish priest, possibly also realising bishops have to negotiate and plan with other church professionals much more than he was doing already. I grew to love Canon Druitt as a grandfather-figure. He gave advice but was also able to take criticism if he felt the person had a point and was not just trying to score points. I and later my husband found him truly sincere and humble. There are those who were hurt by his thoughtless words at times, and came to dislike him. I wish they had seen the side of him that we knew. He officiated at my wedding and baptised my two sons, the eldest of whom was given Druitt as a second Christian name.

To coin a pet word of the 1990s that describes Canon Druitt's congregation it was "inclusive". He seemed to attract a wide section of society to his church services despite the traditional style of worship that he administered. This was probably the reason I found myself so much at home in St Mary's Church. Among the more affluent at the church in the 1960s were Mr and Mrs Graves. They were prominent both in church life and the wider community. Mr Graves was a staunch, upright man with old-school-tie affiliations. He had come from a privileged background, and had had a responsible professional career before retirement. Nevertheless he was approachable and easy to talk to. Canon Druitt in particular got on well with him, but at the same time was dismayed at Mr Graves' membership of the Freemasons, a non-Christ-centred fraternity. Canon Druitt was a vicar of evangelical persuasion and associated with low church practices; he would not condone membership of any group that did not put Christ first and foremost. The two men had several deep discussions on Freemasonry, and both stood their philosophical ground while remaining firm friends. Mr Graves attended nearly all the church services and supported the church in whatever way he could. Outwardly his wife did not give the same upper-crust impression as he did, in fact with her bright lipstick, highly rouged cheeks, and sometimes flamboyant outfits (this is not evident in the following photograph where she is seen standing in a light coloured coat and shoes, with black hat) she looked more like a woman of questionable repute – some would say cheap. Mrs Graves seemed to have few close friends and was sometimes mocked behind her back. She was a shy woman but certainly not faint-hearted. She ignored the negative vibes and did whatever she felt capable of doing to help the church. Her chief contribution was to stand outside the building at the end of the Sunday morning service and sell the church magazine. It was her way of meeting people, especially shy individuals like herself and any new visitors. She made these people feel at ease and spent more time talking to them than selling the magazine.

On one of the few occasions I found myself talking personally to Mr Graves he confided in me how he and Mrs Graves had met. He told me he had noticed her at a post-war dance and found out from friends that she had lost her former partner (fiancé or husband) on active military service. He was also told she was not interested in meeting other men or finding a new partner. This was a disappointment to him as he found himself very attracted to her. He told me he had to work very hard to gain her trust, affection and eventual acceptance of his proposal of marriage. The couple did not have children and were probably in their late sixties or seventies when I knew them. Mrs Graves died before her husband, and following her death Mr Graves was beside himself with grief. He went to stay at the new rectory for a period of time, where Canon Druitt and Violet looked after him until he felt able to move on.

To contrast the different types of people who found themselves at St Mary's Church, Steve Mann is certainly worth a mention, although his involvement with the church came later, around 1967 or 1968, by which time I was a qualified teacher working at Connaught School in Leytonstone. Steve was the complete opposite of Mr Graves in background, attitude and life-style. He looked like a character out of Fagin's Den, and unfortunately some of his involvements matched this image. He was un-groomed, had straggly wild hair, and his clothes looked as though he had just picked them up from the floor. He found himself at St Mary's through a contact he had at the youth club, and despite his odd appearance, non-conformist ways and lack of certain principles he seemed to feel at home with the young people of St Mary's and enjoyed the companionship he found at the youth club. He even went to church on a few occasions, and made more friends there.

Just as Huberta in Freistadt looked on me as an older sister I think Steve may have done the same. When I locked myself out of my flat one day (I was living on my own at the time) he came to my rescue with a bunch of very dubious keys. I dare not ask how he came by these. On another occasion when Steve returned home to Walthamstow from a short stretch in prison or borstal, he came around to see me and presented me with a musical-teapot to celebrate his release – again I dare not ask how he had come by it.

The congregation of St Mary's Church Walthamstow leaving a Sunday morning service circa 1968.

Mrs Graves is in the black hat and white coat, facing the church. Steve Mann is also standing facing the church with his hands in his pockets. The pram and baby belong to an Anglo-Indian couple, the father of whom is holding the hand of their other child. The young woman with slightly longer hair facing away from the church is Mrs Toni Playle, and I am standing to her right.

Steve tried to settle down, and eventually formed a serious relationship with a girl he met through mutual friends at St Mary's youth club. She was quite a catch for Steve, young, sensible, organised and good-looking with lovely long red hair. She and Steve had a baby together and were given a council flat in a tower block on Chingford Hall Estate. For Steve, this was a great achievement. He now had a proper home and a proper family. Unfortunately his unsettled background, bad habits, lifestyle and criminal associates meant the relationship had little chance of long-term success, and the couple eventually split. Years later, I heard on a television news programme that a prison grass had been badly beaten up by the other prisoners. His name was Steve Mann. I hoped this was just a coincidence, but when I saw the picture of the battered face on the screen it looked remarkably like the Steve Mann I had known. I feared the worst and prayed Steve would eventually shake off his real and imaginary gremlins.

With such a wide variety of characters in one congregation, it was not difficult for me, an eccentric, lively, emotionally vulnerable and sometimes rebellious individual, to fit in, although I do believe a few people at St Mary's Church found me difficult to understand. There was an occasion one Harvest Festival when my rather odd contribution to the festivities met with some incredulity from the Reverend Christopher Jenkin, one of the curates. He had come across the boxed orchid I had submitted as he and others sorted through the gifted fruit, vegetables, bunches of flowers and other offerings, ready for distribution around the neighbourhood. He questioned the purpose of the orchid. Fortunately Pat Le May was also in the room helping; knowing the offering was mine, and the thinking behind it, she was able to tell Christopher that the donor hoped it would be given to a recipient who would normally be unable to afford or enjoy such an object, someone like a house-bound pensioner. The Reverend John Knobbs, another curate present in the room praised the sentiment, saying it was a very thoughtful gift. When Pat reported these comments back to me, I was pleased that at least one of the clergy had tried to understand my lateral thinking and dodgy logic.

I have hinted that Canon Druitt's curates did not have an easy time. Canon Druitt sometimes treated them like naughty little school-boys. Nevertheless the four curates in office in 1964 when I arrived in E.17. had characters that could cope with any professional challenge. Despite being very different to each other they gelled together like a bunch of enthusiastic pioneers on a hazardous expedition, and supported each other whole-heartedly. First, there was the Reverend Peter Ashton, the more conventional one. He was a good-looking young man from a stable middle or upper working-class background. He was also married, a disadvantage in Canon Druitt's eyes who liked his curates to be single while training, feeling curates needed to give their full concentration and attention at the induction period of their chosen career, but his mind soon changed where Peter was concerned. Margaret, Peter's wife, proved to be a real asset to the church. She joined in all she could and rigorously assisted her husband with his work. Like her husband she was attractive in appearance and had a sunny disposition. The couple had no problem integrating into the St Mary's community.

Next, there was the Reverend Gary Beswick, a northerner who came from what I imagined to be a more ordinary working-class background. He was short and stocky and retained a strong regional accent. He was very energetic and seemed to spend much of his time rushing between one assignment and the next. The third curate was John Knobbs, who appeared a little slower in wit than the others, but was by no means unintelligent. He was a very sincere and dedicated individual and proved good at comforting the old and the sick who he frequently visited. It was fortunate that John was not oversensitive, because members of the church sometimes joked with him about his absent-mindedness and proneness to accidents. It was John who once fell backwards into the grave while conducting a funeral service, and it was John who created a crisis one year at the annual Sunday school summer outing.

The story goes that John had been among members of St Mary's staff and volunteer parents helping to supervise a Sunday school day-outing to Frinton on Sea one summer. As usual, Canon Druitt was in charge and arranged for the children to be put into groups of twelve. Each group was designated a responsible adult with an assistant to help supervise them. Canon Druitt insisted there were regular counts of children's heads at each stage of the venture. This went well until the end of the day when the party was reassembled back on the platform of the local train station ready to be dismissed. The clergy and volunteer helpers counted the children in their group and John suddenly realised he had miraculously acquired an extra child. Investigation revealed that the thirteenth child had made friends with some of the Walthamstow youngsters in Frinton on Sea and decided to stay with them and travel back with them to Walthamstow. Poor John was immediately despatched by Canon Druitt to go and buy one adult return rail-ticket and one child's single rail-ticket and escort the gate-crasher back to Frinton on Sea where he had to find the parents, return their child and explain what had happened. Only after this could John return to Walthamstow himself. No doubt the police were informed and involved during the process but a single man escorting a child on a journey like that today would be unthinkable, and seen as open to child-abuse. In the 1960s, it was a matter of common sense, and a way of correcting a mistake as quickly as possible.

The fourth curate was Christopher Jenkin (without a final "s" to his surname, as is the more common spelling). He had an aristocratic background, and his family were reputed to own a small island off the Scottish coast. I believe he was the youngest of four brothers, and that his mother died when he was fairly young. One of his brothers, Patrick Jenkin (registered at birth as Charles Patrick Fleeming Jenkin), eventually became a cabinet minister in the Tory government, and afterwards titled as Baron Jenkin of Roding, taking a seat in the House of Lords. Chris (Christopher) was a little eccentric at times, which is surprising considering he was the one who queried my unusual harvest gift offering. He rode around in a bubble car, an icon of the early sixties, and sometimes wore a fancy waistcoat and a redlined cloak or cape-coat. Once or twice he called around to 77, Church Hill to see Susan on church business. I had a feeling he fancied Susan and was trying to make an impression on her. Through the window of our flat I saw him arrive one day on such a mission. He cut a dashing figure as he climbed out of his bubble car in Howard Road at the side of our building, with his cloak billowing out behind him. Chris certainly enjoyed making fashion statements, and with him being tall, good looking and having a reasonably sharp intellect these statements suited him. He seemed a little embarrassed by his public-school accent and upper-crust background, but as a congregation we were not bothered. We knew he was not a snob and was just trying to do his best in his chosen career.

My feeling was that Chris was another of those shy individuals who initially had trouble relating to romance. If he did fancy Susan nothing came of it. Years later I heard he had married Mary Stowe from St Mary's Church. Mary was the youngest of three sisters; Ann and Rita being her older siblings, (there might also have been a brother). Local gossip was that the Stowe family were staunchly and proudly working class and not particularly well read, cultured or au-fais with sophistication and good manners. It was rumoured Mr Stowe could be a little volatile and unpredictable at times. The family had not originally been churchgoers, but at some point Ann had come to personal faith partly due to a miraculous answer to prayer on the matter of her sensory impairment. Rita and Mary became committed Christians soon after their sister and the three girls went on to contribute much to the work of the church. Their background certainly did not hinder them, and their achievements were commendable.

Like her father Mary too was known to be brusque at times, and was thought by some to be the least bright of the three sisters. It was therefore a surprise for me to learn of her marriage to the Rev Christopher Jenkin. Chris may not have registered terribly high on the Mensa scale but he had had an excellent education and possessed a keen intellect. Someone told me Mary had worked very hard to attract Chris's attention, eventually succeeding – whatever the truth the eventual partnership seems to have been a success. Chris's career meant the couple headed and organised the work of several churches while at the same time raising a family. Mary managed to go a fair way with the nursing courses she pursued, and this together with her past childhood austerity meant she must have been a real asset to the parish communities she served with Chris.

Coming of Age Celebrations 1966

In my last year at Church Hill I celebrated my twenty first birthday. A few young people in the 1960s were beginning to change their coming-of-age celebrations to their eighteenth birthday, but many families remained with the traditional twenty first birthday. Being a traditionalist, and having had non-existent dialogue with my family when I was eighteen, twenty-one seemed to be the right age for me to celebrate. Many of my peers in higher education were almost at the end of their core studies, (although I still had a further year and a half to go), and, despite having no permanent boyfriend many of my friends did, and were beginning to settle down with a long-term partner. All in all twenty-one seemed to be the right age for me to arrange a big get-together. I desperately wanted a proper party. There were friends who had helped me through some emotionally painful years, often in very practical ways. I was relieved and grateful that with their involvement, I had come as far as I had with my education and life in general and a party seemed to be a good way of saying thank you to them.

By the end of 1965 I was seeing more of my mother following her cancer scare. This and the fact I had heard her say more than once that there was a sum of money waiting to be released from the endowment policy she had taken out for me (i.e. the Canadian pension) at my coming-of-age, made me brave enough to drop hints about having a twenty first birthday party with some of its proceeds. It goes without saying that with her general aversion to me she was less than quick to take up my suggestion, but I – ever the wilful assertive daughter – pressed the matter home. After many moans and groans she eventually agreed, and we began to plan for a party. I tried to work with her as best I could, hoping to find out exactly how much money there was in the coming-of-age kitty to tailor the party accordingly, but I was made to feel like a grabbing, selfish upstart and did not get a proper answer. I think my father tried to be more helpful in the background. It must have been he who suggested using the co-operative hall where he was caretaker for the venue, and it was he I believe who negotiated the caterers for a buffet supper.

After much planning the day of the party arrived, and there was even a small band of musicians and a Master of Ceremonies to help the proceedings along and ensure all went smoothly. Dad had kept up the Christmas decorations in the Co-op hall for the event, and added some more appropriate ones of his own including the large cardboard key that he covered in silver foil and hung from the ceiling.

It was he who bought me a Bush Transistor Radio as a birthday present, the fashion accessory of the day. I do not think my mother knew about it until the last minute when he presented it to me, which is not surprising considering her passivity through the whole party planning process. She looked a bit put out by Dad's gesture and certainly made no similar gesture herself. On the day, Saturday 29 January 1966, the day after my actual birthday, she gave me a card but no gift, although she arranged for Philip and Jill to give me some bed linen. I suppose I should have been grateful but the items, two single bed-sheets and two pillowcases were of exceptionally poor quality and wore thin in no time. Thankfully, Philip and Jill were too young to be embarrassed by their gift. Bed linen was a very odd thing for my mother to choose anyway. She had always sneered and derided impersonal and practical gifts for birthdays and anniversaries. She felt the recipient should be given some luxury, personal item. If anyone gave her a household item as a present, she would grumble that she should have been given something like jewellery or a good perfume. Now she was doing the same inappropriate thing herself.

Begrudgingly, at my suggestion, my mother had asked her long-term friend Lillian to make me a dress for the party. Lillian as I have said worked in the Rag Trade and was always helping family and friends with her sewing skills. As a child, I once accompanied my mother on a visit to Lillian, at the Peckham sweatshop where she worked. I saw her and others working away on the old-style electric sewing machines, very much reminiscent of a scene from the television comedy series The Rag Trade, broadcasted 1961 to 1963. I bought the material for the dress myself. Lillian unenthusiastically took it from me to begin cutting out the shapes from the pattern that I had also bought and supplied.

197

SOUTH SUBURBAN CO-OPERATIVE SOCIETY LTD.

TOP LEFT Letter to confirm the booking of the Co-op Hall for 29th January 1866
TOP RIGHT Vale Caterer's invoice for the day, the fee being £57.10s.6d
LEFT The Bush transistor radio my father bought me for my 21st birthday.

My mother's negativity was an excuse for Lillian to be hateful too. She made the preparation and fitting of the dress seem like a chore that she had to endure. Her attitude was that it was a liberty in the first place for me to ask her to make this dress. She ignored any requests I made for adjustments at the fitting, and went ahead putting on her own stamp, a cheap nylon flower which she stuck right in the middle of the neckline. Lillian and her husband, John came to the party but made it clear they were coming for my mother not for me. They did not bring along anything to make the occasion happy – not a small present, or even a card. Lillian remained sour-faced throughout the whole evening.

In addition to my mother's negativity and Lillian's attitude, I had one other disappointment at my twenty first birthday party. For some time I had been saving up to have my hair especially styled at a hairdressing salon for the occasion. The previous couple of years I had struggled to grow my hair to the length required for me to have it in the fashionable Lady Pompadour hairstyle of the day. This length had just been achieved and on the morning of my party the salon arranged each tress of my hair in an elaborate curl to stack up on my head. It looked great, but as soon as I left the shop it began to droop. The hairdresser had put masses of invisible pins in my hair to keep it in the required shape but these could not hold the weight of my hair and the style began to sag. Even the front of my hair, where my face had been framed by shorter strands from a former fringe managed to lose shape. I had no time to return to the hairdressers and could only look on in dismay; all the money I had spent was going slowly down the drain. My hair looked clean and presentable, but there was no style and the resulting mess made me look severe and old-fashioned. For my art student image this was particularly disastrous.

198

Everything else on Saturday, 29 January went well; friends from Clapham County School, Camberwell Art School, the S.W. Essex Tech and School of Art, Immanuel youth club, St Mary's Church and other friends, neighbours and relatives of all ages appeared and I was the centre of attention, which I must confess I revelled in. In fact, the party did my ego a power of good. I couldn't believe the presents I was given but my main thrill was having my friends around me and knowing they were enjoying themselves. The fact that many had gone to the trouble of finding and bringing along thoughtful and lovely personal gifts was a bonus. Some of my art student friends had even been creative and made me special customised cards and souvenirs. Dad decided to make a room at the back of the hall available for the storing of these presents among which could be found a bottle of expensive champagne, (a rarity for most people in 1966), jewellery, silk scarves, books, luxury pens, powder compacts (a must for young women of the '60s), hand-made chocolates, perfumes and many other luxuries. One of my cousins bought me an imitation pearl necklace decorated with crystal beads. My mother envied this from the moment she saw it, and started dropping hints that she would like to have it for herself. I didn't think she was serious at first, but when I realised she was, I felt sad that despite all her own boxes of jewellery she wanted one from my treasured hoard. I resisted the request to pass it on but was made to feel selfish and mean once again.

Uncle Cyril and Aunty Phyl bought me a large silver bangle to celebrate the day which I have always treasured. One holiday after my marriage the original one was stolen. It disappeared at a hotel in Corfu and its loss greatly saddened me. Fortunately a few years later, by chance, I saw an identical one in a flea market. Like the original it was sterling silver and had the same pattern – even more exciting was the fact that I managed to purchase it for just eight pounds, a real bargain! I was more than happy with my find and still have and wear the bangle today despite several other wonderful sentimental bracelets having been given to me over the years by family.

Considering her not too distant cancer scare and operation, my mother looked quite well on the day. She always enjoyed a good social gathering and managed to smile for much of the time. I do not think I got a hug from her, or any other sign of love, but that was to be expected. Regrettably, I never forgave my mother for her indifference to me. When she tried to be a little more physical and affectionate towards the end of her life, I responded as coldly to her as she had done to me previously. I have always found forgiveness difficult despite it being a large part of my Christian faith. Thankfully in old age I am beginning to understand some of the problems my mother faced in her lifetime, but I cannot rectify past interactions now.

The band at my party played through most of evening and there was dancing and party games organised by the Master of Ceremonies. The games were fun but only a few guests joined in. Secretly – perhaps because I had inherited my mother's streak of "togetherness" – I wished more would participate but many friends had not seen each other for some time and just wanted to sit or stand and gossip about mutual acquaintances and old times. I do not think there were any speeches at the party, it would have been difficult to know what could have been said in such a dysfunctional family situation, but the atmosphere was happy which was my main aim and there was sufficient formality to suit my sense of tradition.

Parties have repeatedly been emphasised as being high on my list of favourite pastimes. I attended many and enjoyed socialising, but at the same time I continued trying to be sincere about my faith and disciplined myself to regular, short periods of daily personal prayer and Bible study.

LEFT to **RIGHT** Elsie and Ken Lewis, Jack and Elsie Benfield, (aunts and uncles) and the back of my mother.

Uncle Cyril and Aunty Phyl enjoying a dance, with my mother in the background to their right.

Part of the buffet supper laid out in the Cooperative Hall, with the catering manager standing behind.

LEFT to **RIGHT** cousin Brenda, Lea Pehl, cousin Sheila and Colin Dawes

LEFT to **RIGHT** Sheila and David Banks, me, Mr and Mrs Haines (then the back of Karen Fagan and Richard Owen.)

The cutting of my 21st cake, wearing an orchid someone had given me and my silver bangle

When I had to make a decision I prayed for guidance, but with me being so self-willed I suppose I was not always good at recognising the guidance when it came my way – but I did try! On several occasions, I was assured by some sign or coincidence that God was with me and leading me the way I needed to go.

My creative efforts for art school work and other assignments at Walthamstow were not what I considered to be inspiring; I did my best but felt the practical and social odds were stacked against me. I wished I could have had a proper studio to work in, and more money to spend on better equipment. I also believed my network of relationships within the art group was narrowing as the NDD course progressed. My own priorities and preferences seemed to be diverging from those held by most other students within my year group. I sensed an inner crowd was developing who thought and acted alike and I wanted to keep my individuality. This was separating me from peer support and collaboration. The diploma course was marked partly by continuous assessment, and partly by a final exam. Somehow I managed to pass the various stages of continuous assessment. This may have been down to my good attendance, punctuality and reasonable over-all effort because I know the results of my work was at best mediocre. It was the final exam however that caused me the greatest stress. I continued to have nightmares about it for years afterwards. I knew I had to pass the National Diploma of Design to make the past four years of academic struggle worthwhile. For the finals I was expected to write a thesis several thousand words long, design and complete a lithographic print to certain specifications, and produce an oil painting on a given subject.

The subject I chose for my thesis was "The Symbolic Image of Stone as used through the Various Periods of Art and in the Various Schools of Art". It has already been noted that my literacy skills were far from polished. I had to strive really hard to produce the number of words required in a readable and grammatically correct fashion. However the organisation of my ideas was not a problem. I enjoyed being systematic in researching the paintings, sculptures and prints that I used to support my theories; my analysis of the representation of rock and stone was methodical. I took pleasure too in designing the cover of my thesis, using a natural piece of rugged stone to integrate into the hard-backed cover I had chosen. At the age of sixty I discovered my Benfield ancestors were stonemasons in Dorset in the 17th and 18th centuries, and continued as such in London in the 19th century. This has led me to wonder if I might have some inborn affinity with stone. I can think of no other reason or prompting for choosing such an odd and way-out topic.

Added to my interest in stone I also wanted to portray a stretch of rugged, rocky coastline for my lithographic print in this final examination. I intended illustrating cliffs, bays, coves and beaches of coastline similar to that which can be found in Dorset, not knowing then that my stonemason-ancestors lived in such surroundings. They were initially based in the town of Corfe Castle and then moved to Langton Matravers nearer the coast when the headquarters of the Purbeck stone industry shifted to the town of Swanage. These ancestors had several quarries and workshops all along this stretch of coastline. One, George Benfield was a fully qualified stonemason but also operated as a smuggler. He used his quarries to store contraband in and was caught and imprisoned for it in Dorchester Gaol in the year 1803, being accused of assaulting and obstructing customs officers. He was released a year later without charge, (no doubt with a bribe of brandy and "baccy" for the judge!) With this recently discovered family-tree knowledge I am able to link my heritage to one of Mrs Litschi's favourite poems that she taught us in Richard Atkins Junior Girls School. I was never very good at remembering and reciting poetry, but the Smuggler's Song held my attention and I was able to remember a few quotes from it years after leaving the school.

I despaired over my lithographic print depicting the rugged coastline. With my growing dislike of the mess created in this particular medium I had been weaning myself off the idea that lithography or any other form of commercial-art processing was an interesting and edifying activity to pursue. Other students had for some time been using opportunities to research and prepare sketches and ideas for their final print, but I was at a loss to know what to do and how to do it. In the end I had to submit something; I knew it was a poor effort – no definition of line or texture and with smudged colour and little design. I cannot remember the subject of the oil painting I submitted in my finals. If it was based on visual experience it may have fared reasonably well. I loved experimenting and finding ways to mimic texture, movement, colour, perceptive representation and so on, but if it was linked to any abstract interpretation of a given subject, I would have done less well.

I was sure I had failed my NDD, but possibly due to the college wanting a good pass rate I managed to get through my NDD course with a pass-mark. The college was responsible for marking most of the final exam pieces and external moderators viewed only a few specimens, for which I was most grateful. Somehow I managed to gain a national diploma in "Fine Art with Lithography". I was so relieved, but what should I do now? Many artists take up teaching as a way of earning money while continuing with their own personal artwork, but this was not my idea of fun. I had enjoyed teaching in the church Sunday school but did not want the responsibility and commitment of a full-time teaching post. I wanted to be a proper full-time artist, even though my accomplishments in that field to date were minimal. I wanted to develop my artistic ideas further and believed I still had much to say through the medium of Fine Art – but, wanting and reality are two different things! Wanting does not keep you in board and lodging. It then came to my attention that for individuals who managed to acquire a place on one of the post-graduate art courses provided by some colleges, government financial aid would continue to be available. I began writing to various institutions to see if any had such a place to offer me, or perhaps even a fellowship to offer. I think I was given two interviews, both unsuccessful. At this point I had to consider teaching as an option for my future, and re-channelled my efforts in that direction. Following an unsuccessful interview at Nottingham Art School for a place on the Art Teachers' Diploma (ATD) course, I went to Bournemouth and Poole College of Art, and was accepted there. Having been offered this place, and being awarded the associated financial grant, I made plans to leave London for the very first time in my life – that is apart from going on my holidays, or abroad with OM of course.

RUDYARD KIPLING'S "A SMUGGLER'S SONG"

The CHORUS repeated after each VERSE...
Five and twenty ponies trotting through the dark,
Brandy for the parson, baccy for the clerk;
Laces for a lady, letters for a spy,
And watch the wall, my darling, while the gentlemen go by!

Verse 1.
If you wake at Midnight, and hear a horse's feet,
Don't go drawing back the blind, or looking in the street,
Them that asks no questions isn't told a lie.
Watch the wall, my darling, while the gentlemen go by!

Verse 2.
Running round the wood lump, if you chance to find
Little barrels, roped and tarred, all full of brandy-wine, Don't you shout to come and look, nor use 'em for your play.
Put the brushwood back again – and they'll be gone next day!

Verse 3.
If you see the stable door setting open wide;
If you see a tired horse lying down inside;
If your mother mends a coat cut about and tore;
If the lining's wet and warm – don't you ask no more.

Verse 4.
If you meet King George's men, dressed in blue and red,
You be careful what you say, and mindful what is said.
If they call you "pretty maid", and chuck you 'neath the chin, Don't you tell where no one is, nor yet where no one's been!

Verse 5.
If you do as you've been told, likely there's a chance,
You'll be given a dainty doll, all the way from France, With a cap of pretty lace, and a velvet hood –
A present from the Gentlemen, along o' being good!

CHORUS FOR THE FIFTH AND LAST TIME THEN
Them that asks no questions isn't told a lie – Watch the wall, my darling, while the Gentlemen go by!

Chapter 8

Bournemouth and Poole College of Art, 1966-1967

The main building of the Bournemouth and Poole College of Art was sited near the Lansdowne Roundabout in Bournemouth. It was part of a larger multi-disciplinary college of further education and was where undergraduate art students would soon be going to take the new one-year Foundation Art Diploma course. Following this, if successful they would be able to apply for the new three-year Diploma of Artistic Design course at the college (the Dip AD), or seek to pursue their studies elsewhere. These diplomas were the successors of the two I had known, the two-year Intermediate art course and the two-year National Diploma of Design course (the NDD). However the annex for our post-graduate Art Teacher's Diploma course was sited down Bath Road nearing the bottom of the hill, not far from Bournemouth Pier. Most of my lectures and practical work would take place here, with theory and written work being sent to nearby Southampton University for assessment and grading. As an ATD student I would only occasionally attend the main building at Lansdowne Roundabout for a few of my study sessions. The position of our annex was excellent. It took only a couple of minutes to walk from it to the pier and the beach, and was also close to the Winter Gardens, public transport and shopping centres. In fact, it was central for most things in Bournemouth. We as students occupied the top or first floor of the building, while a small bus garage operated on the ground floor beneath us.

The area behind Bournemouth Pier more or less as I knew it in 1966/7.

Bath Road leads uphill from the pavilion. Our ATD annex is the next white building on the left up the hill, with the rounded front. Our studios were on the first floor, with a small bus garage operating below us on the ground floor – all now demolished. The pier is just out of sight to the right. © oldukphotos cc license.

It was a bit of a shock for me, an immature twenty-one-year-old, to realise I had to leave the security I knew – my flat, my friends, my social life and church. These were all based in London. Fortunately the ATD administrators in Bournemouth offered to find digs in or around the town of Bournemouth for any student who required that service. I knew little about the town and was only too grateful to accept their offer. The college found me half board and lodging in a flat above business premises in Old Christchurch Road, Bournemouth. It was within walking distance of the ATD annex. All I had to do to get to the annex was turn left on leaving my lodgings and walk down the hill and a couple of roads – and to get to the main Bournemouth and Poole College building all I had to do was turn right and go a short distance up the hill. I was especially pleased because not only would I be living and studying close to all the town's amenities, but I would also be able to get to and from lectures without having to pay for public transport. On my given day of transfer I arrived at my temporary digs with a few of my living necessities. A week or two earlier I had deposited all non-essential items with Ann and John Smith at their farmhouse in Panfield, Essex. They had kindly agreed to store them for me in their attic space until I had finished my studies in Bournemouth and found a more permanent home. My old school friend Sheila Haines, by then Mrs Sheila Banks, made a special trip to Walthamstow in her Standard 8 car to help me transport these items to the farm. (A few years later, when teaching, I bought this Standard 8 from Sheila and it proved a very reliable vehicle.)

The couple whose Bournemouth flat I was to lodge in were an elderly married couple, originally from Yorkshire. In addition to being my landlord the husband was also caretaker of the ATD annex in Bath Road. Not long after my arrival another female called Mandy came on the scene. She was about to undertake the same course as me and would be sharing my bedroom at the flat. From the outset it looked as though my new room-mate and I would get along well together. We had compatible interests and our expectations for the year were similar. As we unpacked our belongings on to the two beds in our room ready to put into drawers, we chatted and exchanged thoughts and information. The forthcoming year was beginning to look a little less daunting to me.

The landlady was a plump woman, and immediately began to boast about anything and everything. She took particular pride in telling Mandy and me about her previous lodger. Apparently the young woman who had occupied our bedroom the year before was the adopted daughter of the ventriloquist-entertainer Peter Brough and his wife. Like us she had been in Bournemouth to study for an ATD qualification. Our landlady's connection with such a well-known celebrity and his family gave her a great deal of pleasure.

PROFILE OF PETER BROUGH
from details found on the internet................

Peter Brough was born in Shepherd's Bush, London, on 26th February 1916. In 1944 he became a ventriloquist-entertainer on the radio, and is best known for his act with his dummy Archie Andrews. Archie portrayed a mischievous child who was always outwitting his mentor.

Peter Brough's radio performances became very popular, and in 1956 he began working with his dummy on television programmes, first in a sitcom, "Here's Archie" and then in 1958 on the, "Educating Archie" programme. Peter Brough died 3rd June 1999.

In our first week in Old Christchurch Road Mandy and my Yorkshire hosts brimmed with enthusiasm and promises. We were told we would have excellent homemade food; our landlady was a wonderful cook who made the best Yorkshire puddings in the south! We were told we could heat the emersion and have baths whenever we wanted, and were to treat the place as our own home. Concerning the excellent homemade food that we were promised, this swiftly turned into a very basic breakfast and an evening meal consisting of a huge Yorkshire pudding for a starter with a small main course that seemed to shrink each day as the Yorkshire pudding grew bigger. The earlier promise of regular and frequent baths had been especially welcome to us because in addition to theory-work we would be doing a lot of creative practical work on the course. Unfortunately this promise too was soon forgotten. Mandy and I were given excuses such as "We are sorry but we had to use the water for this or that", "We had some unexpected visitors who needed the water", etc. – and when the couple's saint-like prodigy daughter, recently separated from her live-in boyfriend came to stay, we stood no chance of using the facilities.

The couple's daughter was a semi-professional dancer and the idol of her parents. She was – so talented – so accomplished – so beautiful – so professional, yet un-recognised – so misunderstood and unlucky. She had done this and that, had met this person and that person – or so they said! I suppose I was irritated because my own experience was the opposite of our hosts' daughter. My parents had never championed me for anything and I suppose once again I was very jealous.

Being someone who expects people to keep their side of a bargain or contract I became extremely annoyed at the vanishing promises. Whatever excuses we were given by our hosts I was not going to put up with being a second-class citizen and I began to look for alternative accommodation. Jeanette Parry, a friend of mine from Bournemouth College's Christian Union that met once a week at the Lansdowne Roundabout building was also looking for more appropriate digs in the town, and so we joined forces in our effort. Jeanette was a Welsh girl from Ebbw Vale and studying science at the main college. Eventually we heard of a room vacancy in a local hostel run by a charitable non-conformist Christian organisation whose mission was to help young working-ladies in Bournemouth – an attempt I suspect to shield them from abuse and exploitation. The hostel was housed in a large building not far from The Triangle, Bournemouth, near to a wide road junction (possibly in Bourne Avenue). Mandy was not happy with my moving out of the Old Christchurch Road flat. I think she felt I should have weathered the problems and remained there. Even worse for her (if I remember the situation correctly) following my departure the prodigy daughter went in to share the bedroom with her. I think before this the daughter had either been sleeping in the living room, or perhaps in her parents' bedroom. Most serious art students of the 1960s would have found it difficult to relate to a frivolous party-girl with little interest in intellectual pursuits, but Mandy seemed to be a person who would grin and bear any situation. She rarely complained, and kept her disappointments to herself. She never forgave me for leaving and from that time on whenever our paths crossed our dialogue was extremely cool and detached.

Initially Jeanette and I managed to cope with the old-fashioned culture and staff at the hostel. We knew where we stood and only had to conform to the expectations when on the premises. Jeanette and I shared a room and made it as comfortable as we were able. We collaborated, shared ideas and made the most of our new environment. It was during our stay at the hostel that Jeanette had a spiritual experience that compelled her to become a fully committed Christian. Suddenly in the middle of the night she woke me up to share what was happening to her. (This was a dodgy thing to do. I am even grumpier than usual when tired!) She wanted me to witness her asking Christ into her life. This she did and we prayed together. It was 1 May 1967, a date firmly etched in Jeanette's mind, one she has not forgotten. From that moment on Jeanette's life has been geared to following Christ as faithfully as she is able and she has been involved in some really challenging acts of Christian service. Soon after her Christian commitment Jeanette broke-up with her boyfriend Turab, a young Arab student who was studying in Bournemouth. He was a pleasant and handsome young man and the break-up must have caused Jeanette some pain. Personally I was not convinced this action was necessary at that point in her newfound faith, but Jeanette felt it was and it was not my place to comment.

Sometime after Jeanette and I arrived at the hostel the board of governors decided to have a massive reorganisation and set about restructuring management and services. A married couple in their forties were drafted in to run the place for the trustees. Their job-description was to oversee the welfare of residents and carry out all necessary administration; this included oversight of staff and rotas for catering, cleaning and maintenance. The hostel's accounts were firmly in the couple's grasp and it did not take long for me to have a real dislike of the pair, particularly the man. To me he was another control freak, with his wife hanging on to his every word while he himself listened to nobody. Rightly or wrongly I felt his motive for taking the job was to make as much money for himself as possible and that he was not the slightest bit interested in the charitable ethos of the institution he was managing. He began to rearrange work-schedules so that he and his wife did most of the catering, cleaning and maintenance. Many of the original cooks, servers and cleaners were dismissed. Another innovation that worked in his financial favour was to compromise the ingredients in our meals. The hostel provided half board, and residents were given breakfast and an evening meal. For the breakfast we sometimes had cheese on toast. The new practice was to greatly reduce the quota of cheese, thinning it out with a tasteless, cheap, white sauce – just one of the many compromises that helped to reduce the manager's financial outlay.

Once again, I became a rebel and began to speak out which greatly irritated the husband who became extremely oppressive where I was concerned, both in his body language and general attitude. On one occasion he actually followed me into my room, arguing his point with great force. Jeanette was not there at the time and I took offence at having my privacy invaded. This and other incidents that followed the times when I had become assertive led me to be summonsed before the board of governors. At this meeting I took up my case against the manager as best I could, but exaggerated his actions, especially the day he entered my room. Unforgivably and much to my disgrace and regret, I hinted that his intentions were not appropriate when he forced his way into my room. I did not say it in so many words but aroused suspicion and left it to the imagination of the panel as to what really happened. It was an attempt to make the panel of four or five old men and women take me seriously and understand the deep grievance I felt at the manager's imposition. I do not know whether they were sympathetic with me or not. There was no witness as to what happened and they just looked at me with suspicion, but said and did nothing. They could not prove whether the manager's behaviour was appropriate or not, and they could not ascertain whether or not I was an awkward resident. Hopefully they were left with an uneasy feeling that the new manager might not be all they had hoped for. I served the rest of my time at the hostel knowing that at least the manager had not got the better of me, but my dishonest presentation to the panel has remained my regret to this day.

The ATD course at Bournemouth and Poole College of Art was well planned. It covered a wide range of subjects including history of education, philosophy of education, educational psychology, child development, art education, experimental crafts, environmental studies and of course the obligatory teaching practice (TP). There must have been about thirty to forty of us taking the ATD course in Bournemouth our particular year. Once again, similar to Camberwell and Walthamstow, students on this course came from a wide spectrum of society having different backgrounds, ages, family situations, past training, ideologies and attitudes – and similar to my experience at Camberwell we quickly gelled together into a self-supporting collaborative group, this time under the oversight of the annex's principal, Frank Dodman.

I eventually found out that Frank Dodman had made a name for himself in naval design and book illustration. Many years later when I became a collector of Observer Books, (the ones published by Warne,) I discovered that he had compiled the Observer Book of Ships. Mr Dodman, or Frank as we called him, looked more like a bank manager than an art school mentor. He had a fatherly attitude and was a good over-seer of student welfare. He quickly sorted out any problems that occurred within the programme or within individual student situations.

Front cover of Frank Dodman's "Observer's Book of Ships".

Opening pages of this Warne publication

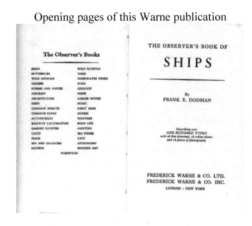

Another lecturer on our course was John Liddell. He was a practical hands-on mentor and loved to use natural ingredients in his creative work, for instance he preferred to use wood blocks for printing rather than artificial plates and advocated the use of natural lichens for dyes in textile crafts.

Some ATD students in our year-group felt a little defensive, knowing that the Art Teachers' Diploma course at Bournemouth would terminate in the town following our graduation. The whole structure of art education in England was under review and development. As outlined the two old art diplomas had given way to two newly constructed ones, and I was concerned that the new arrangement was not for the better. The former two-year art course for an Intermediate qualification that we had known allowed sufficient time to explore many aspects of creativity, and time to get our bearings before making a choice about our future specialisation. The new one-year Foundation course seemed inadequate for this. The old two-year NDD course we knew offered a good kick-start into our subsequent chosen field. We knew our learning curve would continue as we went on to post-graduate courses, apprenticeships, established positions in the art world and so on. I wondered whether the new three years Dip AD might be too conditioning for students, making them too inflexible for future creative development and the art challenges ahead – but then I am an opinionated person!

The ATD courses in England were also being reassessed and reorganised. I came to realise it would be impractical for the authorities to continue with a postgraduate ATD course in such a prestigious holiday town as Bournemouth. The site of our annex close to the town's pier in particular offered prime investment for owners and developers. It was a financial opportunity the council and education authorities could not miss. Knowing of the imminent closure of our Bath Road building our student group made the most of its study-year by the sea. When time allowed, and we could take a break from our lectures and work, we would stroll down to the beach, combing the sand for items of interest that we then used in our creative work, or we would just sit on the pebbles, chat and sunbathe. I had developed an interest in mosaics and loved searching the beach for tiny pieces of coloured glass rounded off by the waves, remnants of old bottles and the like. I then used the beautiful muted colours of this glass in my mosaic designs. Natural creative hobbies in eco-friendly surroundings however were of little interest to the authorities. Their prime objective was to raise capital and fill the town's coffers with proceeds emanating from the holiday trade.

One of the practical crafts we were introduced to on our ATD course was creative weaving. We used wools and other natural yarns that had been dyed with lichens and other organic ingredients. I think the tutor for this module was John Liddell's wife who shared his enthusiasm for natural materials. We were exposed to a variety of arts and crafts during the year. This was intended to increase the options we then had to offer the pupils and students in the institutions where we would eventually teach. If our art syllabus was too limited, and depended only on the skills we had learnt in our specialist NDD course, we would only be able to capture the imagination of the few pupils who had the same interest and skills as ourselves. Of all the practical sessions we undertook, weaving, textiles and dyes was the least I enjoyed. I enjoyed ceramics far better, and for this, we went to the main art school building at the top of the hill that had the equipment we required. On our ceramic days some of us would be tempted over the road in our break, to relax in the huge Fortes Café-Restaurant opposite. It covered at least two floors of a huge building and was geared very much to the holiday-trade. The counters displayed and offered large tantalising ice-cream sundaes, cream cakes, gateaux and the like. Occasionally I found myself with sufficient funds to indulge in a monster-sized fresh cream slice, or a huge knicker-bocker-glory. I was beginning to relish being extravagant and self-indulgent.

FOOTNOTE – I believe the Fortes building has since, at least in part, been taken over by KFC (Kentucky Fried Chicken).

Another luxury I seemed able to afford during my stay in Bournemouth was a regular visit to the TAO Clinic. Ever since being told of my shadow-moustache by a former boyfriend, my upper lip had worried me. Electrolysis at TAO and other beauty clinics in the 1960s was very expensive, but with time, greater popularity and competition it became cheaper to access. I knew the treatment was reputed to remove unwanted hair permanently and felt this was something I had to have done. Initially I went to the clinic once a week, then once a month. Looking back I am not sure how I managed to afford this. Maybe my grant had increased, or maybe my weekly pension from the Canadian government had increased, I cannot now recall, but I do remember my visits to the clinic well. I was treated by a properly trained and registered woman in a professional setting, and received some privileged pampering. Philosophically I believed in temperance and moderation where spending is concerned, but my practice did not always match my principles. I probably excused my growing extravagances with the fact that at least I was not as obsessively self-indulgent as Barbara Madeloff, my Bournemouth TP mentor was. Miss Madeloff owned dozens and dozens of pairs of shoes in every colour and shape you could imagine. This was her self-imposed and self-confessed addiction, and she revelled in it. I met Barbara Madeloff at Kinson Secondary School for Girls where I was sent in the second term of my ATD course to do my teaching practice. As a prospective art teacher I had already spent one week in a primary school studying creativity in the younger child, but most of us on the ATD course would end up teaching in secondary schools or in further education, and so it was necessary to spend a full term – or at least four days a week of it – in the role of teaching-assistant to a fully qualified art teacher in a secondary school or college. Some of the older or more mobile students on our course were sent to institutions in the smaller out-lying towns of Hampshire and Dorset, but those of us without transport, and little knowledge of the area, were kept as close to Bournemouth as possible. Kinson was the place where I was sent. It was a suburb of Bournemouth and I travelled there by bus. On my journey I passed a lovely residential area called Talbot Village. This so-called "village", as it once was, had become engulfed in Bournemouth Town in more recent history. It consisted of pretty little brick cottages around which were neat flower-filled gardens. The village was built in Victorian times by the Talbot family to give local working-class people a better standard of living. The village and its concept left a deep impression on me.

HISTORY OF TALBOT VILLAGE from details found on the internet.

Talbot Village was built between 1850 and 1862, owing to the generosity of two sisters, Georgina and Mary Talbot. With their family, Georgina and Mary were used to dividing the year between living in Surrey and in Hinton Wood House on the East Cliff of Bournemouth. It was while they were staying in Bournemouth that the sisters noticed the many poor who were suffering in the region. They decided to employ some of the poor to clear land and build cottages on it. These workers were then allowed to live in the cottages and slowly a community came together. The original cottages were built on an acre plot and each had a well, animal pens and fruit trees, and residents were charged a rent of between 4 and 5 shillings per week. Georgina Talbot next had 7 alms houses built in the village for the elderly and widowed.

Other than the pretty village of Talbot I found Kinson itself a rather plain dreary region. Most of the pupils at the school where I had been sent lived on local council house estates that in my opinion lacked imagination in planning and development. On the whole pupils at Kinson Secondary Modern School for Girls were well behaved, and the school provided a good all-round education. The headmistress had even taken the trouble to work with the domestic science department to give some work-experience to the senior pupils. On a rota basis these girls would put on white pinafores and headbands and serve refreshments to staff in the morning and afternoon breaks. They were responsible for preparing and distributing tea, coffee and biscuits to teachers and other support staff in the staff room. Proper china crockery was used together with tray-clothes, and catering utensils. To the present-day politically correct educationalists this might seem like child exploitation, but my experience was quite the opposite. The girls enjoyed learning these catering skills and having the opportunity to mix with staff in a non-classroom environment. They felt important and useful and I suspect their following lessons went well with their self-esteem having been raised, and with the staff they served feeling re-charged. This was the one and only time I encountered such a common-sense practice in a secondary school. In all the schools I have visited and taught in since I have found teachers scrambling in unhygienic kitchens trying to make drinks with whatever chipped mugs and lime-silted urns can be found in the few odd minutes they have managed to grab between lessons and their multitude of other extra-curricular duties. Schoolchildren now seem to think they are the only ones who should be waited on and pandered to. Young people are beginning to believe the world owes them a living, and they have a right to complete happiness without effort or responsibility on their part. Thankfully Kinson pupils had a better perspective on life.

ANYWAY............returning to Barbara Madeloff.

Miss Madeloff was the head of the art department at Kinson School, the only full-time art teacher there. At the beginning of my TP I would sit in some of Miss Madeloff's classes to observe. After a while, I began to assist her with a few teaching tasks, and eventually I took over some of her lessons while she discreetly sat at the back of the room taking notes. Finally she left me on my own to teach classes without her or any other professional being present.

Barbara Madeloff had a very strict routine and teaching method. At the beginning of each lesson she expected the girls to stand military style behind their desks, greet her and any other member of staff present in a certain manner, answer to their name on the register and then sit down when told to. Following this she instructed class monitors as to the materials and pieces of equipment that would be required for the lesson. The monitors then collected these and distributed them around to each pupil in turn; all pupils received exactly the same. Miss Madeloff next explained the lesson assignment to the class, and if all was in order the girls could begin. Some minutes later she would walk around the room supervising and offering advice where and when needed, but the girls could only speak to her after raising their hands, drawing her attention and being acknowledged. They were not allowed to speak or leave their seat without permission. Ten minutes before the end of each lesson the girls were told to clean their desktops, brushes, palettes and whatever else they had been using at the sinks around the room. With this done they had to return to their desk, stand and wait for Miss Madeloff to carry out a thorough inspection. She went to each desk in turn, held the pallets up to the light to check for stains and squeezed the bristles of the paintbrushes between her fingers to see if the water that came out was clean, and so on. "Woe betide" any girl who had been negligent! This training method was rare and considered too highly prescribed even for those days, but I think she had a point. Like her I believe responsibility should work alongside privilege, and that individuals can only become truly independent if they are able to clean up their own mess. Perhaps Miss Madeloff did go a bit too far in her expectations – in my eyes she was a little eccentric anyway, especially where her passion for shoes was concerned.

Barbara Madeloff would regularly boast about her large collection of shoes and I often heard her telling colleagues about the meticulous shoe-cleaning regime she had. She took great pride in these shoes. Owing to her surname and slight accent I wondered whether Barbara Madeloff might be of East European origin, and whether she and her family may have escaped from somewhere like Russia or Poland before or during the war. For all I knew Barbara Madeloff may have seen some horrific things which would explain some of her obsessive behaviours. She seemed to keep herself slightly aloof from the rest of the school staff, although she was not reclusive.

FOOTNOTE – I now believe Barbara Madeloff was born in England 1935.

I was treated by Barbara Madeloff the same way as she treated her pupils – with extreme formality. On one occasion towards the end of my TP when I was alone with an art class, I implied to the pupils in my naïveté that my art methods compared favourably to those they had already been taught. Consequently my credibility all but disappeared in Barbara Madeloff's eyes, especially as the implication of what I had said became greatly exaggerated by the time it reached her ears. Thankfully, either because underneath her stern exterior she was an understanding and kind person or because she subscribed to general convenience over revenge, she gave me a reasonable TP report and I passed that part of my ATD course as I was soon to do with my other modules.

Because the ATD course was condensed into one year the programme was very demanding and we students had little time to socialise. Nevertheless I made a few new friends on the course, one being Lesley Johns. Lesley lived with her parents in a bungalow in Charminster Road, to the north of Bournemouth. Her home became a chill-out zone for me and one or two others who would call around now and again to enjoy the benefits of a proper home as opposed to a hostel or lodging environment. Pat Townsend was another ATD friend who frequented the Johns' home.

The Johns were a very hospitable and generous family, but it was noticeable that Lesley lacked confidence, with an indication that she relied on medication to relieve her mental anxiety. A story began to emerge, if I understood it properly, that Lesley had suffered some sort of a mental or emotional breakdown. Putting odd bits of information together I gathered that from a very early age, as an only child, Lesley had been put into the care of relatives because her father, and possibly her mother too, were members of the armed forces and had been posted abroad. I speculated that this separation was the cause of her breakdown. Mrs Johns was very protective of her daughter and seemed to carry a lot of guilt about the whole situation. Outwardly Lesley was positive and cheerful, but she took her artwork extremely seriously. When she talked about it or similar topics, she gave the impression she was a fount of all knowledge. I saw this as a symptom of her low self-esteem because in reality Lesley was not an arrogant person, but to some she sounded conceited with an inflated ego. I knew this was not the case.

| Lesley Johns, Pat Townsend and Mrs Johns at the back of the Johns' bungalow in Charminster Road Bournemouth | Pat Townsend and her much-prized old car. | A photo Pat sent me of her wedding day, following her graduation. |

Pat Townsend's home was in Kettering, Northamptonshire. She was very energetic and full of life, and like Lesley always cheerful and positive. I'm not sure if Pat owned a car while studying in Bournemouth, but if not, she certainly had one soon after. As implied several times few students and newly qualified individuals possessed a car in the 1960s. Most young people had to save up several years to achieve this end.

Another friend I met on my course was Cindy. Cindy was married and lived with her husband in a small Dorset village, possibly Puddletown, within commutable distance of Bournemouth. Several students on the ATD course were married. In the 1960s it was more common for couples who wanted to be together to make their relationship official rather than drift into a casual partnership arrangement. Cindy was very modern in dress and outlook, and seemed to have no hang-ups or inhibitions – until we discovered her proper name was Cynthia. Uncharacteristically she then became very defensive and annoyed. I imagine she supposed we would make fun of the name considering it to be old-fashioned, while we had no intention of doing so. I never actually met her husband. I believe he had links with the world of commercial art and may have been in the advertising business. I was invited to the couple's home once or twice but they lived too far away from the college to make an evening visit practical, and my weekends were usually spoken for. Cindy always came to the annex well-groomed in expensive fashionable clothes which complemented her long, straight, black hair and large jewellery. The age of Flower Power was fast approaching and large beads and flowing hair were becoming the in-thing. Apart from her one show of annoyance, Cindy was a nice person to know, very helpful and caring.

I enjoyed mixing with different types of artist on the ATD course. In addition to qualified fine artists – painters and sculptors – there were potters, dress designers, photographers, illustrators, textilists and so on. I got to know some of my fellow students quite well but once again, similar to Camberwell and Walthamstow, my closest friends tended to come from the college's Christian Union that met once a week at Lansdowne Roundabout college building. Its members like those at Walthamstow came from a variety of subject disciplines including mathematics, science, engineering, music and catering. This is how I came to meet Jeanette Parry. Another of my acquaintances at the CU was a young man who in addition to his college studies was a member of the Bournemouth Symphony Orchestra. I remember him because he was persistent in wanting to take me out on a date but I could not get enthusiastic about the idea. I did not see him as boyfriend material and so did not want to get involved. He was nice enough and very talented, but in my opinion boring. I had my art-student image to maintain, and preferred to associate with less conventional, predictable characters.

Tony Malpas was the leader of the CU and I thought he was a fantastically handsome young man with a wonderful character, not at all the stereotype of a Christian youth leader that one might expect, that is to say a shy, reserved and a shrinking violet sort of person. Tony lived with his parents and brothers in the smart Queens Park area of the town. The family were known to be millionaires in the days when being a millionaire actually meant something. I discovered they worshipped at an Open Brethren assembly and it soon became apparent the home and possessions of the Malpas family were constantly being used to help others, especially those less fortunate than themselves. I think every member of the family owned his or her own car – at a time when even belonging to a one-car family was not standard, as my parents would have confirmed. Vehicles belonging to the Malpas family were frequently seen around and outside the town giving lifts to people who had no transport of their own. The family also had a boat in Poole Harbour that they used on occasions to give trips and outings to boys from the local borstal (or maybe it was an approved school or home). It didn't matter who you were or what you were the family treated everyone with the same respect. If I remember correctly Tony was the youngest of the brothers. I visited his home a couple of times on Christian Union business and to attend a young people's party there one evening – alcohol-free but nevertheless full of fun and laughter. I can still picture myself travelling up the lengthy driveway to the Malpas house on the day of the party, passing the family's vehicles and being met at the door with smiles and a warm welcome by my hosts.

The CU had a social aspect, a worship aspect and a missionary aspect. For the missionary aspect, CU members would sometimes travel to local villages to help small country churches with their community outreach projects. One of these villages was

Wool in Dorset. Tony took me and a couple of other CU members there by car one day to plan and make arrangements for a forthcoming Christian event.

Apart from to my membership of the CU I knew I needed to settle into a local church to support my faith, and so after my arrival in Bournemouth I visited a few places of worship, including a couple of Anglican churches to see which might suit me. I also wondered into an unusual Christadelphian church called Queen's Hall one day. It was situated at the junction of Bath Road and Old Christchurch Road. I believe it is still there today, but with a development of flats beside it.

1966 photograph of the Bournemouth Christadelphian Church.

I learnt later that the teaching of this particular denomination is not exactly mainstream orthodox Christian. Before I had this piece of information, I had found the atmosphere and congregation of the church quite conducive, it was laid-back and friendly, but for some reason I did not settle there. Had I decided to stay and continue worshiping at the hall I might easily have been drawn into their constitution and off-beam Christian doctrine. It is easy in one's teens and twenties to go along with the flow, gradually losing sight of one's fundamental faith and absorbing the practices and ideas of friendship-groups without questioning the central ideology.

Jeanette Parry and I not only attended CU together, and shared the same digs, but eventually chose to worship at the same Bournemouth church. Independent of me, Jeanette too had been looking around and trying to find a suitable place to worship, and somehow we both came to the conclusion that Lansdowne Baptist Church was the place for us. It was where we felt at home, could worship, relate to others in the congregation and maybe contribute in some way.

Lansdowne Baptist Church, Bournemouth. 1966-1967

Having attended a Baptist Sunday school as a young girl in Brixton Hill, having been to two Baptist summer schools with Mary Price while at Clapham County Grammar School, and knowing several people with Baptist backgrounds from OM and elsewhere, the style of service at Lansdowne Baptist Church was not strange to me. Jeanette too was familiar with it having known similar in the Presbyterian and other churches she grew up with back home in Ebbw Vale. Francis Dixon was the minister of Lansdowne Baptist

Church at the time. He was an eloquent speaker and had become internationally famous through the popular Bible School Correspondence Course he ran from his church.

As said, Jeanette and I felt very much at home in Lansdowne Baptist Church. it even had a lively youth group, although we were not able to take advantage of it to any great degree due to our studies and other commitments. We did however make friends with two of the youth club's older members, a married couple called David and Eileen Reckin. Outwardly, David and Eileen appeared very old-fashioned, and possibly gave the impression of being low in intellect, but we soon discovered the couple were quietly and unostentatiously intelligent, modern in attitude, open-minded and more importantly genuine. "What you saw is what you got" with Eileen and David. They had no preconceived ideas or bigoted ways and said what they thought.

David and Eileen Reckin

1967 cover of Lansdowne Baptist Church magazine.

Photograph of Lansdowne Baptist Church Woodbury Avenue, Bournemouth. © Chris Downer – Wikimedia Commons RIGHT Magazine page that recorded Jeanette and my baptism at the church.

David and Eileen lived in a rented flat over business premises at The Triangle, Bournemouth. This was not far from the hostel where Jeanette and I were lodging and close to the centre of town. The area with its surrounding roads and buildings was given this name through the open triangular space at its centre. In the 1960s a small bus terminus operated from this central space. Jeanette, Pat, Lesley, myself and a few others sometimes visited the Reckins when passing, or when we found ourselves with a few spare moments to relax. We were always greeted with a smile and a welcome mug of tea. The Reckins never tried to preach to people like Pat and Lesley who were not regular churchgoers; they were just caring individuals, interested in the lives of others.

It was during our time at Lansdowne Baptist Church that Jeanette and I decided to apply for adult baptism. I had already been christened or baptised as a baby and accepted this as a significant act of family faith, then when a young teenager and wanting to accept the faith personally, I underwent the act of confirmation in the Church of England; now however I felt I had reached the stage where I understand the meaning of Christian discipleship a little better. I wanted to make a public statement that I intended to try and follow in Christ's footsteps as best as I possibly could, and put my own ambitions and desires aside. Adult baptism with total-immersion seemed a good symbolic gesture for this. Jeanette obviously had her own very good reason for being baptised. She wanted a public sign to show she had recently committed her life to Christ, and had experienced his power come into her life. We were baptised together at Lansdowne Baptist Church on 18 June 1967, with some of our Bournemouth friends around us at the church service. Decades later while researching my Dorset ancestry I discovered several of my ancestors had become Baptist worshippers around the year 1790 following their move from Corfe Castle to Langton Matravers. They joined a church that had originally been founded by the Rev Whyatt, a pastor in Oliver Cromwell's army who had established this fellowship when he was stationed in nearby Dorchester.

When I had time to explore during my ATD year, I loved to visit the surrounding countryside. I enjoyed walking in the Purbeck Hills and through the quaint villages of Dorset and Hampshire. I still have a watercolour painting of cottages in Corfe Castle that I painted on one of these trips. It is far from being one of my best efforts, but now that I know of my family link with that town it is greatly treasured.

I remember in particular one cold winter's day walking with some friends in the Purbeck Hills when we came across a lovely old country pub. Inside was a large open log fire burning away in the grate. A few local old farmers were sitting around it dressed as you imagine traditional country farmers should be – old hats, mufflers, well-worn boots, smocks and so on. While sipping their drinks and talking to each other in their strong Dorset accent, one of the group members took a red-hot poker out of the fire and thrust it in his glass of beer making it sizzle. A young man in our group explained that he was mulling his beer. For all I now know this old farmer may have been a distant cousin of mine. In addition to the Purbeck Hills I loved exploring the area around Poole Harbour and Sandbanks. It was also a treat for me to go with friends to little market towns such as Wimbourne, Blandford Forum and to the city of Winchester, and I loved browsing in antique and jewellery shops. There was a special shop in Christchurch, not far from Christchurch Priory, that I especially loved. It had rows and rows of Victorian earrings strung up on cords around its windows. There were earrings made of jet, ivory, pearl, Venetian glass, foiled beads, amber and so on. In following years, when more affluent, I would occasionally return to Christchurch and buy a pair of these earrings from the shop. My Bournemouth year was full and exciting. I used every spare moment I had to explore, but at the same time I worked very hard, knowing of the near miss I had in passing my previous National Diploma of Design.

One of the last assignments I had to complete in the last term of my postgraduate ATD year was to produce an environmental studies project. On one of my early trips out exploring the environs of Bournemouth with Lesley and Pat I had come across the village of Throop with its mill. It was situated to the north east of the town by the River Stour not far from Lesley's home in Charminster Road. In the 1960s it was very rural and laid-back, and it occurred to me that the mill would be an excellent place to study and research for my project. Fortunately it was still a working mill in 1967 and so, in addition to being visually charming and picturesque it also had lots of commercial and human interest. It took me no time at all to get to know Cecil Biles the miller. He was a friendly middle-aged man who was only too pleased to help me with my project. An equally friendly but younger man (whose name I have since forgotten) made regular visits to the mill to bring grain and pick up the processed flour to transport back to Birmingham. I spent many happy days during my last term at Bournemouth and Poole College of Art sketching, painting and writing at Throop Mill. In the breaks I had from art and craft activity I would go and sit on sacks of grain on the ground floor of the building, sipping tea from the miller's old but clean mugs, talking and joking with him and the delivery man. With these two I did not feel like an intruder, I was more like one of their team. I can still remember the laughter we shared looking at the humorous side of life and recalling comical scenes that we had individually witnessed. I believe a little undeclared poaching may have gone on at the mill. I seem to remember traps to catch fish in the river near the weir. I also remember the kingfisher birds and other country creatures I saw as I sat around the mill by the river sketching and drawing the scenes and items of interest. It was a magic place and experience – so removed from the childhood I had known back in London, and the recent pressures I had experienced trying to pass the various stages of my education to become a fully qualified artist and teacher.

The time was fast approaching for the conclusion of my ATD course. I had successfully undergone all assessments and with other students was now in the final stages. The very last task that we as students had was to exhibit our year's practical work for the local Bournemouth community to view. Frank Dodman helped us sift through folders and put our chosen pieces up for display in the annex. After five relatively happy years attending three different art schools, I now reluctantly had to consider future employment. Despite enjoying the ATD course, teaching as a profession continued not to appeal to me, but slowly I began to make enquires to this end. It was rather late in the year for me to forward applications for teaching posts in individual schools; most of the institutions were nearing the end of their selection process and had already appointed the staff they needed to fill their teaching vacancies. I had little knowledge of the individual institutions, while the more enthusiastic ATD students on our course had been researching and sifting through the Times Educational Supplement for weeks. They had sorted out and applied for teaching posts they felt were appropriate to them personally. I decided to apply directly to some of the boroughs, including my old haunt Waltham Forest, where I was called up to the town hall for a general interview and subsequently offered a post as assistant art teacher in Connaught Secondary Modern School for Girls, Leytonstone – later to become Connaught Junior High School for Girls, and later still Connaught School for Girls. It was an unplanned development, but one that proved to be for the best, leading me into a worthwhile and productive future. Trusting as a Christian and praying about my situation had brought about a good outcome. I spent the next thirty-three years teaching in secondary schools, never regretting a moment, despite some very challenging and anxious moments.

My adult life was about to begin. A London War Trophy had survived, and was about to become a self-supporting individual.

Appendices 5. Throop Mill.

UPDATED VERSION OF THE BOOKLET I produced for my Throop Mill Project.

A wonderful experience, a wonderful time and place — unforgettable visual memories!

THROOP MILL, 1966

This booklet is an attempt to relive some happy moments spent at Throop Flour Mills on the outskirts of Bournemouth, in Dorset (or Hampshire as it then was), in the academic year 1966/67. At the time I was a graduate art student undertaking a one-year art teachers' diploma course at the Bournemouth and Poole College of Art, which was affiliated at that time to Southampton University. The curriculum included a module called "Environmental Studies"; one I came to greatly appreciate. In my case it meant taking regular trips to the local flour mill for research, sketching, and passing part of the day in gossip and light-hearted banter with the miller and the delivery driver while sipping heavenly mugs of tea, perched on sacks of grain. Trout swam in the millstream, kingfishers skirted the banks, and clumps of teasels, other weeds and wild flowers hemmed the river. I was too old to be "put upon" by pompous adults, too young to be entangled in complicated relationships and too idealistically philosophical to realise the potential problems of life in general

I am not sure what grading I was given for my final environmental study project, and not sure whether the tutors knew either. The authorities were terminating our particular course that year, and the whole structure of art qualifications, including location of premises and programmes of study, was under "review and reorganisation"; words I continued to hear throughout my following thirty-three years in education. I am however sure of the personal effect this module left on me. Time spent at the mill provided me with an admiration for real people and respect for nature, traditional arts crafts, meaningful occupations and the non-technological life-style.

I consider myself very fortunate to have been able to join in the activity of a manually worked mill before modernisation overtook it. I hope these sketches and drawings executed at the mill, (some of which I must admit have since been technically enhanced,) will capture some of the magic I experienced then, and pass on some of the pleasure I received pursuing this part of my ATD course.

ORIGINS OF THROOP

The village of Throop is found northeast of the seaside town of Bournemouth, and just over one mile to the east of another village, Holdenhurst, the "Mother of Bournemouth".

Holdenhurst's watermill was the cause of a hamlet springing up in its environs which later came to be known as Throop. Former spellings of the hamlet-turned-village are numerous; La Throp and La Throope were used in the fourteenth century, Throupe in the late fourteenth and fifteenth centuries and Throppe in the sixteenth century

"HOLEEST"

Holdenhurst is a village of Hantesure. (Hampshire)

The king holds Holdenhurst which was held by Earl Tosti. It was then assessed at 29 hides ½ yardland, but when granted to Hugh de Port it consisted of 22 hides ½ yardland but was not assessed. There are seven more hides in the island. There are 20 ploughlands, 4½ in desmesne and 37 villeins and 25 borderers with 19 ploughs, also a chapel, 14 servants, a mill worth 15s and 3 fisheries for the use of the hall, 181 acres of meadow and woods for the pannage of 6 hogs. There are 7 hides in the forest where dwell 13 villeins and 3 borderers with 8 ploughlands; with these hides, now detached from the manor there are woods for the pannage of 29 hogs. Its value in the time of King Edward £44, afterwards £34 and now £24 by tale, but it pays £25 reckoning 20d in the ora. The part in the forest is valued at £12.10s. The parish of Holdenhurst which is a chapelry of Christchurch comprises an area of 7280 acres.

Present day villagers of Throop and Holdenhurst are proud that their mill was recorded by the Normans in the Domesday Book, of 1086, under the heading "HOLEEST".

This is the source of the above record after it had been edited and given explanatory notes by Mr Henry Moody of Winchester Museum in the year1862....................

CORN

Corn has been ground at this spot for over a thousand years. Saxons are credited as the original founders of the mill. They chose a good position on the River Stour where it makes a southern loop before turning down to the sea.

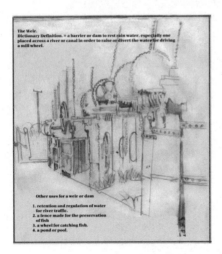

THE WEIR and HATCHES
Seen from the mill.

Blurred sketch of a maker's tab
on machinery

When the mill-race was altered in 1944 ancient stone foundations were uncovered, together with several old coins from the millstream. The coins included ones from the reigns of George III and George IV. Old Spanish and Portuguese coins were also found there.

Water flows under the bridge from the turbine engines downstream.

From "LEE BURN MILL" by
WILLIAM BARNES

An while below the mossy wheel
All day the foamen stream did roar,
And up in mill the floaten meal
Did pitch upon the sheaken vloor
We then could vind but vewhan's still
On veet a resten off the ground,
An seldom hear the merry sound
O' games a play'd at Leeburn Mill.

From "THE MILLER'S
DAUGHTER" by TENNYSON

...... or from the bridge I learned to
hear The mill dam rushing down with
noise,
And see the minnows everywhere In
crystal eddies glance and poise.

WATER WHEELS

Two types of water mills are found in England. One functions with a vertical water wheel, another by the horizontal water wheel or turbine. It is possible that the horizontal wheel, which is the wheel that is used at Throop Mill, is the earliest type. No pre-Norman water mills remain, but the Roman architect, Vitravius, who wrote "De Architectura" circa 16 B.C., gives a detailed explanation of these undershot water wheels.

Whetting a grindstone is synonymous with sharpening it. Both upper and lower millstones are grooved or corrugated on the grinding surfaces; if this were not so the corn would become mashed instead of pulverised. The wear on the stones is such that the grooves require sharpening and deepening about every ten days. A flourmill in Birmingham employs three men exclusively to sharpen the mill stones of its syndicate.

The present turbines were brought to Throop Mill in 1944, and were a development before 45 horsepower. **THESE PARTICULAR MACHINES ARE THE LARGEST IN THE COUNTRY**

THE FOLLOWING SKETCH ATTEMPTS TO SHOW A SWING WHEEL IN MOTION
This wheel used to be an operative swing wheel. There was a belt, which would swing from the main turbine wheel to this wheel, but with electricity it became redundant and is now a "reserve".

Cogs and Wheels

"MILLER'S SPIRITUAL" by JOHN BARCLAY

1

Like the wheel of the watermill,
Yielding to the water's swill
Round and round and round it
wheels As the gushing water it
feels;

2.

So obedient to my soul To the
Holy Ghost's control,
Ever moving by His will' Never,
never standing still,

3.

Let thy grinding millstones bring To
subjection everything:
Grind away my rough and harsh;

Grind my flesh, though bones
should crash.

4.

Grind me o'er, and o'er, and
o'er' Till I fall thy finest flour
Lay me down a mellowy heap,

Make me through Thy bolters
sweep

5.

Sift me, sift, sift me well' Sift me to
approven meal; Give me dust into
the wind, Leaving all the pure
behind.

6.

Stow me up in Thy own vessel,
That no thief Thy store embezzle
Make me, Thou, and make with
speed, Pleasant, pure, unleavened
bread.

7.

A sweet consecrated cake Make me
thou for Jesus sake; That I be not
like Ephraim. bid Thou great I AM!

8.

Ephraim was but singly twin'd;
Ephraim therefore cloudly
mourn'd; Lest I burn me in the
oven,
Draw me soon, O God, to
Heaven.

DUST CONES

It has been estimated that 2% of dust is ejected from the raw wheat. This is expelled outside the mill through the following funnels.

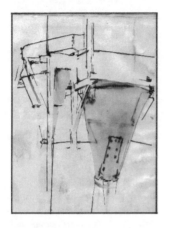 

THE SHAKERS

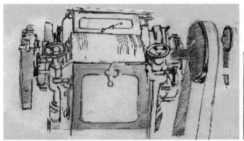

THE SHAKER BELOW grinds the wheat. Shakers in the other half of the mill help to purify the wheat.

1 = **THE SHAKER BELOW** *is on the first floor of the mill, the first of three that purify the wheat, a process of cutting the grain*
2 =The chute that takes the cut grain to the second machine.
3. =The door on which I found the following ornamental handle

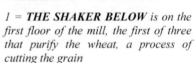
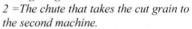

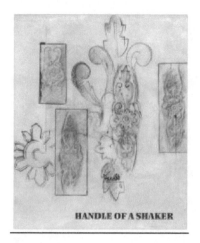

HANDLE OF A SHAKER

LEFT
Ornamental handles and brassware found on the shakers.

DEFINITION of a SHAKER

"An implement or machine used for shaking the flour to a finer more purified state. Gauze and silk mesh is the main material used in this process."

CHIMNEYS

DEFINITION of a CHIMNEY...
A vertical flue to channel air.

DEFINITION OF A CHIMNEY CAP...
A revolving hood turned by the wind to facilitate air currents

RIGHT: *This chimney draws air into Throop Mill to keep the inside machines cool. It operates with an internal fan.*

Wheat is brought to the mill on the ground floor. It is processed and eventually left on the first floor for collection by the delivery lorries. Wheat is taken to the mill in 2 ¼ cwt bags, but leaves as flour weighing only ¼ cwt.

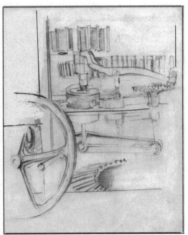

Two samples taken from the process of milling that provide textural inspitation for arts and crafts,

DECORATION

The following designs were found in the mill on various machines.

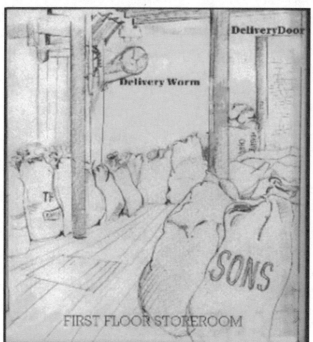

The STOREROOM on the First Floor of THROOP MILL…
This is where my "apparition" will forever remain, sitting on the sacks and sipping mugs of tea with Cecil Biles and the delivery man.

Poor quality photo taken in 1976 of my husband with Cecil Biles the miller on his left.
On this visit Cecil was still smiling and as friendly as ever.

Gratitude for helping me with this Environmental Study Project at Throop Mill goes to Cecil Biles, the miller, the mill's delivery man (whose name has since been forgotten, but friendliness and humour certainly not), Frank Dodman the Bournemouth ATD course director, John Lyddell, the main A.T D. tutor, the Malpas family of Queens Park and the Johns family of Charminster Road, who all but adopted me and a few other student friends of their daughter, Lesley, during our time in Bournemouth,.

Unfortunately many of these individuals have since died, but their kindness will not be forgotten. I hope this weak attempt to capture something of the magic of the Throop Mill has been partially successful.

M. K. Lewis

(Project updated June 2012)